THE
GREAT AMERICAN
HEALTHCARE
HEIST

The Great American Healthcare Heist

WHY WE'RE PAYING MORE AND GETTING LESS

CHRIS DEACON

Copyright © 2025 Chris Deacon

All rights reserved.

No portion of this book may be reproduced in any form without written permission from the publisher or author, except as permitted by U.S. copyright law.

This publication is designed to provide accurate and authoritative information in regard to the subject matter covered. It is sold with the understanding that neither the author nor the publisher is engaged in rendering legal, investment, accounting or other professional services. While the publisher and author have used their best efforts in preparing this book, they make no representations or warranties with respect to the accuracy or completeness of the contents of this book and specifically disclaim any implied warranties of merchantability or fitness for a particular purpose. No warranty may be created or extended by sales representatives or written sales materials. The advice and strategies contained herein may not be suitable for your situation. You should consult with a professional when appropriate. Neither the publisher nor the author shall be liable for any loss of profit or any other commercial damages, including but not limited to special, incidental, consequential, personal, or other damages.

ISBN (hardcover) 979-8-9995314-0-7
ISBN (paperback) 979-8-9995314-1-4
ISBN (ebook) 979-8-9995314-2-1
ISBN (audiobook) 979-8-9995314-3-8

Book Design by Christian Storm

For Marshall Allen

Journalist. Teacher. Truth-teller. Friend.

Marshall gave voice to patients long before most knew they had any power to claim. His work cut through bureaucracy and greed with clarity, moral conviction, and relentless courage. He didn't just expose the failures of our healthcare system—he showed people how to fight back.

Two weeks before he passed, we sat together in Wisconsin and outlined this book. He lit up as he coached me—on voice, on purpose, on how to write not just with knowledge, but with fire. He believed this work mattered. He believed in me. And he offered to walk beside me every step of the way.

That was Marshall: generous, wise, unshakably kind. A man of deep faith and deeper integrity. He saw journalism and justice as intertwined—and lived like that truth mattered every day.

I miss him terribly. But his words, his mission, and his spirit are on every page that follows.

This book is dedicated to him.

May we all fight as hard, write as clearly, and live as boldly.

Contents

Introduction: Standing Alone; The Price of Demanding Accountability 1

PART I

Chapter 1: Setting the Stage 13

Chapter 2: Healthcare Costs as a Drag on American Enterprise 15

Chapter 3: The Human Toll: How Healthcare Costs Crush American Families 24

Chapter 4: The Truth About Hospitals 32

Chapter 5: The Non-Profit Myth 36

Chapter 6: From Charity to Aggression 44

Chapter 7: Where the Money Goes 49

Chapter 8: A Broken Contract 55

Chapter 9: Case Study: Ascension Health – A Sacred Mission or Corporate Ambition? 56

Chapter 10: Case Study: Advocate Health 60

Chapter 11: UPMC Case Study 63

Chapter 12: The Steward Health Care Collapse 67

Chapter 13: The Crisis of Consolidation 77

Chapter 14: Sutter Health—A Case Study in
Anticompetitive Practices 85

Chapter 15: Hospital Consolidations
Across the Nation 90

PART II — THE ROLE OF INSURANCE CARRIERS IN THE BROKEN SYSTEM

Chapter 16: Gatekeepers of the Grift:
Inside the Middleman Machine 105

Chapter 17: Setting the Stage 110

Chapter 18: The "Network" and "Discount" Fallacy . . . 124

Chapter 19: Administrative Costs 128

Chapter 20: Insurance Companies as Healthcare
Providers & Negotiating on Both Sides of the Table . . . 137

Chapter 21: Delay, Deny, Depose: Barriers to Care
in the form of "Utilization Management" 145

Chapter 22: Delay, Deny, Depose: The Public
Outrage Over These Practices 156

Chapter 23: The Billion-Dollar Blind Spot:
Employers and the Cost of Looking Away 160

Chapter 24: The Fight for Healthcare Data:
Employers Writing Blank Checks with No Receipts . . . 167

Chapter 25: The Rules You Didn't Know You
Agreed To: The Unseen Hand Controlling
Employer Health Plans 176

Chapter 26: The Silent Takeover: How TPAs and
Carriers Are Becoming Providers Without
Employer Oversight. 182

PART III — MANIPULATING THE MARKET: PHARMA, PBMS, AND THE COST TO AMERICANS

Chapter 27: A Man Walks into a Pharmacy 191

Chapter 28: The Hidden Profits of PBMs:
Rebates and Spread Pricing 194

Chapter 29: A Billionaire Walks Into a
Broken System: Mark Cuban's Disruption
of the Drug Supply Chain. 207

Chapter 30: Behind the Formulary:
Who Controls Your Medication? 210

Chapter 31: Formularies, Opioids, and
the Architecture of Harm 215

Chapter 32: The Pharmaceutical Machine:
Innovation or Exploitation? 224

Chapter 33: The Pharmaceutical Industry's
Greatest Trick: The Illusion of Expiring Patents. 232

Chapter 34: The Myth of Research and
Development Costs 241

Chapter 35: How Do Companies Decide a Price? 246

Chapter 36: Why Are Drug Prices So Much
Higher in the U.S.? 251

Chapter 37: What Happens When Prices
Are Too High? 254

Conclusion: The Choice We Face 258

Chapter 38: The High Stakes: What Happens
If We Do Nothing? 260

Chapter 39: The Path Forward: Do We Have
the Will to Change? 268

Chapter 40: Labor Unions & Worker Advocacy:
The Sleeping Giant in the Healthcare Fight 275

Chapter 41: The Politicians and Policymakers:
The Architects of the System They Refuse to Fix. 279

The Final Chapter: A System That Breaks Us
Before It Heals Us. 283

Resources 291

About the Author 297

THE
GREAT AMERICAN
HEALTHCARE
HEIST

Introduction

STANDING ALONE — THE PRICE OF DEMANDING ACCOUNTABILITY

I remember that day vividly. Seated in a large boardroom at the heart of the New Jersey Executive Offices, I was surrounded by the state's top brass—Governor's Office officials, the Treasurer, senior staff of the Attorney General's Office and several other senior-level officials. I was there as the Assistant Director of Pensions and Benefits for the State of New Jersey, a role that carried the weight of responsibility for managing the health benefits program for over 820,000 lives. The State Health Benefits Program and School Employees' Health Benefits Program—SHBP for short—encompassed state employees, university faculty, state police, and every local government and school district that had opted into this plan.

The SHBP was far more than a health plan; it was a cornerstone of public-sector compensation, a benefit on which employees and retirees alike depended for security in their working years and counted on for support in retirement. Managing it was a responsibility I approached with a fiduciary duty to every member and the taxpayers funding it. I was determined to be a fiscal steward who didn't just safeguard resources but upheld the promise of high-quality, affordable healthcare for all. For many, this program was a financial lifeline and a source of stability, making our mission not just to manage it—but to transform it.

At the time, healthcare costs for SHBP seemed to be on an unstoppable upward trajectory. By 2019, the SHBP and the School Employees' Health Benefits Program (SEHBP) together were covering approximately 820,000 members at a cost of around $5.79 billion annually, with the state contributing about $3.2 billion—an expenditure representing roughly 8.4% of New Jersey's budget. Local governments and school districts also heavily depended on this program to maintain balanced budgets, especially as healthcare costs grew disproportionately to other expenditures

Health benefits costs weren't just a line item on a budget spreadsheet—they were an albatross around the necks of local governments and school districts. In New Jersey, these costs had become so burdensome that officials faced excruciating trade-offs: should they hire more teachers to address overcrowded classrooms, or should they cut educational programs, extracurricular activities, and even basic resources just to keep up with skyrocketing healthcare premiums? The math was unforgiving. Teachers saw their take-home pay shrink as they were forced to contribute more toward their benefits, and districts scrambled to find funding elsewhere. Strikes and budget fights became common as educators and officials clashed over a system that seemed rigged against them. In Jersey City, for example, a teacher strike erupted in 2018 largely due to the crushing weight of healthcare costs, leaving classrooms empty and parents frustrated. Across the state, schools and municipalities were left in an impossible bind—unable to invest in the future without jeopardizing their present financial stability.

This crisis made one thing clear: the state's approach to procuring health benefits was broken. When I took on the responsibility of overseeing New Jersey's health plan, it was clear that the system was not working for the people it was supposed to serve. The state's request for proposals (RFP) process—the formal bidding process used to select health insurance carriers and administrators—was meant to ensure that taxpayer dollars were spent wisely. Instead, it had become a convoluted exercise that all but guaranteed the same bloated contracts year after year.

Typically, the RFP process in healthcare benefits revolves around vendors offering discounts off their own pricing—pricing that, critically, the state or employer never actually sees. It's like a department store offering a "40% off" sale without ever showing you the original price tag. The end result? You have no idea if you're getting a deal or if the price was inflated to begin with. Carriers would promise discounts on medical services, but those discounts were based on a starting price negotiated in secrecy between the carrier and healthcare providers. And because those prices weren't publicly available, there was no real way to verify whether the "savings" were meaningful or just a shell game shifting costs elsewhere.

That approach made no sense. The vast majority—98% to 99%—of our total healthcare spending wasn't the administrative fee we paid to the vendor; it was the actual medical claims costs. If we were serious about controlling costs, we had to tackle the real driver of spending, not just the sliver of the budget going toward administrative expenses.

So we flipped the process on its head. Instead of relying on vague discounts, the RFP was designed to require bidders to propose actual, guaranteed unit prices for medical services—what they would pay for an MRI, a knee replacement, a specialist visit. This way, we could compare apples to apples, rather than taking their word for it on percentage discounts from an invisible benchmark. Just as a consumer wouldn't sign a cell phone contract without knowing the per-minute or per-gigabyte rate, we sought to ensure that healthcare contracts included fixed, upfront prices for the services our members would actually use.

But price is only one side of the equation. The other critical factor in healthcare spending is utilization—how often and how appropriately medical services are used. Two patients with the same condition might generate drastically different costs depending on whether they're receiving care from the right provider, at the right time, and in the right setting. That's why the RFP aimed to go beyond just unit prices and also address utilization by requiring the implementation of a navigation and advocacy vendor to help members make informed choices about their care.

In the healthcare context, navigation and advocacy mean having a dedicated resource—actual people, not just an app—helping members understand their options, steer them toward high-value providers, and ensure they receive care in the most appropriate setting. Instead of a patient unknowingly going to an expensive hospital outpatient department for a basic procedure that could be done just as well at a lower-cost ambulatory surgical center, the navigation vendor was supposed to guide them to the more cost-effective option. Instead of seeing a specialist without a proper referral or bypassing primary care entirely, they would be directed toward the right provider at the right stage of care.

And this wasn't intended to be based on empty promises. The RFP sought to ensure accountability by requiring vendors to put their money where their mouth was. Under the contract, if the vendor failed to meet the unit prices they had guaranteed for certain services, they were supposed to pay the state back in significant sums. The goal was to create a direct financial incentive for them to actively navigate members toward high-value care. If they wanted to protect their bottom line, they had to ensure that members were making choices that aligned with lower costs and better outcomes.

The intent was to force transparency into a system that had long resisted it. The RFP was designed to make carriers compete on real costs rather than on smoke-and-mirrors discounting. It also sought to ensure that they had a direct financial stake in guiding patients toward the right care, at the right time, from the right provider—because if they didn't, they would face real financial consequences.

Fixing this was never going to be easy, but it was necessary. New Jersey's school districts, municipal governments, and the taxpayers funding them deserved better. If rising healthcare costs were forcing local leaders to make heartbreaking decisions—choosing between hiring a teacher and keeping the lights on—then it was time to stop letting health insurers write the rules.

When the bids were evaluated, Horizon Blue Cross Blue Shield, or Horizon for short, emerged as the winning bidder, securing the contract to administer the state's health plan. Their proposal checked every box: guaranteed unit prices for key medical services, a robust navigation and advocacy program to steer members toward high-value care, and financial accountability mechanisms that put real money on the line if they failed to meet their commitments. On paper, it was the transformative contract the state had been working toward—one that would finally shift power away from opaque pricing schemes and toward real, measurable savings for taxpayers and public employees alike.

A year in, it was obvious something was wrong. Despite Horizon's promises, the terms we counted on to rein in costs weren't being honored. Critical contract services—like steering patients to high-quality, low-cost providers—were neglected, while other essential safeguards went ignored. The state would lose hundreds of millions, if not billions, over the life of the contract if we ignored these contractual deficiencies and grievances. My team and I documented these violations meticulously, escalating memos to my immediate boss, the Treasurer's Office, the Governor's chief of staff, and all the way up the chain to any level of government we believed had authority to hold Horizon accountable, including the State Attorney General's Office. I was pleased that as a result of our alarm-sounding, the situation seemed too egregious to ignore—even with Horizon's deep political ties and pockets.

Then, the moment came. We were all in that boardroom, facing off with Horizon's executive team — a notably uniform group. On our side sat the key state officials: the treasurer, her deputies, senior members of the Attorney General's Office, the Governor's chief of staff and counsel and myself. I was asked to present the case, laying out the breaches of contract and their financial impact on the state. I laid out the service level deficiencies that had been documented not only by division staff, but also independently validated by the state's health benefits consultant and actuary—Aon. My memo circulated beforehand had laid everything out in black and white, leaving little room for Horizon's typical evasions. Forty-five minutes in, we were nearly out of time, and it was clear that Horizon had promised way more than it could (or would) deliver on the contract. Horizon's executives were stalling, repeating phrases about "partnership" and the need for time to "digest" the information. That's when the door opened, and in walked the Governor.

The moment he entered, the atmosphere shifted. Without so much as a glance in my direction, he made his way to Horizon's side of the table, lavishing hugs and backslaps, even declaring his fondness for Ule Diaz, Horizon's chief government affairs officer. "That's my guy, I love this guy," he said with a smile, fully aware of the message he was sending. Only months earlier, Diaz had scored a major victory with the Governor's support for Horizon's governance and corporate structure transformation that would allow it to broaden its business portfolio, reduce its tax burden, and operate more like its for-profit competitors.

Then came the Governor's parting words, delivered with a dismissive tone: "We can figure this out, I'm sure you guys can figure this out." In that instant, I knew our leverage was gone. The message was clear: this issue was to be smoothed over, Horizon was untouchable, and no matter the breach or the cost, the administration would stand by them.

Despite this massive setback, I continued to pursue these issues through the formal complaint process with the contract compliance audit unit within the state. I pushed and pushed what felt like an uphill wheelbarrow piled with boulders. I was given the runaround both by senior brass at Horizon—"We're working a proposal," "We are looking into it ..." and "We value our partnership." I was being given the side eye from internal leadership as well—why did I have to be so difficult, couldn't I just let this go, why did I care so much that I was willing to put my career on the line?

Weeks later, the final blow landed. The assistant treasurer called, urgently informing me that screenshots of texts from my private cell phone were being circulated both in the Governor's Office and the executive offices of Horizon. I was getting too close to the fire and was going to get burned if I didn't move back. For Horizon, hundreds of millions of dollars were at stake, hundreds of jobs and very likely, hefty campaign checks. If you added the savings we stood to gain from New Jersey's largest hospitals into the equation, there was no doubt that there was a bounty on my head.

At a Starbucks in Trenton, where I was asked to meet a treasury official, I was told to stand down. There would be no record of the meeting or anyone else present, just myself and a treasury official that had been given the task of taking care of the situation. Horizon would remain the state's "partner" indefinitely for the SHBP and there was nothing further we could do about the contract or complaints that had been lodged. If I wanted to remain a public servant in the state of New Jersey, I could accept it—or I could walk away.

I chose the latter. And that choice marked the beginning of this mission—to confront the forces that let power and profit overshadow accountability and justice in healthcare.

When I first took on the role at NJ Pensions and Benefits I wasn't a healthcare expert. But I didn't need to be an expert to see that something was deeply wrong. I was willing to question the status quo, to ask why we did things the way we did, and to push for a system that actually served the people it was meant to support. This commitment wasn't about heroism; it was simply what I believe any true public servant should do.

Yet I also know that not everyone in the system has the freedom—or, frankly, the support—to take that moral high ground. For some, the obstacles to meaningful change are simply insurmountable. That's why, for those of us who can choose this path, it's crucial to make that choice meaningful, to push back against complacency, and to insist on accountability and transparency.

What you will read in this book is a deep, unfiltered examination of how the American healthcare system really works—who profits, who pays, and why costs continue to spiral out of control. You will see the hidden forces shaping the industry, from hospital consolidation and opaque pricing schemes to the perverse incentives that allow insurers, pharmacy benefit managers, and consultants to thrive while employers and patients struggle. You will gain the tools to question the system, the insight to recognize when you're being taken advantage of, and the understanding necessary to push for smarter, more effective reforms.

What you will not get is a prepackaged conclusion that the only solution is universal healthcare, a single-payer system, or an NHS-style model. This is not a book arguing for a government takeover of healthcare, nor is it a defense of the status quo. The reality is far more complex than the binary debate between "government-run" and "free market" solutions. What I will show you is that before we can fix anything, we must first acknowledge the deeply entrenched dysfunction that exists today—and understand the ways in which those in power benefit from keeping it that way.

This book is about pulling back the curtain on the industry's worst-kept secrets and forcing a long-overdue reckoning. If you are an employer, a policymaker, a taxpayer, or simply someone trying to afford healthcare in America, you cannot afford to look away.

PART I

Chapter I

SETTING THE STAGE

For decades, Americans have been told the same story: we have the best healthcare system in the world. Modern hospitals, cutting-edge technology, and access to renowned specialists reinforce this belief. Yet for all the pride in these accomplishments, the truth tells a different story. The United States is project to spend an astonishing $4.9 trillion in 2024 on healthcare—more than the GDP of countries like Germany and the United Kingdom, and greater than the combined economies of Brazil, Spain, and Canada. Despite this unparalleled financial commitment, the outcomes we achieve are deeply disappointing.

American life expectancy lags behind that of countries like South Korea, Italy, and even Costa Rica. Infant mortality rates in the U.S. are higher than in nations such as Slovenia and Finland, exposing stark inequalities in access to and quality of care. Chronic diseases like diabetes and hypertension remain widespread, and preventable deaths far exceed those of comparable nations. These failures are not just academic—they impact real people, real families, and the businesses that employ them.

The high cost of healthcare is felt in every corner of American life. For workers, it manifests in stagnant wages, rising out-of-pocket costs, and limited access to quality care. For businesses, it means skyrocketing premiums, constrained budgets, and a diminished ability to compete in a global market. These burdens are not incidental—they are a direct consequence of a system designed to enrich insurers, pharmaceutical companies, hospitals, and middlemen at the expense of everyone else.

This is not about assigning blame, nor is it about deciding whether employers, employees, or even the government should shoulder the cost of this dysfunctional system. The endless blame game—echoed in public discourse and policy debates alike—has been little more than a red herring, skillfully designed to keep us distracted while the real architects of this heist continue to profit unchecked. These diversions have allowed the healthcare industry to flourish at the expense of the very people and businesses it is supposed to serve.

For years, the healthcare industry has pitted stakeholders against one another: pharmacy benefit managers (PBMs) versus pharmaceutical manufacturers, hospitals and providers versus insurance carriers, and employers versus employees. These internal feuds and congressional finger-pointing have created a smokescreen, diverting attention from the $4.6 trillion system that thrives on inefficiency, opacity, and unchecked profiteering. There is no shortage of blame to go around in this $4.6 trillion economy—plenty for everyone—but while these factions squabble over who is at fault, the real victims are the American people and the businesses that employ them.

We must cut through the noise and refocus the conversation. It's not about determining who should bear the weight of this broken system but about understanding why the system is broken in the first place—and, more importantly, who benefits from it staying that way. Only by pulling back the curtain on the industry's deliberate design flaws and exposing the perverse incentives that drive these sky-high costs can we begin to demand the change that both workers and businesses so desperately need.

Chapter 2

HEALTHCARE COSTS AS A DRAG ON AMERICAN ENTERPRISE

American businesses operate in one of the most complex and expensive healthcare environments in the world. The United States spends more on healthcare than any other nation—approximately $4.9 trillion annually, or nearly 20% of GDP—yet consistently underperforms on critical health outcomes like life expectancy and chronic disease management. For employers, this spending represents more than just a line item; it's a growing burden that distorts financial decisions, stifles growth, and diminishes competitiveness.

This cost burden has profound implications for business investment, pricing strategies, employment practices, and global competitiveness. It doesn't just affect large corporations but also small and mid-sized enterprises that struggle to balance offering competitive benefits with staying afloat. While healthcare reform has often been framed as a moral imperative, it is just as much an economic necessity for the U.S. business sector.

One of the most immediate and damaging impacts of high healthcare costs is the suppression of investment. Businesses that are forced to divert resources toward covering healthcare premiums and out-of-pocket costs often sacrifice long-term growth for short-term financial survival. Starbucks, for example, has long prided itself on providing comprehensive health benefits to employees, even part-time workers—a rarity in the service industry. But this commitment comes at a staggering cost. The company has historically spent more on employee healthcare than on purchasing coffee beans, an essential commodity for its core business. While this policy has been credited with attracting and retaining talent, it also highlights the sheer magnitude of healthcare expenses in the U.S. and the trade-offs businesses must make to remain competitive.

The same pressures weigh on industrial giants like General Motors (GM). At its peak, GM was spending more on employee healthcare than on the steel needed to manufacture its vehicles. Former GM executives have directly linked these ballooning costs to the company's declining global competitiveness. In the early 2000s, healthcare expenses for retirees and employees were a major factor in GM's financial troubles, ultimately contributing to its 2009 bankruptcy and government bailout. As foreign automakers operated in countries with nationalized healthcare systems, they were able to produce vehicles at lower costs, while GM was saddled with mounting obligations to cover medical expenses. The company's struggles were a warning sign for American manufacturing as a whole: without serious reform, healthcare costs could continue to undermine domestic industries.

Even the country's largest employer, Walmart, has not been immune to these pressures. With over a million U.S. workers, Walmart has repeatedly revised its approach to employee health benefits in response to rising costs. In 2005, only about 44% of Walmart's workforce was covered by its health insurance, a significantly lower rate than competitors like Costco, which insured around 85% of employees. Facing mounting financial strain, Walmart made several moves to cut back on coverage, first eliminating health benefits for new part-time employees in 2011, then expanding that restriction to all part-time workers in 2013. These cuts forced thousands of employees onto government programs like Medicaid, shifting costs from the private sector to taxpayers.

These examples illustrate a fundamental reality: healthcare isn't just a social or policy issue—it's an economic crisis that is reshaping American business. Whether it's a coffee giant forced to spend more on healthcare than its core product, an automaker struggling to compete against global rivals unburdened by private healthcare costs, or a retail behemoth cutting benefits to manage expenses, the high price of healthcare in the U.S. is actively distorting the decisions of companies large and small. Left unaddressed, it will continue to erode profitability, suppress wages, and force businesses into difficult trade-offs that weaken their ability to compete in the global economy.

REDUCED INVESTMENT: GROWTH ON HOLD

Healthcare costs in the U.S. have been rising at a rate outpacing inflation and wage growth for decades. According to the Kaiser Family Foundation, employer-sponsored health insurance premiums increased by 47% from 2011 to 2021, far exceeding the growth in median household income over the same period. Over the past 20 years, healthcare costs have gone up by 188%, while wages have gone up 84%, according to Milliman, a well known actuarial and consulting firm that specializes in healthcare cost modeling. In fact, the cost of covering a family of four through employer based insurance now exceeds $35,000 —again, nearly triple what it cost 20 years ago. This rapid escalation forces businesses to reallocate funds that might otherwise be used for strategic investments, undermining their ability to grow and innovate.

Every dollar a business spends on healthcare is a dollar it cannot invest elsewhere. This zero-sum dynamic often leads to reduced spending on critical areas such as research and development, technology and infrastructure, and talent development.

Companies across industries, especially in manufacturing and technology, frequently scale back R&D budgets to offset rising healthcare costs. A National Bureau of Economic Research (NBER) study found that businesses facing high employee healthcare costs invest significantly less in innovation, a key driver of long-term growth. For example, a biotech startup in Massachusetts reported that its healthcare expenses doubled over five years, consuming resources initially earmarked for the development of a new therapeutic drug. The company delayed clinical trials by two years, risking its competitive edge in a rapidly evolving market.

Another area where U.S. businesses suffer is in their inability to upgrade technology and facilities, which is critical for staying competitive in many industries. Healthcare costs crowd out these expenditures. A mid-sized logistics firm in the Midwest decided against automating its warehouse operations—a project expected to improve efficiency by 30%—because it needed to cover a 14% increase in employee healthcare premiums.

Businesses often say that their people are their greatest asset. In a services-driven economy like ours, the strength of a business hinges on the strength of its workforce. Yet, the cruel irony is that the very system designed to care for people—our healthcare system—is now one of the greatest barriers to investing in those same people. Healthcare costs, which should be a tool for supporting employee well-being, are instead siphoning resources away from everything else that makes a job more meaningful and a business more successful: retirement benefits, wellness programs, raises, and professional development.

Imagine a small-business owner who genuinely wants to reward their team with raises or expand their workforce training program. Instead, they're faced with a grim choice: absorb a 12% increase in health insurance premiums or cut back on everything else. It's not hard to guess which option wins. Employee training and professional development—investments that build morale, retain talent, and drive long-term competitiveness—are often the first to go. A study by the Society for Human Resource Management (SHRM) found that businesses hit with double-digit increases in healthcare costs are 60% more likely to cut workforce development spending. That's not just a statistic—it's a slow erosion of what makes a workplace thrive.

This isn't just about dollars and cents; it's about priorities. When a system prioritizes profit over people, it forces employers into an impossible bind, robbing them of the ability to fully invest in their greatest asset: their employees. The result is a downward spiral—a demoralized workforce, limited opportunities for growth, and companies that are weaker for it. The saddest part? The very industry that markets itself as essential for our health and well-being is often the reason businesses can't afford to prioritize the very things that make their employees healthier, happier, and more productive. It would be laughable if it weren't so tragic.

IMPACT ON SMALL AND MEDIUM ENTERPRISES

Small businesses are the backbone of the American economy. They employ nearly half of all private-sector workers and generate roughly two-thirds of net new jobs. Yet, for many small and medium-sized enterprises (SMEs), the crushing cost of healthcare has become the immovable obstacle to growth and prosperity. While large corporations may have financial buffers to absorb rising premiums, SMEs often operate on razor-thin margins, leaving little room to maneuver when healthcare expenses spiral out of control. For these businesses, healthcare can easily become their second-largest cost after wages, forcing painful decisions about whether to grow, cut benefits, or even stay in business.

This reality hits close to home for me. My father owned a small construction business in Florida when I was growing up, employing close to 50 people at its peak. For years, he worked tirelessly to provide good jobs and benefits, including health insurance, to his employees. But as premiums climbed year after year, the burden became too great. Expanding the business, which would have created more jobs and opportunities, was out of the question—the cost of insuring additional employees would have been prohibitive. Eventually, the decision was made to keep the company under the 50-employee threshold and end employee health coverage altogether. Instead, the company offered employees a modest cash allowance to purchase insurance on their own through the exchange. While this might have seemed like a lifeline, the reality was stark: employees were left to fend for themselves in a marketplace where plans often came with sky-high deductibles and limited coverage, leaving many effectively uninsured despite paying for a policy.

This story is not unique. In Wisconsin, a family-owned manufacturing business faced a similar dilemma. Despite high demand for its products, the company delayed opening a new production line that would have created 50 jobs. The reason? Healthcare premiums were their single largest barrier to expansion. They simply could not afford to grow while maintaining benefits for their existing workforce.

The stakes are high. Small businesses like my father's and that Wisconsin manufacturer represent 99% of all U.S. businesses. They are vital to innovation, job creation, and the health of local economies. Yet their ability to thrive is being systematically undercut by a healthcare system that punishes their success. Instead of investing in new equipment, hiring more staff, or increasing wages, these businesses are spending more and more on healthcare costs that seem to yield less and less in return.

This isn't just an economic issue; it's deeply personal. For every small business owner who chooses not to expand, for every employee who goes without coverage, there is a ripple effect—on families, communities, and the economy as a whole. When we allow the weight of healthcare costs to crush small businesses, we are undermining the very foundation of what makes the American economy strong. And as premiums climb higher, the consequences for these businesses—and the people they employ—will only grow more dire.

RIPPLE EFFECTS ON THE ECONOMY

The economic consequences of runaway healthcare costs reach far beyond the individual businesses struggling to balance their books. When companies are forced to pull back on spending, the effects reverberate across industries, stifling innovation, slowing productivity growth, and ultimately weakening the very foundation of our economy. Reduced investment in research and development (R&D) means fewer breakthroughs, limited technology upgrades hinder efficiency, and a lack of workforce training erodes the skills needed to compete in a global marketplace. This cascading effect contributes to slower GDP growth and places the U.S. at a significant disadvantage compared to nations with more efficient healthcare systems.

But it's not just about what we're losing—it's about what we're choosing to invest in. What future does this country have if an ever-growing share of its GDP is spent on an industry that produces nothing tangible and delivers substandard outcomes? The U.S. already spends more on healthcare than any other country, yet we rank behind many developed nations in life expectancy, maternal mortality, and chronic disease management. The system demands more money every year, yet the return on that investment continues to decline.

The trajectory we're on is unsustainable. Therapies are becoming increasingly expensive, with the latest gene therapy treatments exceeding $4 million per patient. Medications like GLP-1s, initially developed for diabetes and now being widely prescribed for weight loss, are crippling employer-sponsored health plans. And their use is only expected to grow, with expanded indications and skyrocketing costs on the horizon. Drugs in general are getting more expensive, not cheaper, even as patents expire, thanks to complex schemes by manufacturers and intermediaries to maintain monopolistic pricing.

Meanwhile, healthcare systems, insurance carriers, and pharmacy benefit managers (PBMs) are consolidating at an alarming rate, creating local and regional monopolies. These entities wield unchecked power over entire communities, dictating prices, limiting choices, and extracting wealth from patients and employers alike. In many areas, patients are left with no alternatives, forced to navigate a system designed to prioritize profits over care.

The ripple effects of this consolidation are devastating. Businesses burdened by rising healthcare costs are less likely to invest in capital-intensive projects, such as new manufacturing plants, sustainable infrastructure, or cutting-edge technology—projects that create jobs and stimulate economic growth. According to a report from the RAND Corporation, high healthcare expenditures reduce overall economic productivity by creating inefficiencies at both the employer and employee levels. It's a vicious cycle: businesses spend more on healthcare, invest less in their operations, and ultimately contribute less to the economy.

If we continue on this path, we risk becoming a nation that spends more on sickness than on innovation, infrastructure, or education. What happens when the cost of healthcare outpaces our ability to pay for it, and the system collapses under its own weight? The warning signs are already here. And yet, the industry players—pharmaceutical companies, PBMs, hospital systems, and insurers—continue to

CHAPTER 2

consolidate power and profits, laughing all the way to the bank while the rest of the economy bears the cost.

The question isn't just how much we can afford to spend but whether we can afford to keep propping up a system that drains resources, stifles growth, and fails to deliver the outcomes we deserve. The answer, increasingly, is no. If we want a future that prioritizes innovation, prosperity, and health—not just for individuals but for the entire nation—we must demand accountability from an industry that has taken too much for far too long.

Chapter 3

THE HUMAN TOLL: HOW HEALTHCARE COSTS CRUSH AMERICAN FAMILIES

As healthcare costs in the United States have spiraled upward at an astonishing rate over the past few decades, I am left wondering: how did we get here? How is it that something so fundamental to our well-being has become one of the biggest financial burdens for American families?

For millions of Americans, the weight of healthcare expenses isn't an abstract policy debate—it's a daily reality that dictates financial choices, limits opportunities, and, in far too many cases, costs lives. It's the single mother in Colorado who gets sick, misses a shift at work, and loses not just her paycheck but her health insurance in the process. It's the cancer patient calculating the cost of another round of treatment, realizing the numbers no longer add up. It's the elderly couple choosing between groceries and life-sustaining medication. This is the grim reality of the American healthcare system: the cost of care is not just an economic burden; it's a life-or-death equation.

Take Susan Finley. She worked for Walmart in Grand Junction, Colorado, for ten years. Like millions of Americans, she lived paycheck to paycheck, balancing bills, rent, and daily necessities. One year, she caught pneumonia and took time off to recover. But when

CHAPTER 3

she returned to work, she was handed two things: a ten-year associate award and a pink slip. She had exceeded Walmart's strict attendance policy by a single day. Without a job, she lost her health insurance. And without health insurance, she hesitated to seek medical care the next time she got sick. Three months later, she was found dead in her apartment. Her son, Cameron, later explained that she had been afraid to see a doctor, unwilling to take on medical debt when she was already struggling to keep a roof over her head.

Susan Finley's story is not unique. She is one of millions of Americans who avoid medical treatment due to cost. A 2019 Gallup poll found that 25% of Americans—one in four people—had delayed medical care for a serious condition because they couldn't afford it. That number rises to 33% when including those who skipped treatment for non-serious conditions. And the consequences of these delays are devastating. In a Harvard Medical School study, researchers estimated that 45,000 Americans die each year as a direct result of lacking health insurance—not because their conditions were untreatable, but because they never sought care in the first place.

Over the past two decades, healthcare costs in the United States have surged, placing an increasing financial burden on households. In 2004, the average household spent $2,574 on healthcare, accounting for 5.9% of total expenditures. By 2022, this figure had risen to $5,837, representing 8% of household spending—a 127% increase in dollar terms. These aren't just numbers on a page; they represent real sacrifices families are making—foregoing vacations, cutting back on groceries, delaying home repairs—all to cover an essential service that should be accessible without financial devastation.

And the costs don't stop there. The relentless rise in healthcare expenses has been accompanied by an explosion in out-of-pocket costs, particularly deductibles. A decade ago, a worker with employer-sponsored insurance might have had a manageable deductible of $917. By 2020, that number had more than doubled to $1,945—a

111% increase in just ten years. This means that before insurance even begins to cover costs, families must first come up with nearly $2,000 out of pocket. In an economy where nearly 60% of Americans live paycheck to paycheck, it's not hard to see how a single trip to the emergency room can send a household spiraling into debt.

For some, these rising costs don't just result in delayed care—they lead to outright financial catastrophe. When Anamaria Markle, a longtime clerk from New Jersey, was diagnosed with stage three ovarian cancer, she faced an impossible choice. After nearly 20 years of service, her employer laid her off following her diagnosis, offering one year of severance and continued health insurance. But when that coverage expired, she was left to navigate the maze of COBRA—a program designed to let former employees continue their insurance, but at an exorbitant cost. The premiums alone were financially unsustainable for her family, and that didn't even include copays, deductibles, and out-of-pocket expenses for chemotherapy and surgery. As medical bills piled up, Markle made a gut-wrenching decision: she stopped treatment. She died in September 2018 at the age of 52, after calculating that the cost of staying alive had simply become too much to bear.

Stories like Markle's and Finley's are gut-wrenching, but they are not isolated. Millions of Americans are just one medical crisis away from financial ruin. Many turn to crowdfunding, posting desperate pleas on GoFundMe pages, hoping strangers will help them afford basic medical care. Others take out second mortgages, empty retirement savings, or rack up insurmountable debt just to stay alive.

Imagine a parent whose child wakes up in the middle of the night with a high fever, struggling to breathe. In many parts of the world, that parent would rush to the nearest hospital without a second thought. But in America, they pause. *Is it serious enough to justify the ER bill? Can we wait until morning and try urgent care instead? What if the urgent care sends us to the ER anyway—then we're stuck paying for both?* No parent should have to

— CHAPTER 3 —

weigh the cost of a hospital visit against the health of their child, yet this is the reality for countless families across the country.

This relentless increase in healthcare expenses isn't just an economic burden; it's a profound source of stress and uncertainty. How can families plan for the future when a medical emergency could wipe out their savings in an instant? How did we allow healthcare—something meant to protect us—to become one of the greatest threats to our financial well-being?

At its core, healthcare is supposed to provide security, to ensure that people can access the care they need when they need it. But in America, healthcare has become a financial gamble—one where the house always seems to win. Families are expected to budget for the unpredictable, to save for an emergency that could cost them thousands, all while keeping up with rising premiums, deductibles, and copays. The system is set up to extract, not to protect. And unless something changes, millions of hardworking Americans will continue to struggle under a burden they should never have been forced to carry in the first place.

THE POWERS FAMILY: FROM STABILITY TO BANKRUPTCY

Jim and Cindy Powers thought they were prepared for life's challenges. Living in Greeley, Colorado, they worked hard to maintain financial stability, but their world was turned upside down in 2004 when Cindy required emergency surgery. What began as a routine procedure spiraled into a nightmare. Complications led to a severe infection that kept her in and out of hospitals for years. By 2009, the bills had piled up to a staggering $250,000. Despite their best efforts to keep up with payments, the financial burden was too much to bear. Their savings were depleted, their credit ruined, and their dreams of a secure future shattered. With no other options, the Powers filed for bankruptcy, joining the millions of Americans whose lives have been derailed by unexpected healthcare costs.

BREANNA KENNEDY: A MOTHER'S FIGHT TO SURVIVE

In McPherson, Kansas, Breanna Kennedy was doing everything she could to provide for her family. But when she required extensive head surgery, her world unraveled. The medical bills came fast and furious, each one larger than the last. Soon, she was drowning in debt with no way to pay it off. Filing for bankruptcy was not a choice she made lightly; it was a last-ditch effort to keep her family afloat. Yet even bankruptcy wasn't enough to stave off the threat of homelessness. Breanna and her children were forced to leave their home, seeking refuge wherever they could find it. Salvation came in the form of a tiny home village built by the McPherson Housing Coalition, where Breanna found a small but stable space to regroup. It wasn't the life she envisioned, but it was a start toward rebuilding what had been lost.

IMANI MFALME: A DAUGHTER'S UNEXPECTED BURDEN

In Knoxville, Tennessee, Imani Mfalme faced a shocking financial burden after her mother's passing. Her mother, a trailblazer who won a landmark discrimination lawsuit against Boeing, had purchased her dream home—a symbol of victory and stability. However, after her death, the state's Medicaid office claimed Imani owed $225,000 for her mother's medical expenses and sought a court order to force the sale of the cherished family home to settle the debt. This unexpected claim threatened to erase a significant part of her mother's legacy.

— CHAPTER 3 —

THE HUMAN COST: JOE'S STORY

Okay, Joe isn't real, but he could be. His story captures the everyday struggle of millions of hardworking Americans who face the relentless financial pressures of our healthcare system. A 45-year-old married father of two, Joe works as a mechanic, proud of the life he's built through steady, honest work. His employer offers health insurance, a benefit he's grateful for, but one that comes with a steep price: the average annual premium for family coverage in 2024 is $25,572—roughly the cost of a new car each year. While his employer covers a significant portion, Joe's share is $6,296 annually, a major bite out of his paycheck.

But that's just the starting point. Like many families, Joe's plan includes a deductible of $1,787, which must be paid out of pocket before insurance begins to cover most services. This means routine care like check-ups or prescriptions often comes with hefty bills, to say nothing of unexpected emergencies. For millions of Americans, even these "routine" costs are destabilizing. In fact, 41% of households carry medical debt, a stark reminder that having insurance is no guarantee of affordability.

The system piles on in other, less obvious ways. When Joe's youngest, Abby, comes down with a high fever, he takes her to their trusted pediatrician. Weeks later, the bill arrives—higher than expected. You see, the office of the pediatrician where Joe had been taking his daughter since she first came home from the hospital had recently been acquired by a large hospital system in their community. The office looked the same, employed the same nurses and staff, there were no noticeable differences other than the signage on the office building that now included a small hospital system marking. But there it was, an additional $450 facility fee, which is a surcharge hospitals can add even for simple office visits or even telemedicine visits. Originally intended to offset the costs of specialized hospital care, facility fees are now commonly applied to basic services in doctor's offices and virtual care appointments, inflating costs without improving outcomes. These fees contribute to the $1.3 trillion spent annually on hospital care and are emblematic of a system where consolidation and complexity drive prices ever higher.

And Joe's challenges don't end there. He learns that the imaging center where Abby needs a chest X-ray is no longer in-network after being acquired by another hospital system. Despite verifying his insurance details in advance, he is blindsided by the bill, now two to three times higher than what an in-network visit would have cost. Surprise medical bills like these are all too common; more than half of Americans have received one, often from an out-of-network provider involved in a routine or emergency procedure. These bills push families deeper into debt and erode trust in a system that feels impossible to navigate.

LOOKING AHEAD

Joe's story is emblematic of the American healthcare system—a system where everyone, from small businesses to families, shoulders an ever-growing burden. But how did we get here? Why are premiums rising, facility fees proliferating, and surprise bills still a feature of modern healthcare? Why do we continue to face an ever-increasing tax burden to support "struggling" non-profit hospitals, even as we drive past construction site after construction site of new glass towers and medical office buildings that appear to have spared no expense? These questions aren't rhetorical; they are the key to understanding the structural failures that have led us to this point.

To unpack these issues, we must explore the forces driving this dysfunction. Behind every bill, fee, and inflated cost lies a set of players—pharmaceutical companies, pharmacy benefit managers, hospitals, providers, and insurance carriers—all profiting from the system as it stands. And just as crucial are the government policies and compromises that have allowed these dynamics to take root.

The challenges Joe faces today, indeed the challenges we all face, are the result of decades of decisions in boardrooms and in Congress. Understanding those decisions and their consequences is essential to imagining a healthcare system that works for everyone—not just a select few. It's time to dig deeper.

Chapter 4

THE TRUTH ABOUT HOSPITALS

"The very first requirement in a hospital is that it should do the sick no harm."
—Florence Nightingale

Hospitals hold a sacred place in our communities. They're where lives are saved, where babies are born, where hope and healing intersect. For many, they're also synonymous with charity—places that exist to serve the public, to care for the sick, and to provide a safety net for those in need. But what if I told you, today, that image is largely a myth? That the very institutions we entrust with our health and well-being are among the largest drivers of why American healthcare is so outrageously expensive?

To understand why, we need to take a hard look at hospitals—not as we imagine them, but as they truly operate today. Modern hospital systems are not struggling charities. They are massive enterprises, many of them flush with cash reserves that stretch into the billions. They claim non-profit status while behaving like profit-maximizing corporations, with CEOs earning multimillion-dollar salaries, fleets of private jets, and sprawling administrative bureaucracies that siphon resources from patient care.

CHAPTER 4

And then there's the pricing. It's not just that one hospital charges more than another for the same procedure. Radical price variation exists even within the same hospital system, where one location might charge $600 for an MRI while another charges $3,000, with no clear rhyme or reason beyond what the market—or your insurance plan—can bear. The cost isn't based on quality; it's based on leverage and a willingness to extract as much as possible from patients and insurers.

For-profit motives are so deeply entrenched that even non-profits, including those with religious missions and names invoking sacred religious figures, have been known to pursue ruthless debt-collection practices. Very well-known Catholic hospital systems, for example, have been found foreclosing on patients' homes, garnishing wages, and suing low-income families—often the very populations these institutions claim to serve. These aren't isolated incidents; they are systemic practices designed to protect hospital revenues at all costs, even if it means destroying the financial lives of the people they care for.

Speaking of systemic, consider a federal program designed to help low-income patients by providing hospitals with discounted medications has been turned into a profit engine. Hospitals buy these discounted drugs, meant to lower costs for vulnerable patients, and then charge insurers and patients full price—pocketing the difference. Some hospitals even acquire additional clinics to expand their access to these discounts, not to serve more patients, but to maximize profits. What began as a safety net for the underserved has become a multi-billion-dollar revenue stream, with little benefit reaching those it was designed to help.

Or consider the financial-assistance policies hospitals are required to have for those who cannot afford their medical bills, as a condition of maintaining their tax-exempt status. These policies, known as 501(r) financial-assistance policies, are meant to ensure that hospitals prioritize community care over profit. Yet many hospitals bury these programs in bureaucratic red tape or fail to advertise their existence altogether. Patients who qualify often don't even know help is available, while those who try to apply face mountains of paperwork, confusing requirements, and outright denials. Instead of providing relief, these policies are designed to remain unused—allowing hospitals to claim compliance while continuing to pursue aggressive debt-collection practices against the very people the policies are meant to protect.

As described in the Joe hypothetical above, hospitals routinely exploit practices like facility fees—charges tacked onto bills for services that were once provided at lower-cost outpatient clinics. These fees, justified as necessary to support hospital infrastructure, are now applied to routine doctor visits and telehealth appointments, driving up costs without adding value and leading to further corporatization and consolidation of the industry. Some hospital systems have also been found upcoding, or billing for more expensive procedures than were actually performed, inflating costs for insurers and self-funded employers alike.

Another egregious practice is preventable admissions or tests—unnecessary procedures and hospital stays that are performed simply because they generate revenue. Studies have shown that "overutilization" of services, such as unnecessary cardiac stents or back surgeries, contributes billions to healthcare costs annually while exposing patients to needless risks. We often fault individuals with "overutilization" of the healthcare system and introduce things like co-pays or co-insurance to reduce use of services in the name of efficiency. But this is small peanuts when it comes to both the financial and human cost associated with treating a human's spine like a revenue-generating object.

And finally, relentless hospital consolidations. Over the last decade, mergers and acquisitions have created monopolistic systems that dominate local markets, and increasingly larger cross-regional

CHAPTER 4

markets. When hospitals consolidate, prices rise—often by 20% to 50%—while the quality of care stagnates or declines. Patients have fewer choices, purchasers of healthcare lose negotiating power, and communities lose their local hospitals, replaced by sprawling systems that prioritize profits over care.

These aren't just bad business practices; they're decisions with devastating human consequences. Families are being bankrupted by bills they thought their insurance would cover. Patients are being cut open for surgeries they didn't need. And while your local children's hospital sends home pledge cards for donations, it's sitting on billions in reserves, suing families for unpaid bills, and charging different prices for the same service based on the insurance card in your wallet.

Hospitals are a cornerstone of our healthcare system, and they do save lives. But the public needs to understand the truth about how a majority of the systems operate today—how they exploit loopholes, abuse their non-profit status, and consolidate power to the detriment of patients and the broader healthcare market.

This chapter will pull back the curtain on the modern hospital system. We'll dive into how hospitals generate and protect revenue, the consequences for patients and employers, and the policies that enable this dysfunction. By the end, you'll see why hospitals are both essential and one of the greatest contributors to the unaffordability of American healthcare. It's time to understand the full cost of our hospitals—not just in dollars, but in the lives they impact.

Chapter 5

THE NON-PROFIT MYTH

To understand the modern hospital system, it helps to start with a question: why are so many hospitals classified as non-profits? The answer lies in a series of decisions made decades ago, when the role of hospitals in American society was vastly different.

In the mid-20th century, hospitals were viewed as charitable institutions, deeply embedded in their communities. Most were small, independent facilities often affiliated with religious organizations or civic groups, operating on modest budgets to meet the basic medical needs of their local populations. They relied heavily on donations and philanthropy to keep their doors open and served as a safety net for those who couldn't afford care.

In exchange for their charitable mission, these hospitals were granted tax-exempt status. They were exempt from federal income taxes and often from state and local property taxes as well. The reasoning was simple: these institutions were providing a public good, offering free or reduced-cost care to the needy and improving community health. By removing the tax burden, the government could ensure that more resources were directed toward patient care rather than administrative costs.

The charitable model worked—at least for a time. But as the American healthcare system grew more complex and profitable, hospitals began to shift away from their charitable roots. Advances in medical technology, changes in insurance models, and the increasing demand for healthcare services transformed hospitals into economic powerhouses. By the late 20th century, many non-profit hospitals had grown into sprawling systems with significant financial reserves, sophisticated billing departments, and corporate-style leadership.

Despite this evolution, the tax exemptions remained. Hospitals continued to enjoy the benefits of being classified as non-profits, even as their operations began to look more like those of for-profit corporations. The original bargain—that tax exemptions would fund community care—started to erode.

Today, non-profit hospitals make up nearly 60% of all hospitals in the United States, controlling the majority of the system's resources. Many non-profit hospitals operate more like profit-maximizing corporations than charitable institutions. The financial benefits of their tax-exempt status are staggering. In 2021 alone, non-profit hospitals received an estimated $37.4 billion in tax exemptions. To put this in perspective, this figure exceeds the total combined spending of major federal programs like Medicare and Medicaid disproportionate share hospital (DSH) payments, which provide supplemental funding to hospitals serving a disproportionate number of low-income patients.

These tax benefits include $11.5 billion in federal income tax savings, $9.1 billion in state sales tax exemptions, and $7.8 billion in property tax breaks. The value of these exemptions has grown by 45% over the past decade, from $19 billion in 2011 to $37.4 billion in 2021. This increase far outpaces inflation, reflecting the rising profitability of hospitals and the growing value of their assets.

Yet the benefits of tax exemption are not distributed evenly. A small group of hospitals—just 7%—accounts for half of all tax benefits nationwide. In states like Massachusetts, hospitals receive an average of $159,464 in tax benefits per bed, compared to just $25,098 per bed in Delaware. These disparities highlight the concentration of resources in larger, wealthier institutions, leaving smaller communities with fewer benefits.

THE DISCONNECT BETWEEN TAX BENEFITS AND CHARITY CARE

While hospitals claim their tax exemptions are justified by the community benefits they provide, the reality is often far different. In 2020, non-profit hospitals spent approximately $16 billion on charity care—less than half the value of their tax exemptions that year. This discrepancy underscores a troubling reality: taxpayers are subsidizing these institutions, but the public is not receiving proportional benefits in return. Instead of reinvesting these funds into patient care, many hospitals prioritize capital projects, marketing, and executive compensation under the guise of "community investment." While hospitals claim their tax exemptions are justified by the community benefits they provide, the reality is often far different.

At the federal level, the tax-exempt status of non-profit hospitals costs U.S. taxpayers an estimated $28 billion per year in foregone federal, state, and local tax revenue. But what often gets overlooked is how much these exemptions impact local taxpayers—particularly school districts, municipalities, and county governments that rely on property taxes to fund essential public services.

Unlike for-profit businesses, non-profit hospitals do not pay property taxes, which means cities and towns that host large hospital systems lose out on millions of dollars in potential revenue. This can be devastating for local budgets, particularly for school districts that depend on property tax revenue to fund teacher salaries, classroom resources, and infrastructure improvements.

One of the most significant legal challenges to hospital tax exemptions in recent years came from public school districts in Pennsylvania, which sued Tower Health over its property tax exemptions. The districts argued that Tower Health was operating more like a for-profit business than a charitable institution—expanding aggressively, generating revenue, and paying executives millions while failing to provide a meaningful level of charity care.

In 2022, school districts in Berks County, Pennsylvania, filed lawsuits challenging Tower Health's tax-exempt status, arguing that the hospital system's operations did not align with the legal definition of a non-profit. Tower Health, which had acquired multiple hospitals and expanded its footprint rapidly, continued to claim tax exemptions while making business-driven financial decisions, including layoffs, service reductions, and even closing hospitals in communities that relied on them.

The lawsuit highlighted a growing frustration among local governments: hospitals were reaping the benefits of tax-free status while starving municipalities and schools of critical funding. Without hospital property tax contributions, school districts were left with two options—raise property taxes on homeowners and small businesses to make up the shortfall or cut educational programs. In Berks County, the school districts estimated they were losing millions in revenue every year due to the hospital's tax-exempt status.

The Tower Health case is not an isolated incident. Across the country, school districts, cities, and counties have begun challenging hospital tax exemptions, arguing that many so-called "non-profit" hospitals are indistinguishable from their for-profit counterparts. Hospitals continue to generate massive revenue, pay their executives multi-million-dollar salaries, and build state-of-the-art facilities—all while claiming that their tax-exempt status is justified by the community benefits they provide.

This growing tension between hospitals and local governments highlights a fundamental problem: when hospitals do not pay their fair share, local taxpayers are forced to pick up the tab. Property tax revenue funds essential services like schools, fire departments, and infrastructure. When hospitals claim tax exemptions but fail to provide meaningful charity care, communities lose—both through reduced public resources and higher taxes on homeowners and small businesses.

This issue is particularly egregious in regions where hospitals dominate the local economy. In some cities, hospitals are the largest landowners, occupying prime real estate but contributing nothing in property taxes. As they expand, acquiring physician practices, purchasing new buildings, and converting properties to tax-exempt status, they further erode the tax base—shrinking the revenue available for public services while continuing to operate as high-revenue, business-driven enterprises.

Yet hospitals defend these tax exemptions by pointing to the charity care and financial assistance programs they claim to provide. They argue that these programs justify their tax-free status, ensuring that low-income and uninsured patients receive necessary medical care. But in reality, these financial assistance programs are often more illusion than reality, designed to appear generous on paper while remaining inaccessible to many patients in practice.

At the heart of this issue is 501(r), a provision of the Affordable Care Act that legally requires non-profit hospitals to maintain and publicize Financial Assistance Policies (FAPs). In theory, this means that hospitals must provide free or discounted care to low-income patients and ensure they are aware of these programs. But in practice, hospitals often do the bare minimum to comply—or worse, deliberately make it difficult for patients to access assistance.

A 2022 report by the Lown Institute found that many hospitals fail to proactively inform patients of their eligibility for financial assistance and, in some cases, intentionally obscure the application process. Some hospitals bury financial assistance policies deep within their websites, requiring multiple clicks to find them, while others make applications needlessly complex, demanding excessive documentation or setting unreasonably short deadlines for submission. The result? Many eligible patients never complete the process, leaving them to face enormous medical bills that they should never have been charged in the first place.

And the real-world consequences of this failure are devastating.

In North Carolina, an investigation revealed that from 2017 to 2022, hospitals filed 7,517 lawsuits against patients and their families to collect medical debt. Many of these patients were likely eligible for financial assistance but were never informed of their options. Instead, they faced legal actions that resulted in wage garnishments, property liens, and wrecked credit scores. This aggressive debt collection occurred even as these hospitals received over $1.8 billion in tax exemptions, funds that were supposed to be used to support charity care and community health initiatives. (nctreasurer.com)

In New York, a 2023 Community Service Society report found that five state-run hospitals were responsible for over 80% of all medical debt lawsuits filed statewide. Many of the patients targeted in these lawsuits should have qualified for financial assistance under New York's Hospital Financial Assistance Law—but they were never informed, never screened, and never given a chance to apply before being taken to court.

The inconsistency and opacity of financial assistance policies across non-profit hospitals further exacerbate the problem. A study from Dollar For, a patient advocacy organization, found that many hospitals set arbitrary and restrictive eligibility thresholds, impose excessive paperwork requirements, and apply financial aid inconsistently—sometimes denying patients who qualify while approving others in similar financial situations.

Even when financial assistance is available, hospitals often impose restrictive criteria that exclude a significant portion of low-income and working-class patients. While 501(r) does not specify a universal standard for who qualifies, hospitals set their own income thresholds—often capping eligibility at 200-250% of the federal poverty level (FPL). For reference, that means a single person making just $30,000 a year may not qualify for financial assistance at some hospitals, despite struggling with medical debt. In contrast, states like Illinois require hospitals to provide assistance at up to 600% of the FPL—but such generosity is the exception, not the rule.

And even for those who do qualify, charity care often falls short of providing full relief. Some hospitals offer only partial discounts, leaving patients with large balances they still cannot afford. Others apply financial assistance only to certain types of services—hospital-based care, for example—but not to physician charges, lab tests, or specialty treatments. This creates a false sense of security, where patients believe they are covered, only to be blindsided by massive bills from out-of-network providers operating within the same hospital system.

A 2021 study by *JAMA Internal Medicine*, one of the most well-respected publications in the healthcare space, found that some of the largest and most profitable non-profit hospitals provided less charity care, as a percentage of expenses, than even their for-profit counterparts. While these institutions defend their practices by citing their broader "community benefits," much of what they categorize as a benefit—such as unreimbursed Medicaid expenses or medical training costs—serves their own financial interests rather than directly helping patients in need.

Perhaps most troubling is the fact that many patients who should qualify for financial assistance never even apply—because they are never told it exists. A Health Affairs study found that nearly half of the largest non-profit hospitals fail to properly inform patients of their financial assistance programs. Some hospitals provide information only upon direct request, despite the fact that patients—especially those in medical crises—may not even realize they qualify for help.

CHAPTER 5

This lack of transparency creates a perverse scenario where hospitals claim credit for offering charity care while doing everything possible to minimize its use.

It's a system designed to protect the hospital's bottom line, not the patient. And while non-profit hospitals enjoy tax-free status in exchange for their supposed commitment to serving the public, the reality is that many of them function more like corporations, using every available loophole to limit financial assistance while maximizing revenue.

Hospitals that receive billions in tax breaks every year should not be allowed to bankrupt patients for bills that should have been covered under financial assistance policies. And yet, they do—every single day.

Chapter 6

FROM CHARITY TO AGGRESSION

Hospitals often justify their tax-exempt status by pointing to the financial assistance programs they offer, but their actions frequently tell a different story. While they claim to serve the community, many of these same institutions engage in aggressive debt-collection tactics, taking legal action against patients, garnishing wages, and placing liens on homes. A 2021 study found that hospitals across the country regularly sue low-income families over unpaid bills, even when those patients likely should have qualified for financial assistance. In many cases, hospitals either fail to inform patients of their eligibility or make the process so cumbersome that few complete it. Some require extensive documentation, impose tight application deadlines, or fail to notify patients altogether. Even hospitals affiliated with religious organizations, which publicly emphasize their commitment to compassion and service, have been found to pursue legal action against patients struggling to pay their bills.

At the same time, hospitals have become increasingly sophisticated in how they manage revenue collection, either by building their own in-house revenue cycle management (RCM) operations or by outsourcing to specialized firms. RCM firms handle everything from patient billing to collections, using technology and data analytics to optimize revenue. Many hospitals now own or partner with RCM vendors, giving them greater control over debt collection practices and allowing them to extract as much money as possible before writing off bad debt. The goal of these systems is to improve efficiency and ensure hospitals get paid, but in many cases, they have also led to more aggressive and impersonal tactics in collecting unpaid bills.

Hospitals and their RCM vendors use a variety of methods to increase revenue and limit financial assistance payouts. Some rely on automated systems that flag patients more likely to pay under pressure—those with stable incomes, assets, or positive credit histories—then prioritize collections against them. Some pre-load legal filings, mass-filing lawsuits against patients without reviewing individual financial circumstances. Others use billing software that maximizes the likelihood of claim denials, forcing patients to navigate a complex appeals process that many give up on, ultimately paying out of pocket rather than fighting the charges.

In some cases, these systems go beyond routine billing and actively discourage patients from receiving financial assistance. RCM firms have been known to set up processes that automatically deny charity care applications for minor errors, such as missing a single document or failing to submit an application within an arbitrary deadline. Some require extensive documentation proving financial hardship, far beyond what is necessary, effectively weeding out eligible patients through bureaucratic barriers. By making it harder for patients to access assistance in the first place, hospitals can reduce the amount of money they provide in charity care while continuing to claim they offer robust financial assistance programs.

The increasing involvement of private equity in RCM should serve as a warning about where this trend is headed. Private equity firms have been investing heavily in acquiring and consolidating RCM companies, seeing an opportunity to increase profits in the healthcare billing sector. When private equity moves into an industry, it is usually with the goal of maximizing revenue through cost-cutting, automation, and aggressive billing practices. In healthcare, this means tighter collections, more frequent claim denials, and an even greater focus on ensuring that every possible dollar is extracted from patients before a bill is written off.

Private equity-backed RCM firms use predictive analytics and AI-driven models to identify which patients are most likely to pay and pursue them more aggressively, while deprioritizing financial assistance efforts. Some of these firms specialize in finding legal loopholes to keep bills active longer, preventing them from being discharged as bad debt or limiting a patient's ability to negotiate lower payments. Others streamline litigation, allowing hospitals to file thousands of lawsuits in a fraction of the time it would take under traditional legal processes. As private equity firms seek to increase returns on their investments, these tactics are likely to become more widespread, making it even harder for patients to push back against questionable charges or seek relief from medical debt.

CASE STUDY: UCHEALTH AND THE DISGUISED WAR ON PATIENTS

One of the clearest illustrations of this transformation is the University of Colorado Health system (UCHealth), the state's largest nonprofit hospital network. In 2020, UCHealth stopped suing patients under its own name—but not because it reformed its practices. It simply handed the job to third-party collection intermediaries, allowing it to continue aggressive collections without attaching its brand.

Two firms—CollectionCenter Inc. (CCI) and Credit Service Company (CSC)—brought more than 24,000 lawsuits between 2020 and 2023, with the majority filed on UCHealth's behalf. These cases led to over $67 million in principal judgments—nearly 70% of them through default—and thousands of wage and bank account garnishments.

When questioned in a legal deposition, a UCHealth employee gave the real reason for the shift: *"It would be optically bad"* for UCHealth to appear as the plaintiff. The solution wasn't to stop suing—it was to outsource the blame.

Behind the curtain, the harm was staggering. One grieving mother was sued by UCHealth after her baby died at just three weeks old. Another patient, a disabled veteran, was taken to court after the hospital failed to bill his VA insurance. In one of the most harrowing accounts, a father recounted how debt collectors froze his bank account while he was trying to care for his family. *"It's hell,"* he said. *"I almost lost my family."*

Patients often had no idea who was suing them. In fact, 95.6% of CSC's cases had sealed filings, concealing the identity of the original creditor. In others, patients were sued for balances they didn't understand, couldn't validate, or had already paid—yet still owed 8% interest, court fees, and attorney's fees on a $0 balance.

The bills themselves? Often incomprehensible or flat-out wrong. Studies estimate that 80% of medical bills contain errors, and federal officials put annual medical billing fraud at around $100 billion. Yet UCHealth pursued thousands of these debts through the courts as if every charge was accurate and owed.

And the pricing? All over the map. UCHealth charged between $4 and $1,072 for the exact same routine blood test—a 24,700% price difference, depending solely on who you are and how you pay. For patients trying to understand or contest these charges, it was a losing battle.

As one patient put it: *"You can't fight it. If you're broke, you don't have money for an attorney. Everyone just takes it."*

What happened in Colorado is not confined to one hospital system—it is emblematic of a national pattern. As hospitals increasingly embrace private equity-driven revenue strategies and outsource their billing to third-party vendors, these aggressive and opaque tactics are being replicated across the country. UCHealth may have been especially bold in hiding its hand, but the incentives behind its actions are shared by countless other institutions chasing revenue under the guise of charity.

Hospitals now have two paths: they can either build their own in-house RCM systems or outsource the process to private firms—but the result is the same. The financial assistance programs hospitals promote as a justification for their tax-exempt status are often overshadowed by the aggressive collection strategies these RCM operations employ. Many hospitals receive billions in tax breaks every year based on the idea that they serve the public, yet their approach to billing and collections is indistinguishable from that of a for-profit financial institution. The increasing role of private equity only amplifies these concerns, raising serious questions about whether hospitals are truly fulfilling their charitable mission or simply leveraging their tax-exempt status while operating as businesses focused on the bottom line.

Chapter 7

WHERE THE MONEY GOES

Non-profit hospitals, benefiting from tax exemptions intended to support community health, have increasingly directed their resources toward ventures that resemble corporate enterprises more than charitable organizations. A notable example is the significant investment in high-profile advertising campaigns. In February 2025, NYU Langone Health, a prominent non-profit academic medical center in New York City, faced criticism for purchasing a Super Bowl advertisement estimated to cost $8 million. This expenditure drew backlash from healthcare professionals and the public, especially given the financial challenges within the healthcare system. NYU Langone defended the ad as a means to highlight its quality care and medical advancements on a national platform.

Beyond advertising, non-profit hospitals have engaged in substantial international expansions. The University of Pittsburgh Medical Center (UPMC) exemplifies this trend, having invested heavily in overseas projects. In 2019, UPMC entered into a partnership with China's Wanda Group to co-manage several hospitals, starting with a facility in Chengdu. This initiative marked a significant move by a U.S.-based non-profit health system into the Chinese healthcare market.

These international ventures are not limited to China. UPMC has also established a presence in Europe, managing hospitals and cancer centers in countries like Italy and Ireland. While these expansions aim to bring American-style medical care to international markets, they have sparked debate about the allocation of resources by non-profit hospitals. Critics argue that funds derived from tax exemptions, intended to benefit local communities, are instead being used for global expansion projects.

The financial strategies of non-profit hospitals have also come under scrutiny. Reports indicate that some institutions allocate substantial funds toward executive compensation and luxury expenditures. For instance, UPMC reportedly spent $50 million to lease a corporate jet shortly after announcing significant layoffs. This aircraft was utilized for travel to various international locations, including countries where UPMC operates hospitals.

These practices raise questions about the priorities of non-profit hospitals and the true beneficiaries of their financial decisions. While tax exemptions are granted to support community health initiatives, the diversion of funds to advertising, executive perks, and international projects suggests a shift toward corporate-like operations. This trend prompts a reevaluation of how non-profit hospitals balance their financial strategies with their foundational mission to serve local communities.

THE NUMBERS BEHIND CONSOLIDATION

Non-profit hospitals have increasingly been at the forefront of a wave of mergers and acquisitions that has reshaped American healthcare, consolidating power and shrinking competition under the guise of efficiency and improved care. Today, 58% of community hospitals are classified as non-profits, and many have leveraged their tax-exempt status to fuel aggressive expansion efforts. These mergers, often framed as necessary for financial stability or improved patient outcomes, frequently result in monopolistic control, driving up prices

— CHAPTER 7 —

and limiting patient options—all while these institutions continue to claim they exist for the public good.

Non-profit hospitals argue that consolidation is necessary to keep struggling facilities afloat, ensure continuity of care, and invest in new technology. But in reality, consolidation has led to record-high hospital prices, fewer choices for patients, and shrinking access to critical services. Nearly half of U.S. metropolitan areas are now dominated by one or two non-profit hospital systems. A study by the RAND Corporation found that hospitals in these highly consolidated markets charge employers and patients up to three times more than hospitals in competitive markets, with no measurable improvement in quality.

If this trend feels familiar, it should. Just as consolidation in industries like airlines, cable providers, and technology has reduced competition and driven up prices, non-profit hospitals have followed the same playbook—except in healthcare, the consequences are even more dire. When one hospital system controls an entire region, they don't just dictate prices—they dictate who gets care, when, and where.

Patients in these areas may not immediately recognize consolidation's impact, but they feel it. Have you ever noticed that your local hospital has changed names, or that once-independent doctor's offices now carry the branding of a major health system? These are the signs of consolidation at work. In practical terms, it means fewer choices, longer wait times, and higher prices, with hospitals exerting complete control over everything from the cost of a routine scan to whether an emergency surgery is even available in your town.

One of the most insidious effects of non-profit hospital consolidation is the way it removes the ability to "shop around" for care, even when price transparency laws exist. In most industries, consumers faced with high prices can take their business elsewhere. But what happens when all the hospitals, outpatient centers, and specialty clinics in your region are owned by the same system? The illusion of choice disappears. If every hospital within 100 miles is controlled by a single non-profit entity, patients have nowhere to turn.

And it's not just hospitals. Many of these same non-profit systems have acquired physician groups, imaging centers, and outpatient surgical facilities, extending their reach well beyond hospital walls. The result is that even if you try to seek care outside the hospital, the prices and billing structures are still dictated by the dominant system. Independent physicians are being pressured to join large non-profit hospital networks, knowing that staying independent means being locked out of referral networks or facing financial struggles.

And it's not just prices that are affected. Once a non-profit hospital system dominates a region, it controls hiring, staffing levels, service availability, and even which treatments are prioritized. Entire departments are being shut down, leaving communities without maternity wards, trauma centers, or full-service emergency rooms. It's why, despite record profits and rising executive salaries, rural hospitals are closing at alarming rates, and urban hospitals are cutting services while expanding their real estate footprint.

Hospitals will argue that consolidation leads to greater efficiency, improved patient care, and better access to services. They claim that by merging with smaller hospitals, they can streamline operations, eliminate redundancies, and invest in cutting-edge technology that would otherwise be out of reach for independent facilities. Larger systems point to economies of scale, stating that a larger footprint allows them to negotiate better rates with suppliers, hire top-tier specialists, and provide better coordination of care across different sites.

On the surface, this argument seems logical. If consolidation truly led to greater efficiency and lower costs, patients and employers would see savings reflected in their medical bills. If larger systems were truly focused on patient-centered care, they wouldn't be closing maternity wards, cutting staff, or reducing services in the very communities they claim to serve. But the reality is that these cost savings rarely, if ever, make their way to patients. Instead, non-profit hospital systems use their market dominance to raise prices—not lower them.

Hospitals also claim that large health systems provide a better patient experience, offering seamless access to specialists, more comprehensive treatment options, and the latest medical advancements. But that argument also falls apart when examined more closely. Patients in consolidated markets often face longer wait times for appointments, fewer options for care, and even increased travel times to receive certain treatments. When non-profit hospitals acquire independent physician practices, they frequently reclassify them as "hospital outpatient departments," allowing them to charge hospital-level facility fees for routine office visits. This means patients who once paid a lower rate at their doctor's office suddenly face a much higher bill—overnight.

It's also worth acknowledging that not every hospital merger results in worse outcomes—there are always exceptions. Some non-profit hospital systems may reinvest cost savings into patient care, expand services in underserved areas, or genuinely strive for efficiency without prioritizing financial gain over community health. But the vast majority of consolidations do not play out this way. The prevailing trend in non-profit hospital consolidation is that patients, employers, and communities end up paying more, while these institutions expand their financial and political power.

Despite hospitals' public justifications for consolidation, the data does not support their claims of efficiency, affordability, or improved care. The fundamental issue is that when non-profit hospitals merge, they gain pricing power, not operational efficiency. They don't use their size to drive costs down—they use it to charge more, negotiate harder with insurers, and ensure that patients have nowhere else to go. The result is a system that rewards size over service, dominance over competition, and financial gain over the very patients these institutions claim to serve.

Non-profit hospital systems continue to expand under the assumption that their tax-exempt status protects them from the scrutiny faced by traditional corporations. But in any other industry, a consolidation trend of this magnitude would spark regulatory intervention. In healthcare, despite overwhelming evidence that consolidation raises costs without improving quality, we continue to watch it unfold as though it were inevitable.

So next time you're driving through town and notice another hospital rebranded under a larger system, or hear about a "strategic partnership" between once-independent facilities, ask yourself: what does this actually mean for patients? Because while non-profit hospitals frame these mergers as necessary for stability, the real outcome is clear—fewer choices, higher prices, and a healthcare system that increasingly operates more like a private enterprise than a charitable institution.

Chapter 8

A BROKEN CONTRACT

The social contract that once justified tax exemptions for non-profit hospitals is broken. These institutions are no longer the modest, service-oriented providers they were intended to be. Instead, they operate as billion-dollar enterprises, exploiting their tax-exempt status to pad their bottom lines while providing minimal benefits to their communities.

This systemic failure is not just a matter of mismanagement—it is a deliberate strategy. By prioritizing revenue over service, non-profit hospitals have eroded the trust placed in them by the public. The $37.4 billion in annual tax benefits they receive could have been used to fund public programs, improve infrastructure, or lower the tax burden on working families. Instead, these funds are subsidizing corporate expansion, executive compensation, and aggressive billing practices that harm the very communities these hospitals claim to serve.

Understanding the extent of this disconnect is essential to addressing the broader healthcare crisis. By exposing the financial realities behind the "non-profit" label, we can begin to hold these institutions accountable and demand a system that prioritizes care over profit.

Chapter 9

CASE STUDY: ASCENSION HEALTH – A SACRED MISSION OR CORPORATE AMBITION?

Ascension Health, the largest Catholic hospital system in the United States, often portrays itself as a ministry, guided by its mission to care for the poor and vulnerable. Its mission statement, rooted in the values of compassion and justice, declares: "We are advocates for a compassionate and just society through our actions and our words." Yet beneath this veneer of altruism lies a sprawling, profit-driven enterprise that has become synonymous with aggressive financial strategies, Wall Street-like investment practices, and relentless cost-cutting measures—all at the expense of the communities it purports to serve.

THE PRIVATE EQUITY TURN

In 2015, Ascension took a dramatic turn by partnering with TowerBrook Capital Partners, a private equity firm, to create TCP-ASC, an investment vehicle aimed at pursuing aggressive business strategies. Their first move? A $200 million investment in Accretive

Health, a debt-collection company that had been on the brink of collapse due to allegations of Medicare fraud and lawsuits over illegal billing practices. Minnesota's attorney general had previously banned Accretive from operating in the state for two years after uncovering its attempts to collect money from patients while they were still in the emergency room.

With Ascension's financial lifeline, Accretive rebranded itself as R1 RCM and became the exclusive billing and debt-collection partner for all Ascension facilities. By 2019, Ascension had earned $500 million from its investment in R1, highlighting the stark contrast between its charitable rhetoric and its willingness to profit from a company accused of exploiting vulnerable patients.

SPINNING OFF PROFIT

Ascension's foray into private equity didn't stop there. One of its more audacious moves involved TriMedx, an internal department originally created to manage Ascension's medical equipment and technology needs. Over time, TriMedx grew into a highly profitable entity, prompting Ascension to spin it off into a standalone for-profit company, serving not just its hospitals but over 1,800 healthcare providers across 28 states.

This transition allowed Ascension to monetize its own operational needs, turning what began as a non-profit resource into a revenue-generating enterprise. Critics have noted the ethical implications of using tax-exempt resources to build for-profit ventures, further blurring the lines between Ascension's stated mission and its corporate ambitions.

THE CAYMAN ISLANDS AND CUTS TO SAFETY NETS

Perhaps one of the most striking examples of Ascension's profit-driven priorities came in 2019, when it established a $1 billion private equity fund in the Cayman Islands. This move came as Ascension was facing criticism for closing unprofitable business lines, including a maternity ward in Washington, D.C., that served a vulnerable population. The juxtaposition of transferring resources offshore while cutting essential services highlights the system's prioritization of financial returns over community health.

EXECUTIVE PAY AND STAFFING CUTS

Ascension's leadership has also been a lightning rod for criticism. Former CEO Anthony Tersigni and his successor, Joseph Impicciche, both earned salaries exceeding $10 million annually—among the highest for non-profit hospital executives in the nation. At the same time, the *New York Times* revealed that Ascension had slashed $500 million in labor costs just before the COVID-19 pandemic, leaving hospitals understaffed during a time of critical need. Nurses were forced to work 16-hour shifts, and some were replaced entirely by automation, a move that boosted Ascension's profits but further strained its already overwhelmed workforce.

THE HUMAN COST OF "MISSION-DRIVEN" PRACTICES

Despite its claims of compassion and justice, Ascension has pursued aggressive debt-collection practices that disproportionately affect the poor. Policies at some facilities allow for the denial of non-emergency care to patients with outstanding medical debt. Meanwhile, a recent investigation revealed that Ascension maintained written guidelines allowing it to sue patients, garnish wages, and place liens on homes—practices that starkly contradict its mission to serve the vulnerable.

CONSOLIDATION AND MARKET POWER

Ascension's strategy of acquiring hospitals and clinics has also concentrated market power, allowing it to charge higher prices while eliminating competition. In many communities, Ascension is the dominant healthcare provider, leaving employers and patients with few alternatives. This consolidation has contributed to skyrocketing healthcare costs, with little evidence of improved care quality.

A DARK CHAPTER IN MODERN HEALTHCARE

Ascension's story is emblematic of a larger crisis in the U.S. healthcare system. While claiming the moral high ground as a non-profit, religious institution, it operates like a for-profit corporation, exploiting tax breaks, engaging in aggressive investment strategies, and prioritizing financial returns over patient care. Its actions have not only undermined its stated mission but have also deepened the financial and healthcare disparities in the communities it serves.

Ascension's practices raise an uncomfortable question: how long can institutions like these hide behind the shield of non-profit status while behaving like Wall Street firms? As we examine the broader role of hospitals in America's healthcare crisis, Ascension serves as a cautionary tale—a stark reminder that unchecked power and profit motives can erode even the most sacred missions.

Chapter 10

CASE STUDY: ADVOCATE HEALTH

Advocate Health, born from the 2022 merger of Advocate Aurora Health and Atrium Health, has positioned itself as a behemoth in American healthcare, now spanning six states and generating over **$27 billion** in annual revenue. But beneath its branding as a community-centered, non-profit institution lies a record of practices that prioritize financial gain over patient care, exposing the system as one of the more egregious examples of how non-profit hospitals operate today.

SUING PATIENTS INTO FINANCIAL RUIN

Despite its stated mission to serve communities and vulnerable populations, Advocate has faced repeated criticism for its aggressive debt-collection tactics. In North Carolina, Atrium Health (now part of Advocate Health) has been identified as one of the state's most litigious healthcare providers, suing patients over unpaid medical bills—even those who were likely eligible for financial assistance.

A 2021 investigation by *Kaiser Health News* revealed that Atrium filed thousands of lawsuits against patients in North Carolina courts over medical debt, pursuing wage garnishments and liens on homes. These lawsuits disproportionately targeted low-income patients, leaving many families financially devastated. One particularly egregious case involved a single mother of two who was sued over a $1,200 medical bill, ultimately leading to garnished wages that left her unable to afford rent. These aggressive collection practices, while legal, contradict the principles of care and compassion that Advocate claims to uphold as a non-profit organization.

CHARITY CARE: A HOLLOW PROMISE

Non-profit hospitals like Advocate enjoy substantial tax benefits, ostensibly in exchange for providing charity care and other community benefits. However, studies have shown that Advocate spends a shockingly small percentage of its revenue on charity care compared to its tax-exempt peers. A 2022 report by the Lown Institute ranked Advocate Aurora among the worst offenders in the nation, noting that its spending on charity care and community benefits fell far short of the estimated value of its tax exemptions.

According to the report, Advocate Aurora's charity care amounted to less than **2% of its total** operating expenses—a figure that pales in comparison to the billions it saves annually through tax exemptions. In one egregious example, Advocate Aurora received over $400 million in tax benefits in 2020 while providing a fraction of that amount in charity care. Critics argue that this disparity undermines the very purpose of granting tax-exempt status to non-profit hospitals.

SPORTS SPONSORSHIPS AND MISPLACED PRIORITIES

While Advocate Health claims to prioritize community health, its spending decisions suggest otherwise. Instead of investing in underserved populations or expanding access to care, Advocate has poured resources into high-profile sponsorships, including partnerships with professional sports teams. One such example is its sponsorship of the Milwaukee Bucks, which includes having its name and branding prominently displayed on the team's jerseys. These types of expenditures raise questions about how Advocate allocates its resources and whether its priorities align with its stated mission.

Sponsoring sports teams is not an isolated incident for Advocate. These high-profile marketing deals, while boosting the system's visibility, divert funds that could be used for patient care or community investment. At a time when patients are being sued for unpaid bills and communities are grappling with healthcare disparities, such sponsorships feel especially tone-deaf.

A PATTERN OF BAD BEHAVIOR

Advocate's practices are emblematic of a broader issue within the American healthcare system: the corporatization of non-profit hospitals. By focusing on financial performance, market dominance, and brand-building, systems like Advocate Health have strayed far from their charitable roots. Their actions—whether suing low-income patients, under-delivering on charity care, or sponsoring luxury sports teams—reveal a disturbing misalignment between their stated missions and their operational priorities.

Chapter II

UPMC CASE STUDY

UPMC, the largest healthcare provider in Pennsylvania and one of the most prominent non-profit health systems in the U.S., has transformed into a behemoth that operates less like a charitable organization and more like a profit-driven monopoly. Its staggering growth, aggressive consolidation, questionable business practices, and executive excesses paint a damning portrait of a healthcare giant exploiting its non-profit status while failing to deliver on its promises to communities, employees, and patients. Here's a closer look at some of the most shocking aspects of UPMC's operations.

A MONOPOLY IN THE MAKING

In the last decade, UPMC has expanded from 12 hospitals to a sprawling network of 40 hospitals with 8,800 licensed beds, 4.5 million insurance enrollees, and 92,000 employees. This consolidation has not only given UPMC immense market dominance in Western Pennsylvania but also effectively eliminated meaningful competition. Communities that once had choices in healthcare now find themselves at the mercy of a single provider—a provider that sets the terms for prices, access, and quality.

This dominance has also had dire consequences for workers and patients. With no competition to hold it accountable, UPMC has prioritized expansion and profit over staffing and care quality. Reports from UPMC staff describe emergency rooms operating as de facto inpatient units because there simply aren't enough staffed beds in the hospital. Nurses and aides are overworked, morale is plummeting, and patients are paying the price with delayed care and poor outcomes.

PRIVATE JETS, OFFSHORE CALL CENTERS, AND EXECUTIVE EXCESS

UPMC's leadership seems to live in an alternate reality, one far removed from the struggles of its workers and patients. In 2023, CEO Leslie C. Davis took home more than $10 million in compensation, while her predecessor, Jeffrey Romoff, who retired in 2021, continued to earn millions annually in deferred compensation—$18 million in 2023 alone.

Meanwhile, UPMC executives travel on a $50 million Bombardier Global 6500 private jet, adorned in the health system's signature purple livery. In 2024, this jet was used for trips to Boca Raton, Florida, the headquarters of Omega Healthcare, a company that UPMC has outsourced call center operations to, and destinations like Rome and Dublin, where UPMC maintains clinics. At the same time, UPMC has laid off local employees, replacing them with offshore workers in the Philippines—workers who handle sensitive patient data amid concerns about HIPAA compliance and service quality.

AGGRESSIVE COST-CUTTING AMIDST BILLION-DOLLAR PROFITS

Despite boasting over $1 billion in annual excess revenue, UPMC has relentlessly cut costs at the expense of its employees and patients. During the COVID-19 pandemic, UPMC slashed nurse and aide positions, leaving remaining staff to work 16-hour shifts and leading to severe burnout. In parallel, the system engaged consulting giant McKinsey & Co. to devise additional cost-cutting measures, which included reducing managerial roles and freezing hiring for critical positions.

The irony of these cuts is stark when contrasted with UPMC's simultaneous $1.5 billion expansion of its flagship UPMC Presbyterian Hospital in Oakland. While executives celebrated their growing empire, frontline workers and patients were left to bear the brunt of understaffing and deteriorating care quality.

THE BURDEN ON PATIENTS

Patients, too, are caught in UPMC's profit-driven practices. A common complaint involves facility fees, arbitrary charges tacked onto routine services simply because they're performed in a hospital-owned facility. For instance, Ron Kaplan, a UPMC patient, reported that his routine blood work cost $160 more at UPMC than at his previous primary care provider, with no discernible difference in service quality.

Adding insult to injury, patients have found themselves dealing with outsourced customer service representatives who are often ill-equipped to address their concerns. These interactions leave patients feeling frustrated and underserved by a system that is supposed to prioritize their health.

FAILING COMMUNITIES WHILE EXPANDING GLOBALLY

UPMC has invested heavily in international clinics in locations like Dublin, Rome, and even Kazakhstan. Yet back home, it has shuttered hospitals and services in rural and underserved areas, citing unprofitability. For example, maternity wards and safety-net hospitals in Washington, D.C., and Milwaukee, Wisconsin, have been closed in recent years. These closures disproportionately harm vulnerable populations, forcing patients to travel long distances for care or forgo it altogether.

NON-PROFIT IN NAME ONLY

Despite its non-profit status, UPMC's behavior aligns more closely with that of a for-profit corporation. It avoids paying property taxes on $1.7 billion worth of real estate, depriving local governments of crucial revenue while spending $37 million annually on marketing. For context, in 2021, the City of Pittsburgh sought only $14 million in annual property taxes from UPMC—less than CEO Romoff's deferred compensation.

Additionally, UPMC ranks near the bottom of U.S. hospitals in community investment, according to the Lown Institute. While it claims its profits are reinvested into patient care and community programs, its actual spending on charity care remains shockingly low compared to its immense financial resources.

Chapter 12

THE STEWARD HEALTH CARE COLLAPSE

THE RISE: BOLD AMBITION OR RECKLESS EXPANSION?

In 2010, Steward Health Care emerged as a phoenix from the ashes of Caritas Christi, a struggling Catholic non-profit hospital chain in Massachusetts. Cerberus Capital Management, a private equity giant, acquired the chain, pledging $895 million for debt repayment, infrastructure improvements, and pension stabilization. At the helm was Dr. Ralph de la Torre, a Harvard-educated cardiac surgeon turned CEO, who articulated an ambitious vision: "We will prove community hospitals can thrive in a competitive healthcare market," he declared in 2013. *(Modern Healthcare)*

Initially, the strategy appeared promising. Steward expanded aggressively, acquiring hospitals nationwide. By 2024, it operated 33 hospitals across nine states and held international contracts in Malta and Colombia. Yet the warning signs were there: rapid acquisitions outpaced operational capacity, and profitability took a backseat to expansion. "We were buying hospitals faster than we could manage them," a former Steward executive admitted. *(Boston Globe)*

THE REAL ESTATE GAMBIT

In 2016, Steward Health Care entered into a pivotal "sale-leaseback" agreement with Medical Properties Trust (MPT), a real estate investment trust (REIT) specializing in healthcare properties. Under this arrangement, MPT acquired nine Steward hospitals for $1.2 billion—an astonishing figure nearly nine times the properties' assessed market value. While this deal provided an immediate cash infusion, Steward forfeited ownership of its hospital buildings and committed to leasing them back from MPT at exorbitant rates. The annual lease payments amounted to 75% of the original purchase price of the properties.

"This deal was a financial death sentence," said economist James Henry. "Steward forfeited its most valuable assets—its real estate—while locking itself into unsustainable rent obligations." *(Boston Globe)*

MPT's involvement in Steward Health Care went far beyond that of a typical landlord. While sale-leasebacks are often marketed as a mutually beneficial arrangement, the structure of the deal between MPT and Steward revealed troubling conflicts of interest and predatory practices.

After acquiring nine Steward hospitals in 2016 for $1.2 billion—nearly nine times their assessed market value—MPT locked Steward into leases with exorbitant annual payments. The inflated purchase price not only justified these high rents but also boosted MPT's own earnings and shareholder value. As Steward struggled to meet its rent obligations, MPT provided "bridge loans" to the hospital chain, effectively creating a circular debt structure. Steward used these loans to pay rent back to MPT, perpetuating a cycle that made the hospitals appear profitable on paper while sinking Steward deeper into insolvency.

"MPT behaved less like a landlord and more like an enabler," said Rob Simone, an analyst at Hedgeye. "They lent Steward money to pay

CHAPTER 12

back rent, inflating MPT's earnings while dooming Steward's financial future." (Hedgeye)

The relationship between MPT and Steward blurred the lines of independence expected between landlords and tenants. Documents revealed that MPT's loans and financial dealings with Steward were not always disclosed to shareholders or regulators, raising questions about compliance with securities laws. Senator Elizabeth Warren was among those who expressed outrage, calling the arrangement "a textbook example of profiteering at the expense of public health." In a scathing letter to MPT in 2024, Warren likened the setup to a Ponzi scheme, stating, "MPT and Steward plundered these hospitals for profit, leaving communities in healthcare deserts." (Letter to MPT, 2024)

MPT's dealings with Steward exemplify a broader issue in the healthcare industry, where real estate investment trusts (REITs) increasingly play a significant—and controversial—role. Critics argue that REITs, like MPT, prioritize maximizing shareholder returns over preserving hospitals' financial viability or community access to care. These landlords benefit from inflated real estate valuations, but the long-term impact on hospitals and the communities they serve can be devastating.

"Once the hospital no longer owns the property, they lose not just control, but also the flexibility to weather financial challenges," explained Rosemary Batt, co-author of Private Equity at Work. "These deals create conditions where hospitals are forced to divert limited resources away from patient care just to meet rent obligations."

For Steward, the consequences were catastrophic. The crushing lease payments to MPT drained resources that could have gone toward staffing, facility maintenance, or improving patient outcomes. Instead, MPT and executives enriched themselves while communities suffered, with hospitals shutting their doors and leaving underserved areas without essential healthcare access.

"This wasn't healthcare investment—it was plundering," a critic testified during Senate hearings. (Senate testimony)

EXECUTIVE EXCESS: PROFITS FOR THE FEW, CHAOS FOR THE MANY

As Steward hospitals struggled, its executives thrived. Dr. Ralph de la Torre, the CEO of Steward, enjoyed a salary of $16 million annually—nearly 30 times the average salary of a nurse in his hospitals. His lavish lifestyle included two yachts, a $40 million luxury fishing boat, a $62 million private jet (with a backup jet for personal use), and an $8.8 million Madrid residence, purchased with company funds. In 2016, de la Torre personally received a $73 million dividend, part of the staggering $1.2 billion extracted during the sale-leaseback deal with Medical Properties Trust (MPT). Over the years, he and other executives reaped hundreds of millions more through questionable dividend payouts and loans disguised as "executive compensation."

"While we rationed medical supplies, Dr. de la Torre was flying on private jets and buying yachts," said a former nurse at a Massachusetts hospital. (*Boston Globe*) These excesses fueled public outrage, especially as Steward hospitals fell into disrepair, with reports of broken equipment, delayed surgeries, and patients dying from neglect due to resource shortages.

Steward's bankruptcy filings revealed over $9 billion in total liabilities, including nearly $1 billion in unpaid medical supply bills. "It's unfathomable that a hospital system in such financial distress would prioritize executive excess over patient care," remarked one witness during Senate testimony. (Senate testimony)

The situation culminated in a Senate subpoena for de la Torre, demanding answers about Steward's practices and his role in the chain's collapse. He refused to testify, citing ongoing bankruptcy proceedings—a move widely criticized as an attempt to evade accountability.

Senator Bernie Sanders excoriated de la Torre during a Senate hearing: "You became obscenely wealthy while patients died from neglect and staff worked in deplorable conditions. That's not just unethical—it's criminal." (Senate testimony) Sanders also pointed out the incongruity of Steward's executives enjoying luxury while hospitals serving vulnerable communities, such as Carney Hospital in Boston's immigrant-rich Dorchester neighborhood, were forced to close their doors.

The broader financial practices of Steward only deepened the scandal. Internal emails revealed executives discussing "secret decoder ring" accounting methods to obscure payouts and hide financial mismanagement from auditors. One executive quipped about loan repayments to de la Torre: "Thanks on the 500. I doubt you will be getting it back anytime soon."

Steward's excesses stand as a stark reminder of how misaligned priorities in for-profit healthcare can devastate communities. As one nurse put it, "We were left to mop up the blood while the CEO sailed off into the sunset." (*Boston Globe*)

THE HUMAN TOLL: NEGLECT AND SUFFERING

The collapse of Steward Health Care wreaked havoc on the lives of countless individuals, exposing the devastating consequences of prioritizing profits over people. The once-vital hospitals left in its wake were plagued by deteriorating conditions that endangered patients and demoralized healthcare workers.

At Carney Hospital in Boston's Dorchester neighborhood—a critical lifeline for the local immigrant and low-income population—patients faced unimaginable hardships. Broken medical equipment, outdated technology, and supply shortages became the norm. Stretchers went unrepaired, drinking water was rationed, and patients were left waiting hours for care. "The hospital was falling apart around us," said a nurse who worked there for over a decade. "We couldn't provide basic care, let alone meet emergency needs." (*Boston Globe*)

The tragedies were all too real. In one particularly harrowing case, **Sungida Rashid**, a new mother, bled to death after childbirth because the hospital lacked the necessary equipment to stop her bleeding. The critical device had been repossessed due to Steward's failure to pay its vendors. Rashid's death sent shockwaves through the community and became a rallying cry for accountability. "She should still be here today. Her death was preventable," said her grieving husband. (Senate testimony)

Similar horror stories unfolded across Steward facilities. An internal investigation by the *Boston Globe* found that 15 patients died and more than a dozen were injured in just one year due to neglect, staff shortages, or lack of resources. These included delays in surgeries, failure to administer critical medications, and preventable infections. "Patients paid the ultimate price for executive greed," said a former doctor at Nashoba Valley Medical Center. (*Boston Globe*)

The toll on healthcare workers was equally devastating. Nurses and doctors reported working in what they described as "war-zone conditions," forced to ration supplies, reuse disposable equipment, and forgo proper rest due to chronic understaffing. "I was seeing three times as many patients as was safe," said a nurse from Good Samaritan Medical Center in Brockton, Massachusetts. "We were overworked, overwhelmed, and powerless to advocate for our patients because the system was designed to fail them." (*Boston Globe*)

The emotional burden of witnessing such suffering became unbearable for many. Reports of burnout and mental health crises among healthcare staff surged. "We entered this profession to save lives, but under Steward, it felt like we were set up to fail," shared an ICU nurse from Morton Hospital. *(Boston Globe)*

Communities bore the brunt of the fallout. The closure of Nashoba Valley Medical Center in rural Ayer, Massachusetts, created a healthcare desert, forcing residents to travel long distances for basic medical care. For Carney Hospital, the loss left an already underserved immigrant population without access to critical services. "These hospitals weren't just buildings; they were lifelines," said a local activist. "Now those lifelines are gone, and people are dying as a result." (Senate testimony)

The financial strain on families was equally dire. Steward's mismanagement led to skyrocketing medical bills as patients were charged inflated rates for substandard care. Many families reported being saddled with medical debt they could never repay. One patient, diagnosed with a preventable infection, recounted losing their home after receiving a $70,000 bill for treatment that failed to save their leg. "I trusted the hospital to care for me, not bankrupt me," they said during testimony. *(Boston Globe)*

For many, the betrayal by Steward went beyond the hospitals' collapse—it represented a deeper erosion of trust in the healthcare system. "These were supposed to be places of healing, not profit machines," said one community leader. "The human toll of Steward's greed will be felt for generations." (Senate testimony)

BANKRUPTCY: THE FINAL CHAPTER

By May 2024, Steward Health Care's house of cards collapsed under the weight of its $9 billion in liabilities. The filing listed staggering obligations, including $6.6 billion in rent payments owed to Medical Properties Trust (MPT) and nearly $1 billion in unpaid bills to medical vendors and suppliers. These debts, coupled with mounting losses, made Steward's bankruptcy one of the largest healthcare collapses in U.S. history.

MPT, seeking to shield itself from scrutiny, painted Steward as a victim of adverse market forces, claiming that rising costs and declining revenues left the hospital chain with no options. However, internal documents and creditor testimonies told a different story. Emails revealed that MPT not only extracted exorbitant lease payments but also funneled loans to Steward specifically to cover rent—essentially creating a circular debt scheme that inflated MPT's profits while pushing Steward further into insolvency.

"These leases were never about sustaining healthcare operations," said Rob Simone, an analyst at Hedgeye. "They were financial instruments designed to funnel money to MPT and its investors at the expense of hospitals and patients."

Creditors accused MPT of engaging in "disguised financing," alleging that the REIT's practices violated its legal obligations as a landlord. Bankruptcy attorneys pointed to the inflated property valuations from MPT's sale-leaseback deals as key contributors to Steward's collapse. "This wasn't a healthcare system—it was a financial Ponzi scheme with patients caught in the crossfire," remarked a bankruptcy attorney involved in the case.

For many of the hospitals Steward left behind, the road to recovery remains uncertain. With over 30 facilities up for sale, some communities have been left without any viable healthcare options, further deepening healthcare inequities. "The Steward collapse didn't just bankrupt a company—it devastated communities, families, and the very trust people place in their hospitals," said a former Steward nurse.

CHAPTER 12

WHY STEWARD'S COLLAPSE SHOULD ENRAGE US ALL

The implosion of Steward Health Care is more than a scandal—it's a wake-up call. While Steward made headlines for its egregious mismanagement and executive indulgences, it is not an outlier. It is simply one of the rare cases where the layers of financial manipulation, corporate greed, and operational negligence became too massive to hide. The truth is, what happened at Steward could—and does—happen across the U.S. healthcare system.

Sale-leaseback schemes, bloated executive pay, and the prioritization of profit over patient care are not isolated practices; they are the business model for far too many hospitals, particularly those under private equity ownership. Steward is the warning sign that reveals just how fragile and compromised our healthcare system has become.

Why should you care? Because every patient, every community, and every taxpayer pays the price for these exploitative practices.

- **For patients,** it means worse care, longer wait times, and even preventable deaths as hospitals cut corners to pay the rent.
- **For communities,** it means shuttered hospitals, lost jobs, and the devastating ripple effects of losing critical healthcare infrastructure.
- **For taxpayers and employers,** it means skyrocketing healthcare costs, as the financial burden of corporate greed gets passed along in the form of higher premiums, inflated medical bills, and tax-funded bailouts for failing systems.

This is not just about one hospital chain or one CEO's yachts and jets—it's a systemic issue that drives up the cost of U.S. healthcare while delivering less to the people who need it most.

Steward's collapse erodes more than communities—it erodes the trust that Americans place in their healthcare system. When hospitals are no longer seen as places of healing but as financial playgrounds for investors, we all lose. And the most infuriating part? This isn't an anomaly. It's the predictable outcome of a system that prioritizes profits over patients, balance sheets over bedside care, and greed over public good.

If we don't care, this will keep happening. Steward may have gotten caught with its pants down, but countless other operators continue to profit from the same playbook—quietly siphoning money from a system that is supposed to save lives. The cost isn't just financial; it's human. And until we demand better, we're all footing the bill.

This is your healthcare system. And it's being looted in broad daylight.

Chapter 13

THE CRISIS OF CONSOLIDATION

HOW HOSPITAL MERGERS DRIVE UP PRICES AND REDUCE CARE QUALITY

Hospital consolidation in the United States has profoundly reshaped the healthcare landscape, but the promises of improved efficiency, coordinated care, and better outcomes have largely failed to materialize. Instead, research consistently shows that hospital mergers drive up prices while delivering little, if any, improvement in the quality of care. These dynamics have significant implications for patients, employers, and the overall healthcare system.

Hospital mergers are not a new phenomenon. For decades, health systems have justified these consolidations with grand promises of better care at lower costs. Yet the data tells a different story. For instance, a 2021 analysis found that hospital mergers between entities within the same market led to price increases ranging from 6% to 65% for privately insured patients (Gaynor et al., 2021). Even cross-market mergers—involving hospitals in different geographic regions—have been associated with price hikes of up to 17% (Lewis

& Pflum, 2017). These price increases are not anomalies; they are a consistent pattern.

A 2018 report by the Health Care Cost Institute revealed that inpatient prices rose by 16% over a five-year period in markets dominated by large hospital systems, compared to just 6% in less-consolidated markets. This disparity highlights how dominant health systems use their market power to negotiate higher reimbursement rates from insurers. Such price hikes are typically passed along to employers and patients in the form of higher premiums and out-of-pocket costs, eroding household budgets and employer resources alike.

Increased prices are not limited to inpatient services. Outpatient care, which accounts for a growing share of healthcare spending, is also more expensive in consolidated markets. A study in *Health Affairs* found that prices for common outpatient procedures were 14% higher in highly concentrated markets than in competitive ones. For instance, an MRI scan that might cost $500 in a competitive region could easily surpass $700 in a consolidated market. These increases strain patients who rely on high-deductible health plans, forcing many to delay or forego necessary care due to cost concerns.

Despite claims that mergers result in operational efficiencies and economies of scale, the financial benefits rarely reach patients. A 2020 study from the National Bureau of Economic Research (NBER) found that merged hospitals frequently reduced staffing levels and support services, prioritizing profit margins over patient care. These reductions often lead to longer wait times, reduced access to specialists, and poorer outcomes for patients. For example, in one highly publicized merger in Pennsylvania, patients reported difficulty scheduling timely follow-up appointments due to understaffing, undermining the very care coordination that mergers purportedly aim to improve.

Quality of care also suffers in the wake of hospital mergers. While proponents argue that consolidation enables better integration of services, the evidence is mixed at best. A comprehensive study by Beaulieu et al. (2020) analyzed 246 hospital mergers and found no statistically significant improvements in key quality metrics such as 30-day readmission rates or mortality rates for Medicare patients. Moreover, patient satisfaction scores often declined post-merger, particularly in such areas as communication with nurses and responsiveness to patient needs.

The impact is particularly pronounced in rural and underserved areas, where hospital mergers often eliminate essential services rather than enhance them. Maternity wards, mental health programs, and emergency services are frequently scaled back or closed entirely as health systems prioritize high-revenue service lines like orthopedics or cardiac care. A 2021 analysis by the Chartis Group found that over 130 rural hospitals closed in the preceding decade, with many closures occurring after mergers failed to stabilize finances. This pattern leaves vulnerable communities with diminished access to care, forcing patients to travel long distances for basic medical needs.

The financial toll extends beyond patients. Employers face skyrocketing healthcare costs in highly consolidated markets, limiting their ability to offer competitive benefits and invest in workforce development. A 2022 RAND Corporation study estimated that excessive hospital pricing in consolidated markets costs the U.S. healthcare system over $40 billion annually. These inflated costs contribute to slower wage growth and reduced economic mobility, with small businesses particularly hard-hit. In a survey of small business owners, 42% identified rising healthcare costs as their primary challenge, with many reporting they had to cut jobs or reduce employee benefits to stay afloat.

Policymakers and regulators have started to recognize the dangers of unchecked hospital consolidation, but progress has been slow. While the Federal Trade Commission (FTC) and Department of Justice

(DOJ) have ramped up efforts to scrutinize and block anti-competitive mergers, many deals proceed unchecked. Moreover, reversing the effects of consolidation once it has occurred is exceedingly difficult. Experts argue that stronger antitrust enforcement, along with innovative policies like site-neutral payment reforms, are essential to curbing hospital monopolies and fostering competition.

Hospital consolidation is not merely a business strategy; it profoundly shapes the quality, accessibility, and affordability of healthcare for millions of Americans. Without significant reform, patients and employers will continue to shoulder the financial and human costs of this consolidation wave. To fully grasp the scope of the challenge, it is essential to examine not just local market mergers, but also the rise of sprawling cross-regional hospital systems that operate as empires unto themselves.

CROSS-REGIONAL EMPIRES AND MONOPOLISTIC POWER DYNAMICS

The growth of hospital systems into expansive cross-regional networks has introduced significant monopolistic power dynamics into the healthcare market. These systems leverage their size and geographic reach to dominate markets, negotiate higher prices, and diminish competition, all while framing their expansions as necessary for improving care coordination and financial sustainability. In reality, cross-regional consolidation often results in reduced choices for patients, elevated costs, and a concentration of economic power that undermines market dynamics.

—— CHAPTER 13 ——

THE RISE OF CROSS-REGIONAL HEALTH SYSTEMS

Over the past two decades, large hospital systems have expanded across state lines, creating networks that encompass urban, suburban, and rural areas. This cross-regional expansion often involves acquiring smaller hospitals or merging with other large systems. As a result, the top health systems in the United States now control a significant share of the market. According to a 2021 study by the Health Care Cost Institute, nearly half of all metropolitan areas in the U.S. are now classified as "highly concentrated" hospital markets, as measured by the Herfindahl-Hirschman Index (HHI), a key indicator of market concentration.

These expansive systems wield enormous negotiating power when dealing with insurers, effectively setting the terms for reimbursement rates. Cross-market mergers, in particular, allow hospital systems to use their combined scale to demand higher payments, even in areas where they do not dominate the local market. Research by Lewis and Pflum (2017) demonstrated that cross-market mergers can increase hospital prices by 7% to 10%, compounding the already significant price increases seen in same-market consolidations.

CONSOLIDATION'S IMPACT ON PRICES AND MARKET DYNAMICS

Cross-regional hospital systems benefit from their ability to centralize resources and standardize practices across facilities, but these efficiencies rarely translate into cost savings for patients or employers. Instead, they create monopolistic environments where patients face fewer choices, and insurers are forced to pay higher prices for services. One study found that in regions dominated by large cross-regional systems, hospital prices were 15% to 20% higher than in less consolidated markets (Gaynor et al., 2021).

Further exacerbating this issue, cross-regional systems often implement "must-have" clauses in contracts with insurers, requiring the inclusion of all their facilities in network agreements. This practice leads to increased healthcare costs for employers, insurers, and ultimately, patients. A 2020 analysis published in *Health Affairs* revealed that employers in highly consolidated regions saw their premiums rise by nearly 12% annually, compared to 7% in more competitive markets.

IMPLICATIONS FOR PATIENTS

Patients in regions dominated by cross-regional hospital systems often face restricted access to affordable care. Narrow networks and inflated prices for routine procedures are common in these markets. For instance, an analysis by the RAND Corporation revealed that in states with significant cross-market consolidation, the cost of routine outpatient procedures was 30% higher than the national average. These price hikes disproportionately impact low-income families, who are more likely to forego care due to high out-of-pocket expenses.

Consolidated systems also tend to prioritize high-margin services, such as orthopedic surgery and cardiology, at the expense of essential but less profitable care, like maternity services or mental health programs. Rural hospitals, in particular, often see cuts in critical services after being acquired by large systems, forcing patients to travel long distances for basic care. A 2019 study published in *JAMA* found that maternity care services were eliminated in 12% of rural hospitals that underwent consolidation between 2010 and 2015.

THE BROADER ECONOMIC CONSEQUENCES

The ripple effects of cross-regional consolidation extend beyond healthcare. Higher healthcare costs act as a drag on local economies, reducing disposable income and limiting consumer spending. Employers in highly consolidated regions face increased health benefit costs, which can lead to reduced wage growth and fewer job opportunities. A recent report by the American Hospital Association estimated that excess costs in consolidated markets add $40 billion annually to the U.S. healthcare system, straining families and businesses alike.

Small businesses are particularly vulnerable. In a recent survey by the National Federation of Independent Business, 45% of respondents cited rising healthcare costs as a significant barrier to growth. Many reported scaling back employee benefits or delaying hiring to offset these expenses. "The cost of providing health insurance has become unsustainable," said one small business owner. "We're losing talent to larger companies that can absorb these costs."

ADDRESSING CROSS-REGIONAL MONOPOLIES

Policymakers have started to acknowledge the challenges posed by cross-regional hospital systems. The Federal Trade Commission (FTC) has increased its scrutiny of mergers that create monopolistic dynamics, particularly those involving hospitals with existing regional dominance. Recent lawsuits have highlighted the anti-competitive practices of some health systems, but enforcement remains difficult due to the complexity of undoing completed mergers and the significant resources required to challenge large corporations.

Other potential solutions include strengthening antitrust regulations, promoting price transparency, and reforming payment models to reduce incentives for consolidation. Site-neutral payment policies, which equalize reimbursement rates for similar services regardless of location, could help curb the financial advantages of vertical integration.

Cross-regional hospital empires have reshaped the U.S. healthcare landscape, concentrating power in ways that harm patients, employers, and local economies. While these systems often justify their growth with promises of efficiency and improved care, the evidence overwhelmingly shows that their monopolistic practices lead to higher costs and diminished access to essential services. Addressing these challenges will require bold policy actions and a commitment to fostering competition in the healthcare market.

Chapter 14

SUTTER HEALTH— A CASE STUDY IN ANTICOMPETITIVE PRACTICES

Imagine walking into a marketplace where only one vendor controls nearly all the goods you need. This vendor uses its power to set prices far above what anyone else would charge, blocks competitors from entering, and forces buyers into unfavorable deals. This metaphor mirrors the reality of Sutter Health's dominance in Northern California's healthcare market, as detailed in a 2018 lawsuit filed by the attorney general of California.

Sutter Health, a non-profit healthcare system, grew from a modest collection of hospitals to a regional behemoth controlling 24 hospitals, 35 outpatient centers, and over 5,000 physicians. This scale gave it immense market power, but rather than leveraging this to improve access and affordability, Sutter allegedly used its dominance to stifle competition and inflate prices. Here, we dissect the key practices that led to the state's lawsuit and explore their impact on employers, employees, and the healthcare system.

THE COST OF DOMINANCE

Between 2004 and 2013, hospital prices in California rose by an average of 76%. But at Sutter facilities, prices soared by 113%, far outpacing the state's overall growth. To put this in perspective, imagine grocery prices doubling over a decade—but at your local supermarket chain, they more than triple. The California attorney general's complaint pointed out that these skyrocketing prices were not tied to improved quality of care but were instead driven by Sutter's anticompetitive practices.

For example, Sutter's contracts with health insurers included "all-or-nothing" clauses. These provisions forced insurers to include all Sutter facilities in their networks, even when cheaper or higher-quality alternatives existed nearby. This tactic allowed Sutter to bundle its "must-have" hospitals—those that insurers couldn't exclude because of their reputations or geographic dominance—with less desirable facilities, effectively eliminating any room for negotiation.

THE MECHANICS OF MARKET MANIPULATION

The Attorney General's lawsuit alleged that Sutter's contracts also blocked insurers from steering patients toward lower-cost or higher-quality competitors. For instance, tiered networks—a common tool used to incentivize patients to choose cost-effective care—were off-limits under Sutter's terms. This is akin to a car dealership forbidding customers from test-driving or even considering other brands. By limiting consumer choice, Sutter insulated itself from price competition.

Adding to the opacity, Sutter prohibited insurers from sharing pricing information with employers and patients before services were rendered. Employers, who pay the lion's share of healthcare costs for their workers, were left in the dark about what they were actually buying. Imagine being handed a restaurant bill after dinner without ever seeing a menu—except this bill runs into the tens of thousands of dollars.

THE HUMAN TOLL

For families, the impact of Sutter's practices went beyond abstract percentages. Consider the case of a Sacramento-area teacher who received a $150,000 hospital bill for a routine surgery—an amount that was only discovered after the procedure was completed. This lack of transparency left patients blindsided by costs they had no way of anticipating or avoiding.

Meanwhile, smaller healthcare providers struggled to survive in the shadow of Sutter's dominance. Independent hospitals in Northern California, unable to compete with Sutter's market power and pricing strategies, faced closures or were forced into acquisitions. This consolidation further reduced choices for patients and employers, creating a vicious cycle of rising costs and diminishing options.

A striking example of the financial toll comes from a 2016 study comparing costs in Northern and Southern California. The study found that outpatient cardiology procedures in Southern California cost nearly $18,000 compared to almost $29,000 in Northern California. Similarly, a cesarean delivery in Sacramento cost more than $27,000—nearly double what it cost in Los Angeles or New York. These disparities highlight how Sutter's market power inflated prices for routine medical procedures.

A more recent controversy underscores Sutter's tactics. In 2022, Sutter demanded that employers sign arbitration agreements to resolve disputes. If they refused, employers faced paying 95% of Sutter's full charges for out-of-network care at its facilities. For context, 95% of these charges—based on Sutter's inflated pricing—would be financially devastating for employers and their workers. One health plan representing grocery workers accused Sutter of forcing higher rates, inflating costs that directly impacted union-negotiated health benefits. "The in-network rates at Sutter are already too high, and out-of-network prices are even higher," emphasized Bill Kramer, executive director of the Pacific Business Group on Health.

THE RIPPLE EFFECT ON WAGES AND JOBS

Sutter's inflated pricing didn't just hurt insurers; it had a direct impact on workers and the broader economy. As healthcare premiums rose, employers passed these costs on to employees through higher deductibles, copays, and out-of-pocket maximums. Worse, rising healthcare costs depressed wages. A Harvard study cited in the complaint found that a 10% increase in healthcare premiums leads to a 2-3% reduction in wages. For many families, this meant smaller paychecks and diminished job opportunities, as employers faced higher operating costs.

THE LEGAL FALLOUT

The lawsuit against Sutter was not just about money; it was about breaking the cycle of dominance that stifled competition and hurt Northern California residents. The attorney general's complaint underscored how Sutter's practices violated antitrust laws designed to protect consumers and ensure fair competition. In 2019, Sutter agreed to a $575 million settlement to compensate employers, unions, and others harmed by its practices. The settlement also mandated significant operational changes, including transparency in pricing, limits on out-of-network charges, and an end to "all-or-nothing" contracting deals.

LESSONS FROM SUTTER

Sutter Health's case illustrates how unchecked market power can harm consumers, employers, and the healthcare system as a whole. By blocking competition and raising prices, Sutter turned its dominance into a profit engine at the expense of the very communities it claimed to serve. This case serves as a cautionary tale for policymakers, employers, and patients about the importance of transparency, competition, and accountability in healthcare markets.

The human cost of Sutter's actions is a stark reminder that behind every inflated bill is a person—a parent, a teacher, a worker—struggling to make ends meet. In the end, the Sutter lawsuit is not just a legal battle; it is a rallying cry for a fairer, more transparent healthcare system. By shining a light on these practices, we take the first step toward restoring balance in a marketplace that should prioritize patients over profits.

Chapter 15

HOSPITAL CONSOLIDATIONS ACROSS THE NATION

The story of Sutter Health is just one example of how unchecked hospital consolidation can devastate patients, communities, and local economies. Across the United States, hospital mergers are pitched as opportunities to streamline care, improve efficiency, and lower costs. Instead, they often leave communities grappling with higher bills, reduced access, and heartbreaking consequences for families. Below are stories from across the nation that reveal the profound human toll of hospital consolidations.

ADVOCATE AURORA HEALTH AND ATRIUM HEALTH MERGER

When Advocate Aurora Health merged with Atrium Health in 2022, it created one of the largest hospital systems in the country. But for patients like Beth Jacobson in Milwaukee, the promises of affordability and better care felt like hollow marketing. Beth, a small business owner, saw her family's insurance premiums spike while her plan's network narrowed. Her husband's routine lab work, previously covered, became "out of network" after the merger—leaving the family with an unexpected $1,200 bill. "We were told this would make care more efficient," Beth said. "Instead, it feels like we're paying for their ambition to get bigger."

Meanwhile, the merger's effect rippled into smaller communities. In rural areas served by Advocate Aurora, local clinics shut down, forcing families to drive hours for basic healthcare needs like pediatric checkups or physical therapy. Critics warned that the consolidation prioritized expansion over patient care, leaving vulnerable populations stranded.

PARTNERS HEALTHCARE (MASS GENERAL BRIGHAM)

In Massachusetts, Partners HealthCare (now Mass General Brigham) used its dominance to drive hospital prices in Boston to the highest in the nation. For Jennifer Morales, a public school teacher in a Boston suburb, the impact hit home when her son broke his arm playing soccer. Jennifer's health plan required them to use a Mass General Brigham facility, resulting in a $2,800 bill for a simple ER visit. "I thought insurance was supposed to protect us," she said. "Instead, it feels like we're at the mercy of a monopoly."

Rural Massachusetts hospitals, unable to compete with Mass General Brigham's pricing and market power, faced closures or mergers themselves. This left patients in some areas traveling 50 miles or more for emergency care, further underscoring the disparity created by the system's unchecked consolidation.

UNIVERSITY OF PITTSBURGH MEDICAL CENTER (UPMC)

In Pennsylvania, UPMC's aggressive expansion strategy reshaped healthcare access across the state. Harold Lynch, a Pittsburgh retiree, needed a hip replacement but found himself trapped in a system where UPMC controlled nearly every orthopedic practice. When he discovered that UPMC's prices were double those of an out-of-network provider, his insurance wouldn't cover the alternative. "I saved for retirement, but I didn't save for this," Harold said. "I felt like I had no choice."

In smaller towns, UPMC's dominance meant closures of independent hospitals that couldn't compete. Greene County, for example, lost its local hospital, forcing families like the Thompsons to drive two hours to Pittsburgh for emergency pediatric care when their toddler suffered a severe asthma attack. "Time matters in emergencies," said Emily Thompson, recalling the harrowing drive. "Losing our local hospital put my child's life at risk."

SANFORD HEALTH AND FAIRVIEW HEALTH SERVICES PROPOSED MERGER

Sanford Health's attempted merger with Fairview Health Services in Minnesota raised alarms across the Midwest. Residents in rural towns feared a repeat of Sanford's history in the Dakotas, where smaller hospitals were stripped of essential services. Marla Johnson, a single mother in Willmar, Minnesota, shared how her community lost its maternity ward after a Sanford acquisition years earlier. "I had to drive 75 miles to deliver my baby," Marla said. "If it had been a snowstorm, I don't know what would've happened."

The proposed merger reignited fears of more closures, with local leaders warning that Sanford's history showed a pattern of prioritizing profits over patient needs. "We've seen what happens when they take over," said one local activist. "They cut services, and our communities pay the price."

ASCENSION HEALTH'S MARKET CONSOLIDATION

In Kansas, Ascension Health's acquisition of a small-town hospital initially seemed like a lifeline. But for Amanda and Paul Sanders, it quickly became a nightmare. Ascension closed the hospital's maternity ward, forcing Amanda to travel 90 minutes for prenatal care. "When they closed it, they said there wasn't enough demand," Amanda said. "But how do they expect people to stay in small towns if there's no healthcare?"

The impact wasn't limited to rural areas. In Detroit, Ascension shuttered an emergency department in a predominantly Black neighborhood, leaving uninsured families without a critical resource. James Bell, a local activist, described the devastating consequences: "People in our community are dying because they can't get to an ER in time. It's not just a hospital they closed; it's a lifeline they took away."

THE HUMAN TOLL

These stories illustrate the devastating impact of hospital consolidations on everyday Americans. They reveal a pattern of broken promises and prioritize corporate profits over the health and safety of communities. Behind every shuttered ward and inflated bill are families struggling to make ends meet, patients traveling hours for basic care, and lives endangered by a system that places market dominance above public health.

Hospital consolidations are not just abstract economic events—they are deeply personal crises for millions of people across the country. Policymakers and communities must act to demand accountability, fairness, and transparency in healthcare to prevent further harm.

THE PRICE OF CONSOLIDATION

Inflated costs, diminished access, and communities left in crisis—this is where unchecked consolidation has left us. While health systems promise improved efficiency and quality, the human cost often tells a different story. Patients are left to navigate a system that prioritizes market dominance over patient care, and entire communities are abandoned in the name of "streamlining services." The consolidation of hospital systems is not just a business strategy; it has reshaped the way healthcare functions in the United States, tipping the scales in favor of large hospital systems while leaving employers, patients, and local economies struggling to keep up.

The consolidation of hospitals and healthcare systems has fundamentally altered the balance of power. What used to be a system of negotiation between providers, insurers, employers, and patients has become a landscape where large hospital systems dictate the terms. If one system controls most of the hospitals in a region, it doesn't just set prices—it controls who gets care, where they receive it, and under what financial conditions. Employers that once had the ability to push back on excessive costs find themselves cornered, with no ability to negotiate better rates.

The impact of hospital consolidation has been particularly evident in Northern California, where major employers like Chevron, Wells Fargo, and Intel were locked into Sutter Health's "all-or-nothing" contracts. These agreements required them to include all of Sutter's facilities in their networks, regardless of cost, eliminating the ability to select only the most cost-effective options.

Without competition, pricing power shifted entirely to the hospital system, forcing employers to absorb the costs or pass them on to their employees. The financial consequences of these arrangements ripple outward, affecting workers through higher premiums, deductibles, and out-of-pocket costs.

This pattern is not unique to California. Across the country, major hospital systems have expanded, acquiring independent hospitals, physician practices, and outpatient facilities. With fewer alternatives available, employers are forced to accept price increases year after year, without the ability to seek lower-cost providers. Between 2010 and 2020, the average cost of family health insurance premiums rose by 55%, a trend that coincides with the growing dominance of hospital consolidation. Employers don't absorb those costs alone—they restructure health benefits to offset the burden, resulting in higher employee contributions, increased deductibles, and narrowed provider networks.

The financial strain is even more severe for smaller employers in regions dominated by a single health system. In many smaller cities and towns, local businesses face a harsh reality: rising hospital prices lead directly to rising health insurance costs. An employer with 1,000 employees covering 2,500 people under its health plan, for example, spends an average of $8.8 million per year on health benefits, with hospital services accounting for roughly 44% of that spending. If the dominant hospital system in the area raises its prices by just 10%, that employer faces nearly $400,000 in additional costs. For large corporations, these increases may be absorbed into operational budgets, but for small and mid-sized businesses, they create difficult trade-offs. Employers may have to increase employees' share of premium costs, reduce coverage, limit wage growth, or delay hiring to offset the expense.

When this cycle repeats year after year, the long-term effects become clear. Consolidation removes competition, allowing hospital systems to raise prices with little pushback. Employers that once had leverage in negotiating health benefits are left with limited options, forced to either absorb the cost or shift it onto their workforce. And in regions where a single hospital system dominates, local businesses face financial strain that extends beyond healthcare—higher benefits costs make it harder to compete, invest, or expand.

Even outside of the employer-employee relationship, the effects of hospital consolidation are visible in everyday life. A hospital that once operated as an independent community facility may now bear the branding of a national or regional system. A local physician's office, previously an affordable option for routine care, may now be classified as a hospital outpatient department, resulting in higher facility fees and increased patient costs. Patients who once had multiple choices for specialist care may find themselves limited to one hospital network, with referral options dictated not by medical necessity, but by system affiliations.

Despite claims that hospital mergers lead to improved efficiency and better patient outcomes, the data tells a different story. Instead of reducing costs, consolidation has created a system where hospitals can charge more, leaving patients and employers with no alternatives. The idea that larger systems provide a seamless patient experience often fails to match reality. Many patients find themselves facing longer wait times, higher bills, and fewer choices, while hospital executives continue to expand their market share.

It is easy to overlook these changes in day-to-day life, but the next time a local hospital changes names or a once-independent provider group suddenly becomes part of a larger system, the pattern becomes clearer. What looks like growth on the surface is, in many cases, the consolidation of power. With each merger, the ability to negotiate costs diminishes, and the control over pricing shifts further into the hands of a few dominant players. The effects of these changes are not hypothetical—they are reflected in every rising premium, every higher deductible, and every unexpected hospital bill that employers and workers alike struggle to afford.

PATIENTS: CAUGHT IN THE CROSSFIRE

The consolidation of healthcare providers has profoundly reshaped the landscape of patient care, often to the detriment of those it purports to serve. As hospital systems merge and expand, patients find themselves with fewer choices, higher costs, and diminished quality of care.

Consider the case of Kyunghee Lee, whose experience underscores the financial strain patients face due to consolidation. Kyunghee, who relied on annual treatments for her arthritis, was accustomed to a manageable co-payment of $30. However, after her healthcare provider underwent a merger, she was shocked to find her out-of-pocket expense had skyrocketed to $354.68 for the same treatment. This dramatic increase was not accompanied by any enhancement in care quality; it was purely a financial consequence of the consolidation.

Beyond financial burdens, the quality of patient care often deteriorates post-merger. A study analyzing hospital consolidations revealed that, while clinical outcomes like mortality and readmission rates remained largely unchanged, patient experience scores declined notably after mergers. This suggests that the anticipated benefits of improved efficiency and service quality through consolidation often fail to materialize, leaving patients with subpar experiences.

The closure of essential services in the wake of hospital mergers further exacerbates patient challenges. In Los Angeles, the shutdown of the Martin Luther King Jr. Hospital had immediate and severe repercussions. The closure led to overcrowding in neighboring emergency departments, increased travel distances for patients seeking urgent care, and a significant reduction in accessible hospital beds for the community. This scenario illustrates how consolidation can lead to service reductions, disproportionately affecting vulnerable populations.

Moreover, the financial motivations behind consolidations can lead to the elimination of less profitable services, such as maternity wards and mental health units, forcing patients to travel long distances for essential care. This not only increases the physical and emotional burden on patients but also raises the risk of adverse health outcomes due to delayed or foregone care.

In essence, while hospital consolidations are often justified by promises of enhanced efficiency and improved patient care, the reality for many patients is starkly different. They face higher costs, reduced access to essential services, and a decline in the overall quality of care. These outcomes highlight the need for a critical examination of the true impact of healthcare consolidation on patient welfare.

THE ILLUSION OF CHOICE

Here's the thing: Patients might look at their insurance network and think they have plenty of options, but that's often just smoke and mirrors. Many of those "choices" are owned by the same parent company, which means there's no real competition. Prices stay high, service remains fragmented, and patients get stuck footing the bill without even realizing that the market forces around them have quietly shifted in favor of the health system.

Vertical integration is a key driver of this illusion. Imagine going to your trusted pediatrician's office, only to discover it's now owned by the local hospital system. The same friendly staff, the same waiting room, the same exam table—but now, what used to be a simple office visit comes with a hefty facility fee, doubling or tripling the cost. The

CHAPTER 15

actual medical care hasn't changed, but the bill sure has. Patients don't get an explanation for the increase—they just get a higher copay or a surprise charge weeks later.

Or take your neighborhood imaging center. It used to be an affordable option for an MRI, charging a few hundred dollars for the scan. Then it gets acquired by the dominant hospital system in the region. Suddenly, the same machine, in the same location, operated by the same technician, is billing thousands for the exact same procedure. Why? Because now it carries the hospital's logo, which means it can take advantage of hospital pricing structures—ones that are nearly impossible for insurers to push back on. Patients who would have previously paid a reasonable rate now get hit with inflated costs, and there's no way around it.

Even pharmacies aren't immune. In some cases, hospital systems have quietly acquired independent pharmacies, embedding them into their vertically integrated empires. Patients filling prescriptions might not realize their local pharmacy is now part of the same system that owns their hospital, their doctor's office, and even their physical therapy provider. The lack of transparency makes it nearly impossible for patients to shop around or make informed decisions about their care. One day, a prescription is reasonably priced, and the next, after the acquisition, the cost skyrockets. The same medication, the same dosage—just an entirely different price tag thanks to ownership consolidation.

Even tools like tiered networks, which are supposed to help patients save money by choosing lower-cost providers, don't work in monopolized markets. These networks are designed to steer patients toward high-value providers by categorizing them into tiers based on cost and quality. But when a single system owns all the "must-have" hospitals, specialists, and clinics in an area, insurers can't exclude them, no matter how outrageous their prices are. Patients are told they're in a "preferred network" and might assume they're getting a deal. But in reality, the system has been structured so that there is no lower-cost alternative. The hospital system's dominance ensures that even if you "choose" a different provider, you're still paying the price they set.

This isn't hypothetical—it's happening in real time, in cities and towns across the country. Patients may think they have a say in where they go for care, but when every option leads back to the same hospital system, the illusion of choice disappears. It's not about quality, efficiency, or better patient outcomes—it's about control.

HOW IT ALL HITS YOUR WALLET

When hospital systems consolidate and employers lose leverage, patients end up paying the price—literally. High-deductible health plans (HDHPs), now a common feature of employer-sponsored insurance, force patients to shell out thousands of dollars before their coverage kicks in. For many families, that means delaying or skipping care altogether.

Surprise medical bills are another gut punch. Imagine going to an in-network hospital for surgery, only to find out later that the anesthesiologist wasn't in-network. Now you're stuck with a bill for thousands of dollars. Even with recent legislative attempts to curb these bills, loopholes persist, leaving patients vulnerable.

And then there's the ripple effect on entire communities. When healthcare prices rise unchecked, local governments, school districts, and small businesses—all of which provide insurance for their employees—struggle to keep up. They're forced to cut other essential services or pass the financial burden onto taxpayers. In some cases, local employers simply can't survive, leading to job losses and economic stagnation.

CHAPTER 15

We've spent time unpacking the role of hospitals in driving up healthcare costs, but the story doesn't end there. Now we turn to the insurance companies—the entities often assumed to keep hospital prices in check. In reality, they're not just complicit; they've built a system that profits from these rising costs. Part III exposes how insurers, far from being patient advocates, have shaped a broken system that works perfectly—for them.

PART II:

The Role of Insurance Carriers in the Broken System

"Intermediaries do not just fill gaps in the market; they often create them."
— Thomas Sowell

"It is difficult to get a man to understand something when his salary depends upon his not understanding it."
— Upton Sinclair

Chapter 16

GATEKEEPERS OF THE GRIFT: INSIDE THE MIDDLEMAN MACHINE

When we think about the dynamics between hospitals and insurance companies, the common assumption is that they are adversaries—battling it out in boardrooms to negotiate better prices and keep healthcare costs in check. Many believe insurers act as a counterweight to the rising prices and monopolistic behavior of hospital systems, protecting employers, employees, and individuals who rely on them for coverage. But that narrative, though convenient, doesn't reflect reality. Instead of driving competition and lowering costs, insurance carriers have become complicit in perpetuating the system's dysfunction, thriving in the very chaos they claim to manage.

Insurance companies sit at a pivotal intersection of the healthcare market, wielding influence as payers, administrators, and increasingly, providers. Far from being neutral brokers, they've built a system that works exceptionally well—for themselves. Through mechanisms like vertical integration, opaque administrative practices, and profit incentives tied to rising costs, carriers have consolidated power and shifted accountability away from themselves. For employers and patients, the illusion of control has eroded, leaving them with fewer choices and higher expenses.

Recent events highlight the intensity of frustration with this system. At the time of writing, news broke of the tragic murder of UnitedHealthcare's CEO, allegedly linked to anger at the role insurance companies play in healthcare. While the full motive remains unclear, it underscores the visceral frustration many feel toward a system they perceive as unjust and indifferent to their struggles. This chapter seeks not to sensationalize but to analyze the insurance industry's role in creating these conditions, unpacking the root causes and implications of their growing dominance.

THE INSURANCE CARRIER'S EXPANDING ROLE

Insurance carriers have significantly expanded their roles, moving beyond their traditional functions of pooling risk and reimbursing claims to dominating nearly every facet of healthcare delivery. Through vertical integration, major companies such as UnitedHealth Group, Anthem (now Elevance Health), and Cigna have acquired pharmacy benefit managers (PBMs), urgent care clinics, imaging centers, and physician practices. This strategy enables them to profit from almost every stage of a patient's healthcare journey, while often obscuring the true costs from patients and employers.

A notable example is UnitedHealth Group's acquisition of various healthcare service providers. In 2002, UnitedHealth Group acquired AmeriChoice, a Medicaid insurance company, expanding its reach into government-sponsored health programs. The company also purchased Mid Atlantic Medical Services in 2003, further broadening its market presence. These acquisitions have allowed UnitedHealth Group to integrate services ranging from insurance coverage to direct patient care, creating a comprehensive healthcare ecosystem under its corporate umbrella.

Similarly, Cigna's acquisition of Express Scripts in 2018 for $67 billion exemplifies this trend. Express Scripts, a leading PBM, manages prescription drug benefits for millions of Americans. By bringing a PBM into its fold, Cigna gained greater control over the pharmaceutical supply chain, from determining which medications are covered to influencing their pricing. This consolidation allows Cigna to capture profits at multiple points, from insurance premiums to prescription drug transactions, while potentially limiting transparency regarding medication costs for consumers.

Anthem, now known as Elevance Health, has also pursued vertical integration. In 2015, Anthem announced plans to acquire Cigna for over $54 billion, aiming to create one of the largest health insurance companies in the United States. However, this merger was blocked in 2017 due to antitrust concerns. Despite this, Anthem continued its expansion by developing its own PBM, IngenioRx, launched in partnership with CVS Health in 2019. This move allowed Anthem to manage prescription benefits directly, potentially increasing its influence over drug pricing and patient access to medications.

The implications of such consolidation are profound. When a parent company owns multiple facets of healthcare delivery—such as your local pediatrician's office, the imaging center you visit, and the PBM that determines your medication coverage—patients often face increased costs. Routine doctor visits may incur additional facility fees, imaging services can become more expensive once rebranded under a hospital system, and prescription drug costs may rise due to the PBM's formulary decisions. This vertical integration reduces competition, driving prices higher and limiting meaningful choices for patients.

Moreover, the lack of transparency inherent in these consolidated systems makes it challenging for patients and employers to discern the true costs of healthcare services. With insurers controlling multiple stages of the healthcare process, from service provision to payment processing, there is an increased potential for conflicts of interest and profit maximization at the expense of patient care and affordability.

In summary, the expansion of insurance carriers into various sectors of healthcare delivery through vertical integration has transformed the industry landscape. While these moves may offer operational efficiencies for the companies involved, they often lead to higher costs and fewer choices for patients, underscoring the need for increased transparency and regulatory oversight in the healthcare system.

THE HIDDEN COSTS FOR EMPLOYERS AND PATIENTS

The system's design—whether fully insured, self-funded, or managed through third-party administrators (TPAs)—gives insurance carriers ample room to exploit inefficiencies for profit. Fully insured plans allow carriers to take on financial risk, setting premiums high enough to ensure profitability. In self-funded arrangements, where employers bear the risk, carriers charge administrative fees and manipulate provider networks to maximize their own bottom line.

Legislation like the Medical Loss Ratio (MLR) rule, meant to cap profits by requiring insurers to spend a certain percentage of premiums on care, has had unintended consequences. By linking profits to total spending, the MLR incentivizes insurers to allow costs to rise—because the more dollars they manage, the more they earn.

The consequences ripple outward. Employers see higher premiums and pass these costs onto employees through higher deductibles, copays, and coinsurance. Patients, already burdened by surprise billing and inflated costs, delay or forgo care, leading to worse health outcomes. Communities suffer when local businesses and schools can no longer afford competitive benefits, further straining already fragile local economies.

Chapter 17

SETTING THE STAGE

In this section, we'll delve into the complex role insurance carriers play in the healthcare system. We'll define key concepts like fully insured and self-funded plans, Administrative Services Only (ASO) arrangements, and third-party administrators (TPA) to demystify how insurance works. We'll also explore how insurers have used vertical integration, government contracts for public programs like Medicaid and Medicare, and employer complacency to entrench their position and profit from the chaos.

The story of insurance carriers isn't one of neutral intermediaries seeking balance. Instead, it's a story of unchecked power, strategic consolidation, and systemic incentives that leave patients and employers footing the bill. Let's unpack how we got here.

We've spent time unpacking the role of hospitals in driving up healthcare costs, but the story doesn't end there. Now we turn to the insurance companies—the entities often assumed to keep hospital prices in check. In reality, they're not just complicit; they've built a system that profits from these rising costs. Part II exposes how insurers, far from being patient advocates, have shaped a broken system that works perfectly—for them.

In December 2024, the healthcare world was jolted by a shocking and unprecedented act of violence. Brian Thompson, CEO of UnitedHealthcare, the largest health insurance company in the United States, was gunned down outside a Manhattan hotel. The crime, described by authorities as "brazen and targeted," took place just before Thompson was scheduled to attend an investor meeting. Surveillance footage showed the gunman waiting for Thompson, calmly approaching him, and firing multiple shots before fleeing the scene on a bike.

As investigators unraveled the case, disturbing details emerged. The shell casings left at the scene bore the words "delay," "deny," and "depose"—a chilling nod to criticisms of the insurance industry's perceived profit-driven tactics, such as prior authorizations and claim denials. These words encapsulated the growing sentiment among many Americans: that the health insurance system is not built to serve patients but to maximize corporate profits.

Thompson's death brought renewed scrutiny to UnitedHealth Group, a behemoth in the healthcare sector with revenues exceeding $281 billion annually. The company, which oversees a sprawling network of subsidiaries, including UnitedHealthcare and Optum, has long been a focal point of criticism. From government probes into antitrust practices to accusations of insider trading by top executives, UnitedHealth Group's reputation has been tarnished by controversy.

Just months before Thompson's murder, he and several of his colleagues became the target of a federal lawsuit alleging insider trading. Thompson himself had sold $15 million worth of company stock shortly before news of a Department of Justice (DOJ) investigation into the company's acquisition of another massive healthcare entity became public. This acquisition, which consolidated UnitedHealth's dominance in claims processing and electronic data interchange, had already faced antitrust challenges. The DOJ's renewed probe added fuel to allegations that UnitedHealth was leveraging its vertical integration to stifle competition and prioritize its own interests over those of patients and providers.

Adding to the controversy were lawsuits accusing UnitedHealthcare of using artificial intelligence to prematurely deny claims for post-acute care services, leaving vulnerable patients without coverage for critical treatments. These legal and ethical issues, paired with skyrocketing profits—$16 billion in 2023—painted a picture of a company thriving while many Americans struggled to navigate a system plagued by medical debt, denied claims, and inaccessible care.

Thompson's murder, while a criminal act that cannot be condoned, became a flashpoint for public outrage. Across social media platforms and protest gatherings, a striking mix of grief, anger, and bitter sarcasm emerged. Posts on Reddit and TikTok criticized UnitedHealthcare's practices, with some users going so far as to mock Thompson's death with phrases like "thoughts and prior authorizations." Others shared stories of their own denied claims or the financial devastation wrought by the system.

The reaction was not confined to one political or ideological corner. From leftist activists decrying corporate greed to libertarians suspicious of monopolistic practices, the outrage spanned a broad spectrum. Protestors outside UnitedHealthcare's headquarters carried signs, shared stories, and voiced their frustrations about a system they felt prioritized profits over people. The killing laid bare a profound and pervasive dissatisfaction with an industry that is central to the American healthcare system.

Then UnitedHealth Group CEO Andrew Witty responded to the tragedy in a video message to employees, defending the company's role as a critical player in ensuring safe and appropriate care. He urged staff to "tune out the noise" and focus on the company's mission. But Witty's reassurances did little to quell public anger. Critics viewed his remarks as emblematic of the industry's detachment from the lived realities of patients and providers. In May 2025, Witty was forced to step down from his role as CEO following a devastating series of financial disclosures: the company withdrew its 2025 earnings guidance, admitted to spiraling Medicare costs, and lost over $250 billion in market value.

CHAPTER 17

He was replaced by Stephen Hemsley—UnitedHealth's longtime former chief—who was reinstated by the board with a reported compensation package of $60 million. In his first address to shareholders, Hemsley promised accountability, pledged an internal review of controversial practices like Medicare coding and prior authorization, and asked for "trust." But who, exactly, was he asking? Not the patients burdened by denied claims. Not the providers drowning in administrative red tape. He asked for the trust of shareholders—the people whose expectations for profit the company has always prioritized above all else.

And what kind of trust was he seeking? Trust that UnitedHealth would restore what it had lost—not credibility with the public, but margins. Hemsley wasn't promising to rebuild a healthcare system that works for Americans. He was promising to rebuild the machine that had made UnitedHealth one of the most profitable corporations in America—until the machine cracked under its own weight.

Thompson's murder was a tragic and extreme event, but the rage it ignited offers a stark lens into the broader dysfunction of the healthcare system. It revealed a festering resentment toward insurance companies, which many view as gatekeepers of care and drivers of cost. These companies, despite their marketing of consumer choice and care coordination, are increasingly seen as barriers rather than facilitators of health.

As we transition to exploring the role of insurance companies, this event underscores the deep dissatisfaction and systemic failures that define the healthcare landscape. The next section unpacks how these companies have shaped—and exploited—the system, from their control over pricing and networks to their roles in government programs like Medicare and Medicaid. It's a story of power, profit, and priorities—and one that demands closer examination.

In its earliest form, health insurance emerged out of necessity. The primary driver for its development was the need to cover hospital costs—unpredictable and often catastrophic expenses that individuals and families could rarely afford out of pocket. A single hospitalization could wipe out a family's savings, leaving many unable to access critical care. This financial vulnerability spurred the creation of organized risk-pooling mechanisms, giving rise to modern health insurance.

The first major players in this space were Blue Cross and Blue Shield, non-profit organizations founded in the 1930s. Blue Cross initially focused on prepaid plans for hospital care, offering subscribers the security of knowing their inpatient expenses were covered. Blue Shield followed with a similar model, addressing physician services and expanding the concept of prepayment to include outpatient care. These plans pooled risk among policyholders, spreading the financial burden of serious illnesses across a larger group. By doing so, they helped mitigate the unpredictability of healthcare costs and ensured that more people could access care when they needed it.

The appeal of health insurance grew exponentially during the mid-20th century. Following World War II, employers faced government-imposed wage controls designed to prevent inflation. These constraints made it difficult for companies to compete for workers using traditional salary increases. In response, businesses turned to non-cash benefits like health insurance to attract and retain employees. Providing health coverage offered a dual advantage: it helped companies stand out in a competitive labor market while also delivering a valuable benefit to workers and their families.

This strategy coincided with significant federal tax incentives. Employer contributions to health insurance premiums were made tax-deductible, further solidifying the appeal of offering insurance as a workplace benefit. By the 1950s, employer-sponsored insurance was no longer a novelty but an expectation. The model proved so effective that it quickly became the backbone of the U.S. healthcare system.

CHAPTER 17

By the 1960s, the majority of Americans received health coverage through their jobs. For families, this offered not only access to medical care but also peace of mind, knowing they wouldn't face financial ruin from an unexpected hospital stay. It marked a pivotal shift in healthcare financing, moving from a direct pay system to one dominated by intermediaries—employers and insurers—who negotiated on behalf of patients. The system's success in reducing individual risk would, over time, lay the foundation for more expansive and complex insurance models, ultimately leading to the managed care frameworks that dominate today.

This early model of health insurance—designed to protect against the financial devastation of hospitalization—set the stage for the evolution of the industry. Over the coming decades, the focus would shift from merely covering costs to actively managing them, introducing new complexities and trade-offs that reshaped the relationship between patients, providers, and insurers.

By the 1980s, the American health insurance landscape was undergoing a dramatic transformation. The cost of healthcare was rising at an alarming rate, driven by advances in medical technology, the growing prevalence of employer-sponsored insurance, and an aging population requiring more intensive medical care. In response, insurers and policymakers turned to managed care as a solution to rein in spending.

Health Maintenance Organizations (HMOs), which had existed since the 1970s but were relatively niche, gained traction after the passage of the HMO Act of 1973, which provided federal incentives for their expansion. Unlike traditional indemnity insurance, which reimbursed patients for care received, HMOs controlled costs by restricting access to a network of pre-approved providers and requiring prior authorization for many services. These plans emphasized preventive care and care coordination, but they also introduced gatekeeping mechanisms that limited patient choice and sometimes delayed necessary treatment.

Employers, facing soaring premiums, embraced HMOs and Preferred Provider Organizations (PPOs) as cost-cutting alternatives to traditional fee-for-service insurance. The concept was simple: by directing patients to a defined network of providers who agreed to discounted rates, insurers could reduce overall spending while still covering care. PPOs, a more flexible alternative to HMOs, allowed members to see out-of-network providers—albeit at higher out-of-pocket costs—making them a popular middle ground.

However, these cost-control measures were not always welcomed by patients or providers. Doctors resented the growing influence of insurers in dictating treatment decisions, while patients chafed at the restrictions on where they could seek care. The term "managed care" soon became synonymous with bureaucracy and denial of services, as insurers tightened their grip on medical decision-making.

At the same time, corporate consolidation in the insurance sector accelerated. The 1980s saw the rise of for-profit insurers like UnitedHealthcare and Aetna, which took a more aggressive, profit-driven approach to healthcare financing. Unlike the non-profit Blue Cross and Blue Shield plans of previous decades, these companies prioritized shareholder returns, leading to more aggressive cost-cutting measures and restrictions on care.

THE 1990S: THE MANAGED CARE BACKLASH AND THE RISE OF PBMS

By the early 1990s, managed care had become the dominant force in American healthcare, but cracks were beginning to show. Patients and physicians pushed back against the rigid controls imposed by insurers, leading to mounting political pressure for reform. The controversy over denials of care, preauthorization delays, and restrictions on provider choice created an environment of growing frustration.

Public resentment peaked in the mid-1990s, fueled by high-profile cases of denied coverage and preventable deaths linked to HMO restrictions. In response, states began passing "Patients' Bill of Rights" laws, mandating greater transparency and consumer protections. At the federal level, Congress debated national patient protection laws, though industry lobbying largely succeeded in limiting government intervention.

Despite these tensions, the 1990s also saw the rapid expansion of new cost-control mechanisms, particularly in the realm of pharmaceuticals. The rise of pharmacy benefit managers (PBMs)—middlemen tasked with negotiating drug prices and managing formularies—fundamentally reshaped the economics of prescription drugs. PBMs, originally created to process pharmacy claims, gained immense power as they brokered deals between insurers, pharmaceutical companies, and pharmacies.

Their business model hinged on rebates from drug manufacturers: in exchange for favorable placement on an insurer's formulary (the list of covered medications), drugmakers would provide discounts or financial incentives to the PBM. This led to perverse incentives, where PBMs prioritized high-rebate, high-cost drugs rather than the most cost-effective or clinically appropriate treatments. By the end of the decade, the largest PBMs—like Medco, Express Scripts, and Caremark—had become critical power players in the healthcare system, wielding influence over drug pricing that persists to this day.

Meanwhile, employer-sponsored health insurance continued to evolve, with rising deductibles and cost-sharing mechanisms shifting more financial responsibility onto workers. The traditional model of low-deductible, comprehensive coverage gave way to high-deductible health plans (HDHPs), which required employees to pay more upfront before insurance kicked in. Insurers and employers justified this shift by arguing that greater cost-sharing would make patients more prudent consumers, but in practice, it often deterred necessary care and exacerbated financial burdens for the sickest individuals.

THE EARLY 2000S: CONSUMER-DIRECTED HEALTHCARE AND THE RISE OF MEGA-INSURERS

By the turn of the century, managed care had evolved once again, with insurers adopting new strategies to offload costs onto consumers while maintaining control over pricing and networks. The early 2000s saw the emergence of consumer-directed healthcare, a concept that placed greater responsibility on individuals to manage their own healthcare spending.

One of the hallmarks of this era was the proliferation of Health Savings Accounts (HSAs) and High-Deductible Health Plans (HDHPs). These plans, encouraged by policymakers seeking to curb overutilization, incentivized individuals to shop for care by pairing tax-advantaged savings accounts with higher out-of-pocket expenses. While these tools were marketed as empowering consumers, they largely benefited healthier, wealthier individuals who could afford to accumulate savings, while leaving lower-income and chronically ill patients vulnerable to cost barriers.

Meanwhile, insurer consolidation accelerated at a breakneck pace. UnitedHealth Group, Anthem, Aetna, Cigna, and Humana emerged as the dominant players, acquiring smaller insurers and leveraging their growing scale to negotiate more aggressively with providers. The mergers and acquisitions of the 2000s cemented the oligopolistic nature of the insurance industry, with a handful of mega-carriers controlling vast portions of the market.

At the same time, insurers deepened their involvement in government-funded healthcare programs. The expansion of Medicare Advantage (privatized Medicare plans run by insurers) and Medicaid managed care programs created lucrative new revenue streams. These plans, marketed as cost-saving alternatives to traditional public insurance, gave private insurers an increasing foothold in taxpayer-funded healthcare—a trend that would only accelerate in the years to come.

Yet, despite all these changes, healthcare costs continued to spiral upward. Patients were paying more out of pocket than ever before, employers were struggling to keep up with premiums, and insurers—despite their cost-containment efforts—remained extraordinarily profitable. By the early 2010s, the cracks in the system had reached a breaking point, setting the stage for one of the most consequential health policy battles in American history: the fight for the Affordable Care Act (ACA).

The Affordable Care Act, signed into law in 2010, sought to address these dysfunctions through a combination of regulatory mandates, subsidies, and market reforms. While much of the political and media attention focused on the individual mandate and the expansion of Medicaid, one of the most consequential—yet often overlooked—elements of the ACA was the introduction of the Medical Loss Ratio rule.

Buried within the ACA's thousands of pages was a provision that fundamentally altered how insurers profited from health insurance. The Medical Loss Ratio (MLR) requirement mandated that insurers spend at least 80% of premium revenues, or 85% for large-group plans, on actual healthcare services and quality improvement, rather than administrative costs, marketing, or profits. If insurers failed to meet this threshold, they were required to issue rebates to policyholders.

At first glance, the MLR rule appeared to be a straightforward consumer protection, ensuring that premium dollars were primarily spent on medical care rather than lining corporate pockets. But its long-term impact on the insurance industry was profound.

Before the ACA, insurers could increase profitability by tightening claims approvals and keeping costs low. But with the MLR cap, insurers could no longer artificially suppress medical spending to boost profits—their administrative and profit margins were capped as a percentage of premium revenue. The only way to generate higher profits was to grow total premium revenue, leading to a push for higher overall healthcare spending.

This created an incentive to inflate costs. Under traditional business logic, lower costs drive higher margins. But the MLR rule flipped that dynamic on its head. If an insurer was required to spend at least 80 to 85% on medical care, raising premiums—and thus total healthcare spending—became a more effective strategy for increasing profits than cost-cutting. The higher the premiums, the larger the absolute dollar amount that could be captured within the 15 or 20% allowable for administrative costs and profit.

This also accelerated industry consolidation. With insurers seeking scale to maximize revenue, the ACA supercharged consolidation. Large insurers bought up regional players, acquired pharmacy benefit managers, and even expanded into provider services. The result was fewer competitors, larger networks, and an insurance industry that wielded even more control over healthcare financing.

While the MLR rule forced insurers to issue billions in rebates to consumers over the years, these refunds were ultimately a symptom of higher-than-necessary premium growth rather than a true cost-saving mechanism. Insurers priced their plans conservatively—meaning higher than needed—knowing that overages would simply be refunded, while in the meantime, they benefited from holding and investing the excess funds. Rebates were issued, but they did little to address the broader problem: insurers had learned to price in a way that maximized premium growth while staying within the MLR threshold.

Beyond the MLR rule, the ACA introduced a series of other regulations designed to standardize and expand access to coverage. Insurers were prohibited from denying coverage or charging higher rates based on an individual's health status, eliminating a long-standing practice that had locked sick Americans out of the market. The ACA also mandated a minimum set of essential health benefits that all health plans in the individual and small-group markets must cover, including hospitalization, maternity care, prescription drugs, and mental health services. While this ensured more comprehensive coverage, it also eliminated cheaper, stripped-down plans, contributing to premium increases.

The law also attempted to increase access through Medicaid expansion, though the Supreme Court's 2012 ruling in *NFIB v. Sebelius* made this optional for states, creating a patchwork of coverage gaps where certain states declined to expand Medicaid, leaving many uninsured. To facilitate individual market enrollment, the ACA established online marketplaces, or exchanges, where people could purchase coverage, often with income-based subsidies that softened the impact of rising premiums. While these subsidies helped mask the full extent of premium increases, they did not address the underlying cost problem.

While the ACA dramatically reduced the number of uninsured Americans, it also cemented the power of insurers in ways that many of its architects likely did not anticipate. Despite being framed as a check on insurance industry excesses, the ACA deepened insurers' role in healthcare financing. Rather than reducing administrative bloat, the law entrenched the intermediary-driven system by increasing reliance on private insurers for Medicaid expansion, Medicare Advantage, and subsidized exchange plans.

Premiums continued to rise. The law did not contain meaningful cost controls, and insurers, adapting to the MLR rule, had little incentive to keep premiums low. Instead, they continued increasing rates, justifying hikes through mandated benefits and provider cost trends.

Industry profits surged—just in a different way. Insurers shifted their profit strategies away from underwriting margins and instead doubled down on market expansion, vertical integration, and government contracting. Companies like UnitedHealth Group and CVS Health, which acquired Aetna, turned into sprawling healthcare conglomerates, profiting not just from insurance, but from pharmacy services, provider networks, and even direct patient care.

The Affordable Care Act was a monumental shift in American healthcare, but it did not fundamentally change the trajectory of costs. Instead, it entrenched insurers, solidified the role of private intermediaries, and incentivized higher overall spending—all while delivering critical coverage protections that remain politically untouchable.

For all the debate about the individual mandate, subsidies, and Medicaid expansion, perhaps the most transformative—but least discussed—aspect of the ACA was the MLR rule, which permanently altered how insurers approached profitability.

The ACA has been called many things—a grand bargain, a Faustian deal, the original sin of modern healthcare reform, the most consequential legislation of our time. It expanded coverage, reshaped the market, and enshrined protections that are now politically untouchable. But it also entrenched the very industry it sought to rein in, cementing insurers as the ultimate arbiters of care and costs. For all its ambition, the law did not break the system; it remade it in ways that ensured those with the most power would only grow stronger.

This section explores the high points of that transformation—the regulatory shifts that altered how insurers made money, the financial incentives that shaped their evolution, and the unintended consequences that reverberate to this day. From the introduction of the medical loss ratio, which changed the calculus of profitability, to the mandated expansion of essential health benefits, which reshaped coverage itself, the ACA did more than reform healthcare. It rewrote the rules of the game. And those rules affect everyone. Whether as taxpayers funding Medicare and Medicaid, as employers navigating rising costs in self-funded plans, or as individuals purchasing coverage on the exchange, no one interacts with the healthcare system without passing through the hands of these massive entities. They don't just sell insurance—they administer government programs, process claims for self-funded plans, and negotiate the rates that determine what hospitals, doctors, and drug companies get paid. In many ways, they are the system, their influence woven into every financial transaction in healthcare.

Chapter 18

THE "NETWORK" AND "DISCOUNT" FALLACY

Insurance companies have spent decades convincing Americans that their value lies in their ability to negotiate discounts. The message is clear: without their networks, healthcare costs would be even higher, and access to care would be uncertain. But when you look at how these "negotiated rates" actually work, the entire premise falls apart.

In theory, networks exist to create savings—insurers pool together covered lives, promising hospitals and doctors a steady stream of patients in exchange for lower prices. But in practice, negotiated rates are often far from the lowest available price. Many times, the cash price—the amount an uninsured patient or someone willing to pay out of pocket might be charged—is substantially lower than the insurer's negotiated discount. This runs directly counter to the notion that insurers leverage their market power to secure better deals for the people they cover.

Recent price transparency data has confirmed that this is not an isolated phenomenon. Studies analyzing newly available hospital pricing data have found that in nearly half of U.S. hospitals, the reported cash price for common shoppable services—like MRIs and lab tests—is lower than the median insurance-negotiated rate. In some cases, the cash price is even lower than the minimum price negotiated by an insurer within the same hospital. This dynamic is not limited

CHAPTER 18

to elective or planned procedures. A study of trauma activation fees in emergency rooms found that cash prices were consistently lower than insurance-negotiated prices across all levels of trauma care, with discounts ranging from 18 to 46%.

The fact that cash prices are often cheaper than insurance-negotiated rates raises an obvious but uncomfortable question: what exactly are insurers negotiating, and for whose benefit? In a rational system, insurers—who supposedly possess far more bargaining power than an individual patient—should be able to secure lower rates than what a cash-paying customer could get on their own. But that is not what happens. Instead, insurers negotiate rates within the context of their business relationships with hospitals and providers, ensuring that all parties continue to profit, rather than driving prices down to what is reasonable or affordable.

For employers, this means they are often paying far more for care than they realize. Self-funded health plans, which cover the majority of working Americans, rely on these rates to determine what they will reimburse. But plan sponsors rarely have the ability to verify whether the rates they are paying are truly competitive. Contracts between insurers and hospitals are deliberately shielded from scrutiny, with employers blocked from auditing claims data or questioning why their plan is being charged certain amounts. Even when price transparency rules expose negotiated rates, the results often confirm the worst suspicions—major insurers are not driving costs down so much as ensuring that they and the providers they contract with both continue to profit.

This dynamic plays out most obviously in high-cost claims, where the illusion of negotiation completely falls apart. When an employer sees a $400,000 hospital bill and is assured that their insurer's "discount" has reduced it to $320,000, they are led to believe they have benefited from a powerful negotiation. But in reality, that discount is meaningless without understanding the starting price. If the insurer has allowed the hospital to set an absurdly inflated chargemaster rate to begin with, a 20% reduction is not a savings—it is theater. And because self-funded employers do not have direct access to the real numbers behind these agreements, they are entirely reliant on their insurer to tell them whether they got a good deal or not.

At the same time, insurers have another reason to keep these rates high: their own compensation structures. Many third-party administrators—who process claims for self-funded health plans—take a percentage of the total healthcare spend as their fee. This means their revenue grows as healthcare costs rise, creating a built-in disincentive to truly lower prices. Instead of driving toward more affordable care, they benefit from maintaining the appearance of aggressive negotiation while ensuring the underlying costs continue to escalate.

The idea that networks provide value by securing better rates is one of the biggest scams in American healthcare. Patients are told they must stay "in-network" to get coverage, that venturing outside these insurer-controlled networks will result in exorbitant out-of-pocket costs. But in many cases, going out of network—paying cash instead of using insurance—can result in a lower total cost than what the insurer would have negotiated. The supposed value of the network is, more often than not, an illusion.

Consider how absurd this arrangement is in any other industry. No one would sign up for a credit card that forces them to shop at a specific set of stores and charges them extra for shopping elsewhere—especially if it turned out that some of the non-approved stores were actually offering better prices. Yet in healthcare, this is exactly the system insurers have built. Networks do not exist to protect patients from high costs; they exist to ensure that insurers, hospitals, and other players in the system control pricing, steer volume, and maintain their revenue streams.

The negotiated rate fallacy is one of the great misdirections in modern healthcare—an industry-wide sleight of hand where

CHAPTER 18

insurers convince their customers they are securing savings while actually presiding over a system that ensures prices remain artificially high. It is not just that negotiated rates are flawed; it is that the entire concept of insurer-driven price containment is a myth. The system does not work for the purchasers of healthcare—it works for the middlemen extracting value at every stage. And as healthcare costs continue to rise, employers, patients, and taxpayers are the ones left footing the bill.

Chapter 19

ADMINISTRATIVE COSTS

Administrative costs are one of the most overlooked yet significant drivers of U.S. healthcare spending. Unlike medical costs—what is actually spent on patient care—administrative costs encompass the vast and growing web of billing, claims processing, compliance, network management, prior authorizations, marketing, and other non-clinical functions that add no direct health value. These costs are a defining characteristic of the American healthcare system, yet they remain largely hidden from the public.

The rise of administrative costs in U.S. healthcare has been a slow but relentless trend, one that has accelerated over the last half-century as private insurance companies have cemented their role as intermediaries between patients and providers. In 1970, administrative costs accounted for about 5% of total U.S. healthcare spending. By 2000, that number had climbed to nearly 15%, and today, estimates suggest that administrative expenses make up between 25% and 34% of all healthcare expenditures in the U.S.

This is a uniquely American problem. In other wealthy nations with universal healthcare systems, administrative costs are dramatically lower. The United States spends an estimated $1,055 per person per year on healthcare administration, while the next-highest country, Germany, spends just $306 per capita. Canada, which operates a single-payer system, spends $180 per person—one-sixth of what the U.S. does. The difference is staggering: if the U.S. reduced its administrative costs to the level of Canada or Germany, it would save over $600 billion per year.

So what drives these excessive costs? The bulk of administrative spending in the U.S. comes from the fragmented, multi-payer structure of the healthcare system and the layers of complexity introduced by insurers. Unlike single-payer systems, where there is a uniform billing and payment structure, the American system is a chaotic landscape of thousands of insurance plans, each with its own set of rules, networks, reimbursement rates, and preauthorization requirements. This complexity generates waste at every level, requiring armies of coders, billers, auditors, and compliance officers just to navigate.

The complexity of claims processing and billing in the U.S. healthcare system is staggering, but before diving deeper, it is important to note that this is not an exhaustive account of every aspect of the billing process. Entire books could be—and have been—written on the subject. The goal here is simply to highlight some of the key points that illustrate how this system has evolved into an administrative behemoth that benefits insurers and providers while leaving patients and employers drowning in costs they cannot control or even begin to understand.

One of the largest components of administrative spending in U.S. healthcare is claims processing and billing, a system that is inefficient by design, generating waste on both the provider and insurer sides of the equation. Unlike in other industries where a transaction is straightforward—a service is provided, a bill is issued, and payment is made—the U.S. healthcare system has created a labyrinthine process that involves multiple layers of documentation, coding, review, and negotiation before a claim is actually paid.

At its core, this complexity is driven by both sides of the transaction—providers and insurers—each engaged in a tug-of-war over payments. Hospitals, physician offices, and outpatient facilities employ vast billing departments whose sole function is to navigate the byzantine rules of insurance reimbursement, ensuring that claims are coded in a way that maximizes payment while avoiding outright denial. On the other side, insurance companies employ equally massive teams whose job is to review, adjudicate, and, in many cases, find reasons to deny or reduce payment. The result is a costly administrative arms race, where neither side is incentivized to simplify the process, and both sides invest heavily in navigating its inefficiencies.

Hospitals and physician groups employ huge billing operations, often with entire teams dedicated to managing insurance claims for each department or specialty. In large hospital systems, it is not uncommon for there to be one billing or revenue cycle employee for every two to three physicians—a staggering ratio that highlights just how burdensome the system has become. These teams are responsible for coding services correctly, submitting claims, tracking denials, filing appeals, and resubmitting claims when insurers push back. But this is not just a matter of following standard procedures—billing errors, whether intentional or unintentional, are rampant.

Hospitals and providers often upcode services, meaning they bill for a more expensive version of a procedure than what was actually performed, in order to increase reimbursement. They also engage in unbundling, where procedures that should be billed as a single service are instead broken into multiple line items, each with a separate charge. Other common practices include duplicate billing (submitting the same charge multiple times, hoping one gets through) and miscoding (where a service is deliberately misclassified in a way that increases reimbursement). While some errors are accidental, many are calculated, designed to take advantage of the system's inherent complexity in order to maximize payment.

On the insurer side, the response to this chaotic billing environment has been to create ever-more complex claims review processes, requiring layers of approval, preauthorization, and verification before a bill is paid. Insurers employ tens of thousands of claims processors, auditors, and review specialists, each tasked with scrutinizing claims for inconsistencies, coding errors, and suspected fraud. This is not an altruistic effort to control healthcare spending—it is a cost-containment strategy designed to protect insurer profits by limiting how much is actually paid out in claims. Every denied or reduced claim represents retained revenue for the insurer, making these processes not just a defensive mechanism, but a core part of the industry's business model.

The numbers behind this administrative bloat are staggering. The U.S. employs an estimated 1.5 million people in medical billing and claims processing, a workforce larger than that of entire industries like mining or utilities. Within insurance companies alone, there are hundreds of thousands of employees dedicated solely to handling claims—filing, processing, adjudicating, appealing, and reviewing every step of the payment process. These workers do not provide medical care, improve patient outcomes, or contribute to public health—they exist purely to manage the inefficiencies created by a system that thrives on complexity.

A significant driver of this complexity is the coding and classification system that dictates how services are billed and reimbursed. Medical claims are not submitted in plain language but are assigned specific codes under systems such as the Current Procedural Terminology (CPT), the International Classification of Diseases (ICD), and the Healthcare Common Procedure Coding System (HCPCS), among others. The number of codes is vast—more than 68,000 diagnosis codes and 87,000 procedure codes—each requiring precise documentation and coding expertise. This complexity results in an endless cycle where providers must document and classify every aspect of care to avoid underbilling, while insurers comb through these claims looking for errors, mismatches, or discrepancies that justify a denial or reduction in payment.

Adding to this dysfunction is the deliberate opacity of medical billing. The vast majority of Americans—even those with extensive education—find their healthcare bills incomprehensible. Unlike a restaurant receipt or a credit card statement, a hospital bill is rarely a simple list of services rendered and their corresponding charges. Instead, it is a series of cryptic line items filled with codes, abbreviations, and jargon that obscure what is actually being billed. Patients frequently receive multiple bills for the same episode of care, as hospital services, physician services, imaging, anesthesia, and lab tests are often billed separately, each from a different provider group.

The lack of transparency is not a mistake; it is a design feature. It allows hospitals and insurers to maintain control over pricing and avoid scrutiny. Patients have no way of knowing whether they were charged a fair price, whether they were billed for something unnecessary, or whether their insurer actually paid what it claimed to. Even employers—who foot the bill for most private insurance in the U.S.—struggle to access claims data and verify whether they are overpaying.

This opacity also makes it nearly impossible for patients to advocate for themselves. In many cases, a patient will not even see the total cost of their care until weeks or months after the service was provided, by which point they have little recourse to challenge an incorrect or excessive charge. Surprise billing practices—where patients unknowingly receive out-of-network care and are charged exorbitant fees—flourished in this environment, further demonstrating how the system preys on complexity to extract more money.

The sheer scale of resources dedicated to billing and claims processing is an unavoidable cost borne by every participant in the system—patients, employers, and taxpayers alike. Hospitals and providers pass their administrative costs onto the people they treat, insurance companies bake theirs into premium pricing, and self-funded employers see these costs reflected in inflated claims expenses. The end result is a system where administrative waste is not

CHAPTER 19

just tolerated—it is deeply embedded, ensuring that money continues to be extracted at every step.

Over the past two decades, high-deductible health plans (HDHPs) have become a dominant feature of employer-sponsored insurance, presented as a way to reduce premiums and encourage employees to become more "cost-conscious" consumers of healthcare. In theory, these plans lower overall spending by requiring enrollees to pay a significant portion of their medical costs upfront before insurance coverage kicks in. But in practice, HDHPs have created a financial trap—one that shifts more costs onto employees while delivering little actual savings for employers.

At its core, the purpose of insurance has always been to pool risk—to allow a group of people to contribute manageable amounts over time so that when they need care, they can access it without financial ruin. The earliest modern health insurance plan in the U.S. followed this model. In the 1920s, a group of teachers in Dallas agreed to pay 50 cents a month to Baylor Hospital in exchange for guaranteed hospital care when they needed it. This was the foundation of Blue Cross, an arrangement built on the idea that the financial burden of medical expenses should be shared to ensure that no one was left without care.

Fast-forward a century, and the model has been completely inverted. Americans today still pay massive amounts for insurance—whether through employer-sponsored plans, marketplace premiums, or payroll deductions for government programs—but when they actually need to use their coverage, they find that care is out of reach. Instead of pooling risk to ensure affordable access, the system now requires individuals to bear enormous out-of-pocket costs before their insurance actually begins covering anything. The result is that many people are functionally uninsured despite having insurance, forced to pay thousands of dollars out of pocket before their policy provides meaningful benefits.

The rise of HDHPs was driven by a combination of economic pressures and shifting cost-containment strategies. As healthcare premiums soared, employers sought ways to keep costs down without eliminating benefits altogether. HDHPs seemed to offer a solution: lower monthly premiums in exchange for higher out-of-pocket expenses when care was needed. These plans also came with the option of Health Savings Accounts (HSAs), tax-advantaged accounts designed to help employees set aside money for medical expenses.

From 2006 to 2023, enrollment in HDHPs surged, particularly among self-funded employer plans. In 2006, only 4% of workers were enrolled in an HDHP; by 2023, that number had climbed to over 55% of employees in large firms. In many cases, workers are given little choice—high-deductible plans are often the only employer-sponsored option available.

While these plans have been sold as a tool for making healthcare more affordable, the reality for many employees is quite different. The promise of lower premiums often obscures the significant financial burden placed on individuals when they actually need care.

- **Higher out-of-pocket costs**: Employees in HDHPs routinely face annual deductibles of $2,000 to $7,000 for individuals and upwards of $15,000 for families, meaning they must pay out of pocket for routine doctor visits, medications, and procedures before their insurance coverage takes effect. A single hospital visit can quickly leave someone with thousands of dollars in medical bills, even if they have an HDHP with a lower premium.

- **Delayed or foregone care**: Studies have consistently shown that employees in HDHPs are more likely to delay or skip necessary medical care—not just discretionary treatments, but also preventive screenings, chronic disease management, and even emergency care—because they cannot afford the upfront costs.

One study found that 42% of adults with HDHPs delayed or avoided medical care due to cost concerns, a significant increase compared to those in traditional lower-deductible plans.

- **Minimal employer contributions to HSAs**: While HSAs are often touted as a benefit, many employers contribute little or nothing to these accounts, leaving employees to cover their deductible entirely out of pocket. And for lower-income workers, the idea of setting aside money in an HSA is simply not feasible. A Federal Reserve survey found that nearly 40% of Americans would struggle to cover an unexpected $400 expense—making it highly unlikely that they are able to fund an account meant to offset a multi-thousand-dollar deductible.

For employers, the expected cost savings from shifting workers to HDHPs have often failed to materialize. While these plans reduce the amount employers pay in premiums, they also lead to decreased employee productivity, higher long-term healthcare costs, and greater financial instability for workers. Employees who avoid care due to cost concerns often end up sicker and more expensive to insure over time, driving up costs for self-funded employers who ultimately bear the burden of more severe and costly claims down the line. Employers who initially saw HDHPs as a way to control spending often find themselves paying more in lost productivity, absenteeism, and expensive hospitalizations that could have been prevented with earlier intervention.

Adding to the problem is the fact that HDHPs do not actually control the underlying cost of care—they merely shift who pays for it. The same inflated hospital prices, opaque negotiated rates, and administrative burdens remain in place, meaning that employees are simply absorbing more of the cost without any structural change to pricing or efficiency. A visit to the emergency room, for example, does not suddenly become cheaper just because an employee has a high-deductible plan—it simply means that the first several thousand dollars of that bill will come directly from their pocket instead of the insurer's.

Meanwhile, the insurance companies offering these plans continue to profit. Unlike a traditional insurance model where the insurer takes on financial risk, HDHPs transfer much of that risk onto employees while still collecting monthly premiums. Many workers go months or even years without meeting their deductible, meaning insurers receive regular premium payments while paying out very little in claims. In effect, employees are paying for coverage they cannot afford to use, leaving insurers with lower claims costs and higher margins.

For individuals, the impact of this shift is profound. Healthcare has become a financial gamble: do you pay thousands upfront for the security of knowing your care is covered, or do you opt for a high-deductible plan, hoping you won't get sick or injured? The entire concept of health insurance—protection against financial devastation—has been flipped on its head.

In the end, the high-deductible model has proven to be a financial squeeze for employees while offering limited upside for employers. It is a cost-shifting mechanism, not a cost-containment solution. A system that once guaranteed access to care when it was needed has now become one where insurance itself is an obstacle, forcing people to navigate financial hurdles before they can even begin to use the coverage they have already paid for. Employees and their families are paying more, getting less, and shouldering more risk than ever before—while the insurance industry continues to thrive in a system that was once designed to protect people, not profit from them.

Chapter 20

INSURANCE COMPANIES AS HEALTHCARE PROVIDERS & NEGOTIATING ON BOTH SIDES OF THE TABLE

For decades, health insurance companies were largely seen as financial intermediaries —entities that process claims, negotiate provider contracts, and design benefits for employers and individuals. But in recent years, the nation's largest insurers have expanded their reach far beyond traditional insurance roles, acquiring physician groups, clinics, urgent care centers, surgical centers, and even home health agencies, transforming themselves into vertically integrated healthcare conglomerates.

This transformation is most pronounced with UnitedHealth Group, which has become the largest employer of physicians in the United States. Through its subsidiary Optum, UnitedHealth has systematically acquired healthcare providers across the nation, managing over 90,000 physicians. Optum's reach extends into primary care practices, urgent care centers, specialty groups, surgical centers, and even behavioral health services, effectively making UnitedHealth both a payer and a provider. This expansion allows UnitedHealth to direct patients into its own facilities, capturing more of the healthcare dollar at each step of the patient journey.

CVS Health, leveraging its acquisition of Aetna, has aggressively entered the provider space as well. CVS owns Oak Street Health, which operates primary care clinics in underserved communities across 21 states, targeting the lucrative Medicare Advantage market. Additionally, CVS acquired Signify Health, a company specializing in home health assessments, further embedding itself in the delivery of care. The MinuteClinic model, with over 1,100 retail clinics inside CVS pharmacies, serves as another touchpoint, providing accessible but limited care directly in their stores.

Cigna, through its Evernorth subsidiary, has expanded its provider footprint with acquisitions in telehealth, behavioral health, and pharmacy services. By integrating these services, Cigna positions itself as not just an insurer but a full-spectrum health service provider, controlling more aspects of patient care directly.

Humana has also invested heavily in expanding its provider capabilities. The CenterWell brand, Humana's primary care platform, is growing rapidly, focusing on senior-focused primary care clinics and home health services. These clinics are designed to capture Medicare Advantage members, enhancing Humana's control over both the financing and delivery of care. Humana's acquisition of Kindred at Home, the nation's largest home health and hospice provider, further strengthens its position as a direct care provider.

Anthem, recently rebranded as Elevance Health, has joined the ranks of insurers expanding into direct care delivery. Elevance launched Carelon, its healthcare services subsidiary, which focuses on home health, behavioral health, and advanced primary care. Through Carelon, Elevance is aiming to integrate services across the care continuum, offering everything from telehealth visits to in-home care, directly managing patient health beyond traditional insurance roles.

These expansions into the provider space represent a strategic

CHAPTER 20

shift for insurers. By owning and operating healthcare facilities and services, they increase their ability to control patient flow, capture more revenue, and influence care decisions directly. The vertical integration of these massive entities allows them to steer patients into their networks, ensuring that healthcare dollars circulate within their ecosystems, ultimately boosting their profitability.

This consolidation is not just about efficiency or care coordination—it is about control. Insurers are no longer simply processing claims on behalf of employers, individuals, or government programs; they are now on both sides of the transaction—acting as both payer and provider. This allows them to direct patients toward their own physicians, clinics, and services, capturing revenue at every step. When a UnitedHealthcare member sees an Optum doctor at an Optum clinic, undergoes imaging at an Optum-owned facility, and fills a prescription at an Optum-affiliated pharmacy, UnitedHealthcare keeps nearly every dollar spent on that care within its own corporate structure. The same dynamic plays out with CVS-Aetna, Cigna-Evernorth, Humana-CenterWell, and Elevance-Carelon—the result is a system where insurers aren't just paying for healthcare; they are running it.

This structure squeezes out independent providers who are unable to compete with massive, insurer-owned medical groups. As these conglomerates expand their control over primary and specialty care, independent physicians and clinics are finding themselves locked out of insurer-controlled networks or forced into acquisition. The bargaining power of independent providers has eroded, with many left with little choice but to sell to the very insurers that once merely negotiated their reimbursement rates. This cycle of acquisition and consolidation is systematically reducing competition, choice, and provider autonomy, all while giving insurers greater leverage to dictate the terms of care.

For employers and patients, the consequences are profound. Employers who self-fund their health plans often assume they are independently managing their benefits, but their third-party administrator (TPA)—often UnitedHealth, Cigna, or another major insurer—has a vested interest in directing members toward its own, more profitable services. The same companies that negotiate provider contracts and determine network access are steering employees into their own provider networks, creating a closed-loop system that maximizes their own revenue. Employers, thinking they are securing competitive pricing for their health plans, often lack insight into how much of their healthcare dollars are being funneled into insurer-owned entities rather than the open market.

One of the most underappreciated financial levers in this consolidation is how insurers manipulate the MLR requirement. As noted previously, under the Affordable Care Act, insurers are now required to spend 80% to 85% of premium revenue on actual medical care, leaving *only* 15% to 20% for administrative costs and profit. However, by owning the providers, clinics, and services delivering that care, insurers can shift profits from their insurance business to their healthcare subsidiaries, effectively circumventing the cap. This is done through eliminations—accounting maneuvers where payments made between an insurer and its wholly owned providers are counted as medical expenses rather than administrative costs. The insurer still profits, but now under the guise of "care delivery" rather than insurance margins.

This practice obscures true profitability and allows insurers to appear compliant with MLR regulations while still maximizing earnings. If a traditional insurer negotiates a rate of $100 for an office visit with an independent physician, only a fraction of that money is retained as profit. But when the insurer owns the clinic, employs the doctor, and controls the entire financial flow, that $100 stays within the company, counted as a medical expense rather than a profit center. This allows insurers to hide margins, artificially inflate medical spending, and continue raising premiums—all while appearing to operate within regulatory constraints.

As the boundaries between payer and provider blur, the implications for patients and employers become increasingly significant. The same entities responsible for determining coverage, negotiating prices, and managing networks are now the ones delivering care, setting rates, and deciding treatment pathways. This creates fundamental conflicts of interest, where the incentive to minimize claims payouts conflicts with the role of a provider that should prioritize patient care.

This massive consolidation is accelerating at breakneck speed, reshaping the healthcare landscape with only a handful of voices raising alarms about the consequences. While some policymakers and industry experts have begun to recognize the risks, most of the transition is happening in plain sight, with little pushback and even less public awareness. If history is any guide, the time to act is before the market becomes so consolidated that reversing course requires sweeping—and often painful—government intervention.

This is not without precedent. We've seen this play out before, in industries that once seemed untouchable—railroads, oil, airlines—where unchecked vertical integration allowed a handful of dominant players to consolidate power, eliminate competition, and manipulate markets to their advantage. Eventually, public and regulatory pressure forced change, but not before massive economic distortions, consumer harm, and a loss of market freedom.

A historical parallel to what is happening in healthcare today can be found in the early days of the railroad and oil industries in the late 19th and early 20th centuries, when vertical integration and monopolistic practices led to market distortions that forced government intervention. The clearest example is Standard Oil, the company founded by John D. Rockefeller, which, much like today's major insurers, did not just sell a product—it controlled every part of the supply chain, allowing it to dominate an entire sector of the economy.

In the late 1800s, oil refining was a fragmented industry, with numerous independent refineries competing to process crude oil. Standard Oil began acquiring these refineries, but its most powerful move was its vertical expansion—instead of just refining oil, it also took control of the pipelines, railroads, and storage facilities that transported and distributed petroleum products. By doing so, it could dictate prices, cut off competitors from access to distribution channels, and steer all oil-related revenue back into its own ecosystem—very similar to how UnitedHealth, CVS-Aetna, and Cigna are now taking control of both the financing and delivery of healthcare.

One of Standard Oil's most notorious tactics was offering preferential railroad shipping rates to its own subsidiaries while charging competitors higher prices, effectively forcing them out of business. If an independent oil producer wanted to ship crude oil via rail, it had to pay far more than Standard Oil's own subsidiaries, making it financially impossible to compete. This mirrors what insurers are doing to independent doctors and hospitals today—as they buy up more providers, they steer patients into their own networks, offer more favorable reimbursement rates to their own clinics, and make it increasingly difficult for independent providers to survive. Over time, this forces consolidation—not because it improves efficiency, but because independent players are being suffocated out of the market.

The government eventually stepped in with antitrust actions, culminating in the landmark 1911 Supreme Court case *Standard Oil Co. of New Jersey v. United States*, which led to the forced breakup of Standard Oil into 34 separate companies. The case established the legal precedent that vertically integrated monopolies—where a single company controls multiple stages of an industry—can be inherently anticompetitive and harmful to consumers. The parallels to healthcare today are striking: insurers are no longer just paying for care; they are dictating where patients go, what doctors can charge, and even how care is delivered.

Another historical analogy comes from the airline industry in the late 20th century, when major carriers began controlling not only flight routes but also airport infrastructure and reservation systems. In the 1970s and 1980s, airlines began to dominate key airports and use their control over gates, baggage handling, and ground services to block out smaller competitors. Additionally, large carriers owned and controlled the computerized reservation systems (CRS) that travel agents relied on to book tickets, giving them the ability to manipulate search results and favor their own flights over competitors' offerings. This created a closed-loop system where the largest airlines could dominate access to customers and force smaller airlines to operate at a disadvantage—similar to how insurers today control provider networks, dictate reimbursement rates, and limit patient choice by funneling them into their own vertically integrated healthcare facilities.

The federal government eventually stepped in with new regulations, including the Airline Deregulation Act of 1978 and later antitrust scrutiny of CRS abuses, to ensure that large carriers could not use their infrastructure dominance to eliminate competition entirely. However, many of the airline industry's structural problems remain today, particularly in markets where one or two airlines control most of the available flights, leading to higher prices and limited options for travelers—exactly what is happening in healthcare as insurers continue to buy up provider networks, reducing competition, and controlling access to care.

These historical examples serve as a warning for what happens when dominant players vertically integrate and eliminate meaningful competition. In both cases, the government eventually had to step in to curb the abuses—but not before enormous economic damage was done. Healthcare is now facing a similar inflection point, and the question remains: will policymakers intervene before insurers consolidate even further, or will the market reach a point where it is virtually impossible for independent providers and employers to push back against these corporate behemoths?

Chapter 21

DELAY, DENY, DEPOSE: BARRIERS TO CARE IN THE FORM OF "UTILIZATION MANAGEMENT"

At its core, prior authorization and medical necessity reviews were created as guardrails to prevent overuse of healthcare services. In a system where providers are paid based on the volume of services they perform—rather than outcomes or necessity—there is a legitimate concern that unnecessary tests, procedures, and treatments could drive up costs and expose patients to unnecessary risks. Insurers argue that these oversight mechanisms are designed to ensure care is both appropriate and evidence-based, and in principle, that is a valid and important function. When used effectively, they can also serve as a moment of intervention—redirecting patients to more appropriate sites of care, steering them toward Centers of Excellence, or connecting them with benefits programs that improve quality and reduce out-of-pocket costs.3

However, what started as a tool to protect patients from unnecessary interventions has evolved into something far more obstructive. Today many, insurers use prior authorization and medical necessity reviews as powerful cost-containment tools, inserting themselves between patients and providers in ways that often delay or deny necessary care, create administrative burdens, and leave patients with few options when they are most vulnerable.

And increasingly, these decisions are not even being made by doctors or medical experts, but by algorithms and artificial intelligence—systems designed to reject claims and shift the burden of proof onto patients and providers.

HOW PRIOR AUTHORIZATION AND MEDICAL NECESSITY REVIEWS FUNCTION IN PRACTICE

When a doctor determines that a patient needs a particular medication, imaging scan, procedure, or specialist referral, the assumption might be that the next step is scheduling the care. But in many cases, that's just the beginning of the process.

Prior authorization requires providers to submit detailed documentation to justify why a treatment is needed before an insurer will agree to cover it. Medical necessity reviews allow insurers to determine, based on their own criteria, whether a service is "appropriate"—even if the treating physician believes it is essential. Insurers may require patients to try and fail on cheaper treatments before approving more expensive or advanced options—a process known as step therapy, which can be frustrating and even harmful for those with complex conditions.

These systems are time-consuming for doctors and overwhelming for patients, especially when coverage is denied and appeals are required. And while insurers argue that these tools prevent wasteful spending, data suggests that they are being used far more aggressively than necessary, leading to harmful delays in care.

A 2022 American Medical Association (AMA) survey found that:

- 94% of physicians reported that prior authorization caused delays in care.
- 80% said they had patients abandon recommended treatments due to authorization obstacles.
- 34% said that prior authorization had led to a serious adverse event, including hospitalization or even death.

A separate Kaiser Family Foundation study found that in Medicare Advantage alone, insurers denied over two million prior authorization requests in a single year, with nearly 75% of denials overturned on appeal—suggesting that many of these initial rejections were not medically justified in the first place.

THE RISE OF AI-POWERED DENIALS: ALGORITHMS OVERRULING DOCTORS

The latest evolution of these oversight mechanisms has been the widespread adoption of AI-driven claim review and prior authorization systems. Instead of a trained medical professional reviewing claims for appropriateness, artificial intelligence models are now making split-second determinations on whether care should be approved, denied, or questioned.

UnitedHealth Group has been at the center of this controversy, particularly due to its use of AI through its subsidiary NaviHealth to review and reject claims for post-acute care services. Investigative reporting from *ProPublica* and lawsuits from patients and providers have revealed disturbing patterns:

- The AI was overriding physician recommendations and predicting shorter recovery times than doctors deemed appropriate.
- Denials were issued automatically—sometimes in mere seconds—without meaningful review by a human expert.
- Patients recovering from major surgeries, strokes, and other conditions were forced to leave care facilities prematurely, often before they were physically ready.

This practice is not unique to UnitedHealth. Cigna has been investigated for using AI to automatically reject thousands of claims at a time—with some reports indicating that doctors working for Cigna spent just 1.2 seconds "reviewing" each claim before issuing denials.

The scale of these denials is staggering. A 2024 report by the Senate Finance Committee highlighted that major insurers, including UnitedHealthcare, Humana, and CVS Health, denied prior authorization requests for post-acute care services at significantly higher rates than other types of care.

- UnitedHealthcare and CVS Health denied post-acute care requests at rates nearly three times their overall denial rates.
- Humana's denial rate for post-acute care services was more than 16 times higher than its general denial rate.

These statistics raise serious questions about whether AI-driven denials are being used as an aggressive cost-containment strategy rather than a tool to ensure appropriate care.

At the same time, AI-driven decision-making has largely outpaced regulation. Congress has attempted to address these issues through legislative proposals, such as the Improving Seniors' Timely Access to Care Act, which seeks to impose greater oversight on prior authorization processes within Medicare Advantage plans. The bill has gained bipartisan support but has yet to meaningfully alter the way insurers deploy AI-driven denials in real time.

This convergence of payer and provider roles within large healthcare conglomerates further complicates the issue. As insurers acquire physician groups and healthcare facilities, they are not just setting coverage policies—they are determining how, when, and where patients receive care. Prior authorization decisions made by insurers increasingly funnel patients into their own, more profitable services, creating a closed-loop system that maximizes revenue while limiting external competition.

The consequences of these trends extend beyond individual denials and delayed treatments. The rapid expansion of AI-driven utilization management, vertical integration, and prior authorization bureaucracy has fundamentally altered how Americans access healthcare. Patients no longer interact with insurers simply as payers—they are dealing with corporate healthcare behemoths that not only decide whether their care is covered but also increasingly dictate where that care is received.

This shift has drawn increasing attention from lawmakers, patient advocacy groups, and medical organizations. But as investigations into AI-driven denials continue, and insurers expand their control over care delivery, the question remains: will these practices be reined in before they become too entrenched to reverse?

THE JUSTIFICATION FOR PRIOR AUTHORIZATION? FRAUD, UPCODING, AND THE NEED FOR OVERSIGHT

While prior authorization and claims review processes have drawn widespread criticism, insurers argue that these measures are necessary to prevent fraudulent billing, overutilization, and unnecessary treatments that inflate healthcare costs. One of the most prevalent issues insurers point to is upcoding—a practice where healthcare providers submit claims for more expensive procedures or services than were actually performed, leading to inflated reimbursements.

A classic example of upcoding might involve an emergency room visit that, in reality, required only a basic evaluation and treatment but is instead billed as a high-acuity, high-intensity encounter. Under the standardized Evaluation and Management (E/M) coding system, a simple visit for a minor issue (such as a mild fever or minor wound cleaning) might be billed at Level 2 or 3, whereas a critical, resource-intensive visit (such as a patient experiencing a heart attack or severe trauma) would be billed at Level 4 or 5—with significantly higher reimbursement rates. If a provider routinely bills Level 4 and 5 visits when Level 2 and 3 care was actually provided, they are effectively defrauding the payer—whether it's an insurer, an employer, or the government.

This issue has been at the center of ongoing litigation between UnitedHealthcare and TeamHealth, one of the nation's largest physician staffing companies. In 2021, UnitedHealthcare sued TeamHealth, alleging that the company systematically upcoded emergency department claims, inflating charges and overbilling UnitedHealthcare for services that were far less complex than what was represented in the claims. According to the lawsuit, TeamHealth's upcoding resulted in overpayments exceeding $100 million since 2016, with UnitedHealthcare arguing that it had been fraudulently billed for emergency visits that did not meet the level of severity claimed.

TeamHealth, in turn, countersued UnitedHealthcare, accusing the insurer of intentionally downcoding legitimate claims and underpaying providers for necessary emergency care. In 2021, a Nevada jury sided with TeamHealth, awarding $60 million in punitive damages, finding that UnitedHealthcare had willfully reduced payments for emergency services—a strategy that many providers argue is simply the other side of the same coin: insurers suppressing reimbursements in an effort to contain costs, whether or not the claims were appropriate.

This legal battle is part of a much larger debate about the delicate balance between preventing fraud and ensuring timely patient access to care. On one hand, cases like TeamHealth's upcoding practices support the argument that insurers must have robust claim reviews and oversight before issuing payments. Without such measures, bad actors can take advantage of the system, inflating costs not just for insurers, but for the employers, taxpayers, and patients ultimately footing the bill.

Healthcare fraud is a major issue, with estimates from the National Health Care Anti-Fraud Association (NHCAA) suggesting that financial losses due to fraudulent claims could account for anywhere from 3% to 10% of total healthcare expenditures. These figures include everything from phantom billing (billing for services never provided), falsified diagnoses, unbundling (charging separately for services that should be billed together at a lower rate), and upcoding. In an employer-sponsored health plan, every fraudulent claim directly increases overall spending—ultimately driving up premiums, deductibles, and out-of-pocket costs for employees.

Because of this, many employers are actually supportive of rigorous claim review processes—at least in principle. When it's their money being spent on overbilled claims, they demand cost containment and oversight. But when those same processes start denying necessary care to their own employees—causing frustration, lost productivity, and even worsened health outcomes—their perspective shifts. Employers find themselves in an impossible position: they want claim reviews to prevent waste, but they also don't want to see their employees caught in an endless web of denials and appeals.

Another reason insurers argue that utilization management is necessary is the troubling overuse of unnecessary medical procedures, which not only inflate costs but also expose patients to risks they should never have faced in the first place. How many people have undergone surgery they didn't actually need? How often do hospitals and doctors recommend procedures that offer little to no benefit—or worse, create complications that make a patient's condition even worse?

Consider spinal fusion surgery, a procedure that permanently joins two or more vertebrae to stabilize the spine. While it can be life-changing for certain conditions, such as severe scoliosis or spinal instability, it has also become one of the most overused procedures in the U.S. healthcare system. In fact, a review of Medicare billing data found that more than $2 billion was spent over a three-year period on spinal fusion surgeries that were later deemed unnecessary. Even more startling, a prospective observational study found that 60% of patients who were recommended spinal surgery didn't actually need it—meaning that for every 10 people told they required a major back operation, six might have been better off without it.

A similar story plays out with coronary stents, tiny mesh tubes inserted into arteries to improve blood flow in patients with heart disease. Stents are lifesaving in emergency situations, such as during a heart attack—but what about when the patient is stable? A large international study led by researchers at Stanford and New York University found that for patients with stable heart disease, stents provided no greater benefit than medication and lifestyle changes. Yet, despite mounting evidence that stents offer little benefit for stable patients, they continue to be widely used—not always out of medical necessity, but because the system financially rewards their use.

It is important to note that the issue of unnecessary medical procedures isn't just a financial concern that costs the system millions—it has harmed patients, and shattered trust in the healthcare system. Among the most shocking cases is that of Dr. Mark Midei, a once-respected

CHAPTER 21

cardiologist in Maryland whose name is now synonymous with one of the worst stent-fraud cases in U.S. history.

For years, patients trusted Dr. Midei with their hearts—literally. He was the go-to cardiologist at St. Joseph Medical Center in Towson, Maryland, and had a reputation for performing cutting-edge heart procedures. But what many of his patients didn't know was that they were undergoing completely unnecessary stent placements, receiving metal implants in their arteries for blockages that didn't exist or were too minor to require intervention.

The scope of the fraud was staggering. A federal investigation found that Dr. Midei had implanted over 500 medically unnecessary stents, falsely telling patients that they had dangerous arterial blockages. One patient was informed he had a 90% artery blockage when, in reality, his artery was only 10% blocked. Another patient, believing his life had been saved, later discovered through legal proceedings that his stent had been implanted for no valid medical reason.

The hospital itself was complicit, benefiting from the revenue generated by the procedures. In 2010, St. Joseph Medical Center agreed to a $37 million settlement with the U.S. Department of Justice for its role in the fraudulent billing scheme. Patients who had trusted their doctor's word were left with unnecessary implants, lifelong medical risks, and a profound sense of betrayal. Dr. Midei lost his medical license and became a national symbol of how financial incentives can drive overuse in medicine.

But Maryland isn't the only place where stent overutilization has turned into a high-profile scandal. In Orlando, Florida, cardiologist Dr. Ashish Pal found himself at the center of a federal investigation after performing hundreds of questionable procedures.

Dr. Pal didn't just implant unnecessary stents—he also allegedly performed risky ablations, vein treatments, and other cardiovascular procedures on patients who didn't need them. One patient underwent multiple vein ablations for a condition she didn't actually have, only to suffer from severe complications afterward. Others were told they required invasive interventions for circulation issues that could have been treated with far less aggressive methods—or not at all.

The government alleged that Dr. Pal knowingly submitted false claims for these unwarranted procedures, raking in millions from Medicare and private insurers. In 2022, he agreed to pay a $6.75 million settlement to resolve the fraud allegations. While he never admitted wrongdoing, the case underscored the financial incentives that drive overuse in medicine—and the role insurers claim to play in stopping such abuses.

These cases lay bare the difficult reality at the heart of utilization management: How do we stop bad actors like Midei and Pal while ensuring that legitimate care isn't delayed or denied? How do insurers distinguish between genuine medical necessity and profit-driven overtreatment?

The answer, so far, has been to cast a wide net—one that catches fraud but also ensnares thousands of patients who truly need care. And in this battle between overutilization and under-approval, it is always the patient who pays the price.

These examples, from upcoding to extreme overutilization, highlight why insurers often insist on stringent oversight—without some level of review, payers argue that the system would simply be writing a blank check for procedures that might not be in a patient's best interest. But where is the line between necessary oversight and obstructing legitimate care? How do we prevent unnecessary spinal surgeries and stents while ensuring that patients who truly need these interventions don't get trapped in a bureaucratic nightmare of denials and appeals?

The reality is that bad actors exist in every corner of the healthcare system, from hospitals that push unnecessary procedures to insurers that deny legitimate claims. The challenge is not just stopping fraud

CHAPTER 21

or overuse—it's whether we can create a system where patients aren't collateral damage in an endless tug-of-war between cost containment and provider incentives. If every effort to regulate spending ends up harming access to legitimate care, perhaps the problem isn't just too much or too little oversight—it's that we have built a system where these competing forces can never be balanced in a way that truly benefits patients.

If there is no middle ground—if every effort to rein in costs through prior authorization, utilization management, or claims reviews ends up harming patient access—then perhaps the real question isn't how to strike a better balance, but whether the model itself is fundamentally broken.

Chapter 22

DELAY, DENY, DEPOSE: THE PUBLIC OUTRAGE OVER THESE PRACTICES

As noted earlier in Chapter 1, the increasing frustration with denials, delays, and bureaucratic hurdles boiled over in 2024 when UnitedHealthcare CEO Brian Thompson was murdered in New York City. The accused shooter left three bullets with the following words: "Delay, Deny, Depose."

"Delay, Deny, Depose" is a phrase that originated as a play on words based on David Berardinelli's 2006 book, *Delay, Deny, Defend: Why Insurance Companies Don't Pay Claims and What You Can Do About It*. The book explored how major insurance companies developed systematic strategies to delay payouts, deny claims, and defend against policyholders who challenged them, effectively making it as difficult as possible for people to access the benefits they had paid for.

Berardinelli's work focused primarily on property and casualty insurance, particularly how Allstate Insurance adopted McKinsey & Co.-designed playbooks that instructed adjusters to delay processing claims, deny as many as possible, and aggressively fight back against those who dared to challenge them in court. The result? Policyholders often gave up, accepted lower settlements, or found

CHAPTER 22

themselves financially ruined—all while insurance companies padded their bottom lines by holding onto unpaid claim dollars for as long as possible.

The same tactics Berardinelli described in *Delay, Deny, Defend* have now become deeply embedded in health insurance, where insurers have perfected the strategy of making care access so difficult, cumbersome, and exhausting that many patients either give up or go bankrupt in the process.

Over time, the phrase evolved from "Delay, Deny, Defend" to "Delay, Deny, Depose" in the healthcare context—highlighting not just the bureaucratic and financial barriers, but also the legal and procedural roadblocks that insurers place in front of patients, doctors, and employers who try to fight back:

- **Delay**: Stringing out the claims process, forcing patients and doctors to jump through administrative hoops, resubmit paperwork, or wait weeks (or months) for approval.

- **Deny**: Rejecting claims outright, often based on vague criteria, internal guidelines that contradict medical best practices, or AI-generated denials that lack meaningful human review.

- **Depose**: If patients or providers fight back, insurers leverage their legal teams, administrative exhaustion, and drawn-out appeals processes to wear them down, knowing that only the most persistent—and well-resourced—can afford to keep challenging denials.

This three-step process has become so routine that it was immortalized in legal battles, patient advocacy forums, and whistleblower complaints, before resurfacing in public discourse following the 2024 killing of UnitedHealthcare CEO Brian Thompson. The accused shooter's social media posts referenced "Delay, Deny,

Depose," bringing national attention to the widespread frustration with insurers and their obstructionist tactics.

While no act of violence can ever be justified, the killing of Brian Thompson put a global spotlight on the depth of public outrage toward UnitedHealth and the insurance industry as a whole. The news was met with a surge of online discourse, as patients and providers shared their own horror stories of denied care. The reaction was visceral—some called it a tragic but predictable consequence of a system that prioritizes profits over lives, while others saw it as a wake-up call to lawmakers, employers, and the broader public about the unchecked power of insurers.

UnitedHealth issued statements condemning the violence and emphasizing its commitment to patient care, but the damage was already done—this tragedy exposed just how deep and widespread the resentment toward insurance companies has become.

NOT JUST A BAD SYSTEM—A MISALIGNED ONE

There is a fundamental reality that cannot be ignored: the American healthcare system operates on misaligned incentives. Insurers, hospitals, and providers are all structured to extract as much money as possible from the system, but they are not structured to ensure that people receive the right care, at the right time, in the right setting.

Utilization management—the broader category under which prior authorization and medical necessity reviews fall—exists because of legitimate concerns about unnecessary procedures, overtreatment, and waste. The U.S. healthcare system, largely built on fee-for-service payments, financially rewards hospitals and providers for doing more, not necessarily for achieving better health outcomes. Insurers were originally meant to act as a check against these perverse incentives, ensuring that care was cost-effective and appropriate.

But over time, insurers have manipulated this function into a tool for revenue extraction rather than responsible cost control. Instead of preventing unnecessary care, they have built layers of bureaucracy that stand in the way of necessary care—forcing patients and providers to navigate a labyrinth of rules, AI-driven denials, and endless administrative burdens.

The solution isn't simply stricter utilization management or better enforcement of billing transparency—both are necessary but insufficient on their own. The reality is that both sides of the transaction—insurers and providers—are engaged in a relentless effort to extract more revenue, leaving patients caught in the middle. Providers push for higher reimbursement, while insurers erect ever more complex barriers to payment—and in the end, patients are the only ones truly paying the price.

Until the system is structurally realigned to prioritize patient care over financial maneuvering, delays, denials, and endless appeals will persist—not because they are medically necessary, but because they are financially advantageous for those controlling the system.

Chapter 23

THE BILLION-DOLLAR BLIND SPOT: EMPLOYERS AND THE COST OF LOOKING AWAY

For tens of millions of Americans, the "insurance company" denying a claim, setting network prices, or requiring prior authorization isn't actually the one paying for their healthcare. Instead, these insurers are often nothing more than glorified and extraordinarily wealthy middlemen, acting as administrators for employer-sponsored health plans. The real payer? Their employer.

This distinction is critical—because while insurers are often blamed for rising costs, the real purchasing power in the U.S. healthcare system lies with employers who sponsor these plans. And yet, despite their financial stake, most employers have ceded control to the very same insurers and consultants whose business models thrive on runaway spending.

The numbers speak for themselves. Starbucks spends more on employee healthcare than it does on coffee beans. General Motors' annual healthcare bill rivals what it spends on steel. Across corporate America, health benefits are one of the largest—and fastest-growing—expenses. And yet, for all this spending, most employers have shockingly little insight or control over where their dollars go.

To truly understand the mechanics of the system—and why efforts to rein in costs continue to fail—it's essential to explore the role of self-funded employers, the largest purchasers of healthcare in America, and perhaps the most underutilized force for change.

The backbone of the American healthcare system isn't government programs or individual insurance markets—it's employer-sponsored health plans. Today, nearly 160 million Americans receive their healthcare coverage through their employer, making these plans the single largest source of health insurance in the country. And within this system, self-funded employer health plans dominate.

Unlike traditional fully insured plans, where an employer simply pays an insurance company a fixed premium to cover employees, self-funded plans operate more like large-scale risk pools. In a self-funded arrangement, the employer itself pays for medical claims directly, using a combination of company funds and employee contributions. Rather than purchasing a one-size-fits-all insurance plan, employers hire third-party administrators (TPAs) or insurance carriers to process claims, manage networks, and handle administrative functions—but the financial risk remains with the employer.

This structure gives employers tremendous purchasing power, far greater than that of individual policyholders, and in theory, it should incentivize them to aggressively negotiate for better pricing, demand transparency from vendors, and ensure employees receive high-value care. Because they are spending their own money—rather than paying premiums to an insurer that assumes the risk—self-funded employers should be among the most engaged, informed, and cost-conscious participants in the healthcare system.

THE ERISA FRAMEWORK: EMPLOYERS AS FIDUCIARIES

Fiduciary duty is one of the oldest and most sacred legal obligations, originating from the Latin word *fiducia*, meaning "trust" or "confidence." It is the legal and ethical expectation that someone managing another's money or interests must act solely in that person's best interest—loyally, prudently, and with absolute care. This principle is deeply embedded in law and business, from investment management to estate planning

If you have a 401(k), you expect the people overseeing it to be making decisions that benefit you, not themselves. Your employer selects financial managers to invest those funds wisely, minimize fees, and maximize returns for your future retirement. If they fail—if they allow excessive fees, make reckless decisions, or cut deals that benefit themselves over plan participants—they can be sued for breach of fiduciary duty because they have a legal responsibility to prioritize your financial well-being above all else.

Or think about a trustee managing an inheritance. If a parent leaves money in a trust for their children, the trustee doesn't get to use those funds for personal gain, take unnecessary risks, or cut deals that diminish the value of the estate. If they do, they can be sued for violating their fiduciary duty to protect those assets for the beneficiaries, not themselves. The entire purpose of fiduciary law is to create guardrails, ensuring that when someone is entrusted with managing assets on behalf of others, they don't exploit that responsibility for personal or financial gain.

So what does this mean in the world of health benefits plans?

Governance of these plans falls under ERISA (the Employee Retirement Income Security Act of 1974), a federal law designed to ensure that employers act as responsible stewards of the health benefits they provide. Under ERISA, employers who self-fund their health plans are not just picking a health insurance option from a menu—they are fiduciaries, responsible for managing health benefits in the best interests of their employees. That means they have a legal and ethical duty to make smart purchasing decisions, ensure costs are reasonable, and demand transparency from vendors.

The intent behind ERISA was to create a system where employers, acting as plan fiduciaries, would have both the incentive and the obligation to ensure that every dollar spent on healthcare was used wisely. Unlike fully insured plans—where an employer simply pays a premium to an insurance carrier and offloads the financial risk—self-funded employers retain direct control over the funds used to pay employees' medical claims. This means they are not just buying a health plan; they are managing their employees' healthcare dollars more directly.

The stakes couldn't be higher. Employees don't negotiate their own healthcare plans—they rely on their employers to do it for them. Just as an investment manager is expected to maximize returns on a retirement plan, an employer sponsoring a health plan is expected to maximize the value of every healthcare dollar spent on behalf of their employees. If those decisions are careless—if vendors are allowed to extract excessive fees, if waste and inefficiency are ignored, if backroom deals inflate costs—then employees are the ones who suffer.

They pay the price in higher premiums, reduced wages, and rising out-of-pocket costs. They pay it in denied claims, restricted networks, and inflated hospital bills. Just as no one would tolerate a 401(k) manager squandering retirement funds, no one should tolerate a healthcare fiduciary failing to ensure that employees get the highest quality care at the most reasonable cost.

This is why fiduciary duty in health benefits matters. It is the mechanism that ensures accountability in a system where employees have no direct say in how their healthcare dollars are spent. Without it, the balance of power shifts entirely to third-party administrators, insurers, and vendors—entities that profit when costs rise, not when they are contained.

Yet despite the clear fiduciary obligations under ERISA, many employers remain passive participants in the management of their health plans, trusting vendors to act in their best interests without adequate oversight. But trust is not a strategy. Instead of leveraging their fiduciary power to demand better prices, transparency, and accountability from their vendors, many employers have handed over the keys to the very entities responsible for the runaway costs of the healthcare system.

And when they do wake up? They're often met with a carefully curated response—one that discourages scrutiny, reassures them that their vendors have everything under control, and steers them back toward the very system that has led to skyrocketing costs in the first place. For decades, self-funded employers have trusted their consultants, brokers, and third-party administrators to act in their best interest—but what if those entities are actually profiting from the very inefficiencies they claim to manage? What if, instead of working to reduce costs, they are taking a cut of the excess, padding their own margins while telling employers there's nothing they can do?

Employers, the financial backbone of American healthcare spending, have been turned into pawns in a rigged game—one where the rules are written by the very industry players profiting from their inaction. And now, for the first time, some of them are being forced to answer for it.

For years, lawsuits over 401(k) mismanagement exposed how employers turned a blind eye to excessive fees and failed to challenge bad deals that siphoned workers' savings into the pockets of financial firms. Those same cracks are now forming in employer-sponsored health plans, and employees are starting to take notice. If employers have a legal obligation to ensure their retirement plans aren't riddled with hidden fees, why shouldn't they have the same duty when it comes to their health benefits?

A growing wave of lawsuits is beginning to test that very question. Employees are suing their employers, arguing that they have failed in their fiduciary duty by allowing insurers and PBMs to drive up costs unchecked. Just like in the early days of 401(k) litigation, these cases are at the starting line, but the implications could be massive. If the courts begin ruling in favor of employees, it could permanently reshape how employers engage with their health plan administrators. For now, however, the wave is not yet tidal as judges have been reluctant to allow these cases to proceed beyond the motion to dismiss stage.

Even as employers start to grasp the legal risk and are trying to face it head on, many are discovering they have little recourse. Some have attempted to hold their trusted vendor partners accountable, suing their Administrative Services Only (ASO) carriers, PBMs and consultants. Several prominent cases involve employers suing companies like UnitedHealthcare, Cigna, and Blue Cross Blue Shield—arguing that these insurers should share fiduciary responsibility for managing plan dollars. Courts were reticent to find any fiduciary liability on the part of these entities, ruling that unless the ASO carriers expressly agreed to being a fiduciary for plan purposes in their contract with the group health plan client, they were not fiduciaries for purposes of ERISA liability.

At least one Circuit Court has ruled in favor of the group health plan as of the publication of this book. In late May 2025, the 6th Circuit ruled that the plaintiff, a self-funded health plan, had adequately established that Blue Cross Blue Shield of Michigan was a fiduciary for purposes of ERISA because they exercised discretionary authority over plan assets when they knowingly continued to pay claims in error and in amounts that were well above what their clients had agreed to pay as part of their plan benefit document. Given the ramifications of the court's finding, and the emerging circuit split on this issue (the First Circuit ruled in an earlier case involving a BCBS entity and a labor fund that the BCBS entity was not a fiduciary under ERISA, even if they made determinations like how much the plan would pay providers, whether they would recover overpayments, etc.

While we await more clarity from the courts on these issues, specifically whether these third party administrators/carriers are functional fiduciaries given their role in determining plan payment amounts, accuracy, validity, and whether or not to recover claims paid in error, the legal distinction has left employers in a precarious position. The very vendors they relied on to manage their healthcare plans may be shielded from fiduciary accountability, while employers are now squarely on the hook for ensuring those plans are being run prudently. The parallels to the 401(k) lawsuits are undeniable. Employers failed to monitor excessive fees in retirement plans, and employees sued. Now they are failing to monitor excessive spending in healthcare—and the lawsuits are beginning.

Whether these cases succeed remains to be seen, but one thing is certain: the days of employers blindly trusting their consultants, insurers, and PBMs to act in their best interest are coming to an end. Employers have a choice—take control of their health plans, or wait until a judge forces them to.

Chapter 24

THE FIGHT FOR HEALTHCARE DATA: EMPLOYERS WRITING BLANK CHECKS WITH NO RECEIPTS

Imagine you run a global logistics company, and you contract with a firm to manage your entire fleet of trucks, shipping routes, and fuel costs. Every month, you receive a single invoice with a giant total—millions of dollars—but no itemized breakdown of how that money was spent. You ask for details: How much was spent on fuel? Which routes were the most expensive? Are we overpaying on maintenance? But instead of answers, your vendor tells you, "That information is proprietary. Just trust us."

Or imagine you're a major retailer, and your procurement team signs a contract with a vendor to source all your raw materials and manufacturing services. At the end of the quarter, you get a bill for tens of millions of dollars, but no insight into how much you paid for each component, whether prices were competitive, or where the markups occurred. When you ask to see the details, you're told, "We can't disclose that information—it would be disruptive to our supplier relationships."

Would any CFO in these industries accept such an arrangement? Would a board of directors allow this level of opacity in one of the company's largest expense categories? Of course not. Yet this is exactly how self-funded employers purchase healthcare—blindly, with little to no visibility into where their money is going, how prices are set, or whether they're being taken advantage of by the very vendors they hired to manage their plans.

DATA IS POWER—AND THEY KNOW IT

One might assume that, as the ones footing the bill, employers would have unrestricted access to detailed receipts of their healthcare spending. In any other industry, a business making a multimillion-dollar purchase would expect to see exactly where its money was going, who was getting paid, and whether the costs were justified. But in healthcare, that logic doesn't apply. Insurers and third-party administrators treat claims data—the raw information about what services were provided, to whom, at what cost, and how much was actually paid—as proprietary property. They restrict employer access to this data using vague contractual language about confidentiality and trade secrets, all while turning around and selling de-identified versions of the same information for enormous profits.

Healthcare claims data is one of the most valuable assets in the industry, and for good reason. It provides a window into the entire system, revealing who is getting care, where they are going for it, what they are being charged, and how much of that cost is being passed through various intermediaries before it reaches the provider. This information is so powerful that insurers, PBMs, and healthcare analytics firms have built an entire secondary market around it, selling it to pharmaceutical companies, private equity firms, and research institutions eager to extract insights that can be monetized. The very data that employers and patients are denied access to is being repackaged and sold behind closed doors, reinforcing the reality that healthcare is not just a service—it's a marketplace where information itself is a commodity.

Consider how this plays out. A hospital might charge wildly different prices for the same procedure, and that discrepancy would be obvious if employers had access to full claims data. They would see that a simple MRI costs $600 at one facility but $4,000 at another just a few miles away. They would know exactly which hospitals and physician groups are padding their bills with unnecessary services. They would be able to trace the money flowing through middlemen—the PBMs, insurers, and third-party administrators that all take a cut before the provider even sees a dime. Instead, they are handed summary reports, redacted figures, or outright refusals when they request full transparency, all while insurers quietly package this same information and sell it to the highest bidder.

UnitedHealth Group provides a prime example of how this system operates. The company owns Optum, a massive data and analytics arm that generates billions of dollars by analyzing and selling healthcare data. Optum, in turn, markets this intelligence to pharmaceutical companies looking for prescribing trends, private equity firms scouting profitable acquisition targets, and even hedge funds seeking investment opportunities in the healthcare sector. In one particularly egregious case, data firms working with insurers were found to be selling de-identified patient data to life insurance companies. This allowed insurers to assess health risks based on real-world medical claims rather than self-reported health history, meaning that consumers who had never disclosed a preexisting condition could still be flagged as high-risk and face higher premiums—or even denial of coverage—without ever knowing why.

Pharmaceutical companies are another major buyer of claims data. By analyzing prescribing patterns, they can tailor their marketing efforts to target doctors who are most likely to prescribe their drugs, sometimes even adjusting sales strategies based on which competitor's medications are being prescribed in a particular region. PBMs, which are supposed to negotiate drug prices on behalf of employers, often simultaneously sell aggregated prescription claims data to the very drug manufacturers they are negotiating with—giving those manufacturers the upper hand in pricing discussions.

Meanwhile, the employers actually paying for this care remain locked out of the system. They are given heavily redacted reports, partial data sets, or outright refusals when they request full claims data under the guise of contractual limitations or patient privacy concerns. Yet these supposed concerns seem to vanish the moment a pharmaceutical company, hedge fund, or private equity firm comes knocking with a check in hand.

This isn't just a minor inconvenience—it's a fundamental power imbalance. Employers are expected to make multimillion-dollar purchasing decisions with no visibility, while the same information that could empower them to negotiate better rates or detect fraud is being monetized elsewhere. If this sounds absurd, that's because it is. In any other sector, transparency is a prerequisite for smart purchasing. In healthcare, secrecy is the business model.

The real question is why this continues. Why have regulators not stepped in to ensure that the payers of the system—employers and patients—have full transparency into where their money is going? The fact that insurers and third-party administrators are willing to go to such great lengths to restrict access to claims data while simultaneously profiting from it elsewhere tells you everything you need to know about the incentives at play. The less employers and patients know, the more the system can extract from them.

WOULD ANY OTHER INDUSTRY OPERATE THIS WAY?

Would any other industry operate this way? Imagine an airline contracting with a third-party fuel supplier that refuses to disclose how much it pays for fuel at each airport, instead providing a lump-sum invoice with a vague assurance that the pricing is competitive. Or picture a technology company outsourcing its supply chain management but being denied access to the cost breakdown of components, manufacturing fees, or shipping expenses. No rational business would accept these terms—yet this is precisely how the vast majority of self-funded employers operate when it comes to healthcare.

If a major retailer were to sign a sourcing contract without knowing the per-unit price of the goods purchased, shareholders would demand accountability. If a construction firm hired a subcontractor who refused to disclose labor costs or material expenses, executives would be fired. Transparency is a baseline expectation in nearly every sector because businesses cannot make informed decisions without data. Yet in healthcare, the opposite is true. The lack of transparency isn't a flaw in the system—it is the system.

Employers don't just allow this; they perpetuate it by continuing to operate in the dark, trusting vendors who have every incentive to keep them uninformed. When they push for access, they are met with resistance—complex contractual barriers, exorbitant data fees, and outright refusals under the guise of confidentiality agreements. Meanwhile, the very data they are blocked from seeing is being sold behind their backs, fueling an industry that thrives on opacity.

The consequences of this blindfolded approach are staggering. Employers spend billions of dollars annually on healthcare, yet most have no idea whether they are overpaying, subsidizing inefficiencies, or funding outright fraud. They trust that the administrative fees they pay to their insurers and third-party administrators are reasonable, never questioning the layers of markups embedded in the claims process. They assume that the negotiated rates for hospital services reflect genuine cost savings, when in reality, these rates are often the product of backdoor deals that prioritize carrier profits over employer savings.

Even those who begin to suspect they are being taken advantage of often struggle to break the cycle. If an employer dares to demand better terms—full access to claims data, the ability to audit beyond a few hundred cherry-picked claims, or transparency into pharmacy rebates—they are frequently told that such requests are impossible or will result in higher administrative fees. They are warned that pushing too hard could jeopardize their network access or disrupt employee coverage. The message is clear: play by the industry's rules, or risk being left without options.

But is that really the case? The fight for healthcare data isn't just about spreadsheets and cost breakdowns—it's about power. It's about whether employers will finally start behaving like the sophisticated purchasers they are in every other aspect of their business, or whether they will continue outsourcing one of their largest expenses to entities that profit from their ignorance. It's about whether they will take back control of their own spending or remain complicit in a system designed to extract as much money as possible while providing as little transparency as necessary.

The problem isn't just that employers lack access to data. It's that most haven't yet realized how much it's costing them. And until they do, the industry has no reason to change.

Once an employer finally gains access to their healthcare data—after months or even years of battling their insurer or third-party administrator—they expect to finally be in control. They imagine combing through claims history, pinpointing waste, renegotiating contracts,

CHAPTER 24

and finally ensuring that their employees receive high-value care at reasonable prices. But instead of wielding newfound power, they find themselves shackled by an entirely new set of restrictions—buried deep in the fine print of agreements they never fully realized they had signed.

Audit restrictions. Confidentiality clauses. Vendor approval requirements. Instead of transparency, they encounter a labyrinth of roadblocks designed to keep them from using their own data in any meaningful way.

Even the ability to audit claims—a fundamental practice in nearly every industry—becomes a controlled, performative exercise. A self-funded employer spending $75 million annually on healthcare, covering over 10,000 employees, should be able to review any and all claims to ensure accuracy and root out waste. But their administrative services agreement tells them otherwise. Many contracts limit audits to just 250 or 300 claims per year—barely 0.25% of the total claims processed. In financial terms, that means auditing only $187,500 out of a $75 million spend. Would any company allow this level of oversight in their procurement, payroll, or supply chain? Would a publicly traded company tell its shareholders that only 0.25% of financial transactions were being verified? Of course not. Yet, in healthcare, this is the norm.

Employers who dare to question these constraints are often met with another hurdle—the cost of access itself. Some insurers charge employers six-figure fees just to obtain their claims data, demanding upwards of $100,000 per month for visibility into spending. That means an employer could be paying over a million dollars a year just to access records that should already belong to them. Others impose additional requirements, such as cybersecurity insurance policies of $50 million or more, arbitrary barriers that further restrict access and discourage employers from even attempting to review their data. And if they do manage to get the data, it often arrives in fragmented, unstructured formats, requiring additional payments just to make it usable.

Meanwhile, the same insurers and third-party administrators who block employers from accessing their own data have no qualms about monetizing it for themselves. De-identified claims data is regularly packaged and sold to pharmaceutical companies, research firms, and private equity investors. Employers are told their data is "proprietary" and therefore off-limits—until someone else is willing to pay for it.

Even after overcoming these initial obstacles, employers find that their ability to act on the data is just as restricted. If they want to benchmark costs against other companies of similar size, they are often told that their insurer must approve the benchmarking methodology—ensuring that no unflattering comparisons emerge. If they want to bring in an independent auditor to assess waste and identify opportunities for savings, they may discover that their contract requires the insurer's explicit approval of the auditor—giving them veto power over anyone likely to uncover excessive costs. If they attempt to remove a high-cost hospital from their network, their contract may grant the insurer sole discretion over network changes, effectively blocking any efforts to steer employees toward better-value care.

And when an employer pushes too hard, the industry has a ready-made solution: its own in-house consultants, analytics teams, and self-service dashboards. On the surface, these tools appear to provide useful insights—trend reports, cost breakdowns, utilization metrics—but they are carefully curated to serve the interests of the insurer, not the employer. Certain data fields are omitted, cost comparisons lack real benchmarks, and the insights provided are just enough to make employers feel informed, but never enough to empower them to make fundamental changes.

Even when employers hire their own independent consultants, they often discover that those consultants are operating under their own restrictions. Many of the largest benefits consulting firms have explicit agreements with insurers and TPAs that limit what they can analyze, report, or recommend. In some cases, consultants are contractually prohibited from providing claims data to third-party auditors without insurer approval. Others are barred from extrapolating audit findings to identify systemic overpayments or fraud. Some agreements even prevent consultants from conducting independent financial modeling that could expose excessive administrative fees or hidden cost-shifting tactics.

The result? Employers pay for access, pay for consultants, and still find themselves locked into a system where oversight is carefully managed and real accountability is nearly impossible. The firms employers trust to protect their interests are often bound by agreements designed to serve the very entities they should be scrutinizing.

In any other industry, this would be considered a fundamental failure of corporate governance. But in healthcare, it's just another day in a system designed to keep employers paying without questioning.

Chapter 25

THE RULES YOU DIDN'T KNOW YOU AGREED TO: THE UNSEEN HAND CONTROLLING EMPLOYER HEALTH PLANS

By now, it should be clear that employers are not actually in control of the health plans they fund. Even when they secure access to their claims data—after fighting through contractual barriers and consultant limitations—they quickly discover that their ability to act on what they've learned is severely restricted by the fine print in their administrative agreements.

Employers might quickly realize that simply knowing where their money is going doesn't mean they can do anything about it. Insurers and third-party administrators (TPAs) don't just process claims. They dictate the terms of reimbursement, control which providers can be prioritized, and even forbid employers from steering their employees toward lower-cost, higher-quality providers.

This is the power of anti-tiering and anti-steering clauses—contractual provisions that rig employer-sponsored health plans in favor of dominant hospital systems, forcing employers to treat all in-network hospitals the same, regardless of how much they charge or how well they perform.

To put it in perspective, imagine running a business where you negotiate deals with multiple suppliers. One vendor offers a high-quality product at half the price of a competitor. It seems like a no-brainer—you should be able to highlight that supplier as the best choice for customers, right? Not in healthcare. Anti-tiering clauses prevent employers from doing exactly that. They force employers to keep all in-network hospitals on the same playing field, even when one is twice the cost for the same service.

Anti-steering clauses take it even further. Suppose a hospital is charging exorbitant rates for a simple procedure, but another hospital just a few miles away offers the same service for thousands of dollars less with better patient outcomes. If you were running a business, you'd direct your customers to the better-value option. But in healthcare, you can't. Anti-steering clauses prohibit employers and insurers from incentivizing or even recommending that patients seek care at the more affordable, high-quality provider.

I saw this play out firsthand when I was running the New Jersey State Health Plan, covering more than 800,000 public employees, retirees, and their families. Given the plan's size, we should have had unmatched leverage to negotiate better deals.

We approached our TPA with a simple request: Help us steer members toward high-quality providers who delivered excellent care at a significantly lower cost.

Their response?

"No, we can't do that."

Why not? Because they had a side deal with the largest hospital system in the state that forbade them from steering members to lower-cost alternatives.

This wasn't written in our contract. This was an undisclosed agreement—one that dictated how our health plan had to function, despite our billions in spending.

Naturally, I pushed further. What made this particular hospital system so special? Was there any quality data, cost transparency, or outcomes justification that made them more worthy of being in the preferred network?

Their answer?

"We can't disclose that. The terms are proprietary."

Think about that. A taxpayer-funded health plan was contractually prohibited from steering members to lower-cost, higher-quality providers—and we weren't even allowed to ask why.

THE CASE OF 32BJ AND NEWYORK-PRESBYTERIAN

This isn't just a New Jersey problem. 32BJ Health Fund, which covers tens of thousands of Service Employees International Union (SEIU) workers across the Northeast, found itself in the same fight.

They had a simple goal: improve maternity care while reducing unnecessary spending. Their research identified hospitals that provided better maternal outcomes, fewer complications, and significantly lower costs. Naturally, they wanted to steer their members toward these hospitals.

But when they approached their TPA to implement this program, NewYork-Presbyterian (NYP), one of the most dominant hospital systems in the country, issued an ultimatum.

NYP flat-out refused to accept any designation other than "preferred."

CHAPTER 25

They didn't care that other hospitals had better outcomes. They would not allow any financial incentives that encouraged members to choose a lower-cost, higher-value alternative.

It was a power play—one that most employers would never challenge.

But 32BJ called their bluff—and kicked NYP out of the network entirely.

This kind of bold move is extremely rare, because most employers are conditioned to believe they have no other choice but to accept these demands. The reality is that employers aren't even allowed to consider alternatives because the system is built to keep them compliant, paying, and in the dark.

If employers needed even more proof that the system is stacked against them, the Department of Labor's (DOL) lawsuit against Blue Cross Blue Shield of Minnesota (BCBSM) makes it impossible to ignore.

According to the lawsuit, BCBSM quietly charged employers $66.8 million in provider taxes—taxes that were meant to be paid by hospitals and doctors, not employers.

BCBSM pulled this off by baking those taxes into provider reimbursement rates—essentially passing the cost off as a legitimate claim expense.

When employers caught wind of what was happening and demanded answers, BCBSM didn't deny it.

Their response?

"It was in the contract. If we agreed to pay the providers' taxes, then you, the employer, are bound by that agreement."

Let that sink in.

A major insurer signed a deal on behalf of employers—without their knowledge or consent—that forced them to pay someone else's tax obligations.

And when they were caught, their response was essentially: "Too bad. You signed the contract."

SUTTER HEALTH'S MONOPOLY POWER

If you think these tactics are exclusive to insurers, dominant hospital systems are just as bad—if not worse.

Take Sutter Health, the largest hospital chain in Northern California.

For years, Sutter used its sheer market power to force insurers into all-or-nothing contracts, meaning if an insurer wanted access to any Sutter facility, they had to contract with all of them—no cherry-picking based on cost or quality.

Sutter also implemented anti-steering and anti-tiering provisions to prevent insurers from directing patients toward lower-cost hospitals—even within their own network.

When patients sought care at Sutter hospitals, they were often stuck paying massively inflated prices for services that could have been 50% cheaper just a few miles away.

After years of legal battles and investigations, Sutter was finally hit with a $575 million settlement in 2019 for engaging in anticompetitive practices that led to higher costs for millions of Californians. But that didn't stop them—new lawsuits have already surfaced, proving just how embedded these tactics are in the system.

The deeper you dig into the mechanics of employer-sponsored healthcare, the clearer it becomes: the system is designed to keep employers locked into high-cost arrangements with minimal control. Even when they finally access their claims data—after cutting through layers of red tape and legal roadblocks—they quickly realize that their ability to act on that data is just as restricted as their ability to obtain it in the first place. The game is rigged in ways most employers don't fully grasp until it's too late.

At every turn, they find themselves constrained by anti-tiering clauses that prevent them from steering employees to lower-cost, high-quality providers, anti-steering provisions that force them to treat every hospital in a network as equal regardless of price or outcomes, and hidden financial agreements that siphon millions from their health plans without their consent. Employers are conditioned to believe they are managing a competitive benefits plan, but in reality, they are operating under terms dictated by insurers, TPAs, and dominant health systems—entities that profit off the inefficiencies they create.

And yet, this is only one piece of the puzzle. As infuriating as these restrictions are, they are just the beginning. Because in recent years, insurers and TPAs have taken their control a step further—not just managing networks and negotiating rates but becoming direct providers of care themselves. Through acquisitions, partnerships, and strategic expansion, the same companies responsible for overseeing employer-sponsored health plans are now delivering healthcare services, from primary care to specialty treatment.

At first glance, this might sound like a step toward efficiency—after all, wouldn't it make sense for the entities paying for care to also be involved in delivering it? But as with everything in healthcare, the reality is far more complicated. The rise of insurer-owned and TPA-controlled providers is not about improving patient outcomes or driving down costs. It is about control. It is about consolidating market power. And, most importantly, it is about making sure employers and patients have fewer alternatives, fewer opportunities to push back, and even less transparency than before.

If employers thought they had little leverage before, they are now facing an entirely new playing field—one where the referee, the rule-maker, and the opposition are increasingly one and the same.

Chapter 26

THE SILENT TAKEOVER: HOW TPAS AND CARRIERS ARE BECOMING PROVIDERS WITHOUT EMPLOYER OVERSIGHT

While we've already touched on the growing vertical consolidation in healthcare, it's important to highlight just how much self-funded employers stand to lose in this rapidly changing environment. TPAs and insurers—long positioned as neutral administrators of employer health plans—are no longer just processing claims and negotiating provider contracts. They are becoming the providers themselves, integrating deeply into the delivery of care in ways that create direct financial conflicts of interest.

And no company has executed this takeover more aggressively than UnitedHealth Group.

UnitedHealth isn't just an insurance company. It owns Optum, one of the largest healthcare delivery systems in the country, which employs more than 90,000 physicians, owns surgical centers, operates urgent care clinics, and manages home health services. It also owns OptumRx, one of the three largest pharmacy benefit managers

(PBMs), giving it massive control over drug pricing and distribution.

For self funded employers, this vertical consolidation creates an inherent conflict of interest. The same company managing your claims and negotiating provider rates is also profiting from the services being billed to your plan. And, as expected, UnitedHealth's ownership of providers hasn't led to lower prices for employers—it's led to higher payments for its own subsidiaries.

A recent study found that UnitedHealthcare routinely pays Optum-owned physicians more than independent doctors for the same services. Instead of using its massive scale to negotiate lower prices, United is using its position to funnel more money into its own provider network—directly increasing costs for self-funded plans.

The same self-dealing exists in its pharmacy business. CVS Health, which owns Aetna, has been found to pay more for prescriptions filled at its own CVS pharmacies compared to other in-network pharmacies. Cigna, through its Evernorth subsidiary, has expanded into telehealth, behavioral health, and pharmacy benefit management—consolidating its grip over key parts of the healthcare supply chain.

For years, self-funded employers have been constrained by opaque pricing, limited access to claims data, and restrictive contracts. Now, with major insurers transforming into fully integrated healthcare behemoths, they have even less control. The very companies they trusted to administer their plans are now in the business of maximizing revenue at every possible level—managing the money, owning the providers, controlling the drug supply, and steering patient care toward their most profitable assets.

As this trend continues, the opportunities for insurers to extract profit from self-funded plans will only grow. When the entity paying the claims also owns the hospitals, the doctors, the pharmacies, and the surgical centers, it blurs the lines between payer and provider—allowing these conglomerates to raise prices, steer referrals, and squeeze out competition with virtually no pushback.

The result? Self-funded employers—who represent the largest source of private healthcare spending in the country—are left paying the bill for an increasingly rigged system. And by the time they realize just how much leverage they've lost, it may already be too late.

Everything covered so far—the unchecked consolidation of hospitals, the financial games played by insurers, and the powerlessness of employers in managing their own healthcare spending—only scratches the surface of the dysfunction embedded in the American healthcare system. This book was never meant to be a comprehensive ledger of every abuse, loophole, or bad actor in the industry. Rather, it aims to provide the reader with a clearer understanding of why their premiums keep rising, why their employer might be forced to drop coverage, why local hospital expansions don't translate into better access, and why, despite spending more than any other country on healthcare, our actual health outcomes continue to deteriorate.

At the core of all of this is a perverse set of incentives. Whether it's called fee-for-service, value-based care, or some other reform-friendly buzzword, the system is structured not to improve health, but to extract as much financial value as possible from sickness. Every player—hospitals, insurers, consultants, TPAs—has built a business model around maximizing revenue at every step. The one thing that is missing from this design? A true incentive for anyone to actually create a healthcare system—one designed to keep people well, rather than one built to profit from keeping them just sick enough to need care indefinitely.

And when anyone dares to challenge this system, to question why we are sustaining a model that serves shareholders better than patients, the immediate response is that "it's complicated." That cost containment is difficult. That changing the system would be disruptive. And most importantly, that the industries making billions from this structure—hospitals, insurers, PBMs, and pharmaceutical companies—have too much money and too much political power to be meaningfully challenged.

Our policymakers—the people who should be safeguarding public interest—haven't just allowed this to continue; they have actively enabled it. Legislators refuse to push back against the industry money that floods their campaigns. Every attempt at reform gets neutered, delayed, or manipulated in ways that ensure the financial interests of the biggest players remain untouched. We are told that this system is "unsustainable," but history has shown that it will, in fact, continue to sustain itself—just at a devastating cost to American families, businesses, and communities.

Yet, there is still one more piece of this puzzle to explore—perhaps the most powerful and politically entrenched of them all. The pharmaceutical industry and the PBMs that control access to medicine sit at the center of some of the most consequential and least understood cost drivers in healthcare. They dictate what drugs are covered, who can afford them, and how much they cost—not based on patient need, but based on their own financial interests.

If hospitals and insurers have built a system that profits off sickness, PBMs and pharmaceutical companies have mastered the art of monetizing it. Understanding how they operate—and why the system allows them to extract billions in profits while millions struggle to afford basic medications—is essential to grasping the full scale of what's at stake.

PART IV: PBMS AND PHARMA: A SYSTEM OF MANIPULATION

If hospitals and insurers have created a system designed to generate revenue from illness, PBMs and pharmaceutical companies have taken it a step further—turning essential medications into profit centers with little regard for affordability or access. Understanding how they operate—and why they're allowed to extract billions while patients ration life-saving drugs—is critical to grasping just how deeply entrenched these financial incentives have become.

The United States spends more on prescription drugs than any other country in the world—more than $600 billion annually and growing. On a per capita basis, that's nearly twice what other high-income nations pay. The cost of certain life-saving medications in the U.S. defies logic: a cancer drug that costs $1,200 in Australia is priced at over $10,000 here; an insulin vial that costs $8 in Germany is nearly $100 in the U.S. And with the emergence of gene therapies and next-generation biologics, drug prices in the future will likely make today's costs seem modest. Some of these treatments already carry price tags north of $2 million per patient.

Faced with these soaring prices, PBMs and pharmaceutical manufacturers point fingers at each other. Pharma insists that PBMs are the problem, claiming that they manipulate formularies, inflate costs through rebates, and block access to lower-cost drugs. PBMs, in turn, blame manufacturers for setting exorbitant list prices and gaming the patent system to delay competition from lower-cost generics and biosimilars.

To be fair, legislators have been hammering both sides in reports, congressional hearings and proposed (if not yet passed) legislation. Congress has dragged PBM executives and pharma CEOs into press-laden committee rooms, scolding them for their roles in the drug pricing crisis. States have passed transparency laws targeting PBM practices, while the federal government has made incremental attempts to rein in drug prices through policies like Medicare price negotiations. Yet, for all this scrutiny, prescription drug costs continue to rise.

The truth is, both PBMs and pharmaceutical companies are to blame. And more importantly, so is the system that enables them to profit from this dysfunction.

For all the attention on their infighting and blame-shifting, the bigger issue is that they both operate in a system that allows them to extract billions while patients, employers, and taxpayers foot the bill.

Take GLP-1 drugs like Ozempic and Wegovy, which have become some of the most sought-after medications in the world. Originally developed for diabetes treatment, these drugs are now being mass-marketed as weight-loss solutions, fueling skyrocketing demand and record-breaking profits for manufacturers. Novo Nordisk, the maker of Ozempic and Wegovy, saw its market value surge past $500 billion as sales exploded. But these drugs come at an astronomical cost—especially in the U.S. A one-month supply of Ozempic costs approximately $936 in the U.S., compared to just $169 in Japan. It's the fact that employers, taxpayers, and the healthcare system as a whole are making an enormous financial commitment to a drug that has not yet been subject to the kind of long-term, rigorous studies one might expect given its widespread use and staggering cost. With limited data on long-term efficacy, potential risks, and the economic sustainability of covering these medications at scale, the healthcare system is being asked to bet billions on a treatment whose true value and impact remain uncertain.

And then there's Humira, the poster child for how drug companies exploit the patent system to block competition. Since its approval in 2002, AbbVie has made over $200 billion in revenue from Humira, using an aggressive patent-evergreening strategy to delay cheaper alternatives. By stacking over 100 patents on minor tweaks—formulation changes, delivery device modifications—AbbVie was able to extend its monopoly for years, preventing biosimilars from entering the U.S. market. The Humira saga isn't just about one drug—it's a blueprint for how pharmaceutical companies and PBMs collaborate to keep lower-cost options from gaining traction.

This section will explore the ways in which PBMs and pharmaceutical companies manipulate the system to maximize their profits—often at the expense of access and affordability. From spread pricing and rebate games to patent evergreening and biosimilar suppression, we'll break down the tactics that drive up drug costs, the legislative responses that have failed to fix the problem, and the real-world impact of these schemes on patients, employers, and government programs alike.

PART III

Chapter 27

A MAN WALKS INTO A PHARMACY...

You walk into the pharmacy to pick up a prescription. Maybe it's one you've been taking for years. But today, something has changed. The pharmacist tells you it's no longer covered by your insurance. Or that it now requires prior authorization. Or that it'll cost triple what you paid last time—but if you use a coupon, it might be cheaper.

If you've ever experienced this, you weren't dealing with your insurance company—you were dealing with a pharmacy benefit manager (PBM).

Of course, that distinction is largely meaningless in today's healthcare system. Because while PBMs are technically separate from your medical insurance provider, there's a very good chance they're owned and controlled by the same parent company. If you have UnitedHealthcare, your prescriptions are likely managed by OptumRx. If you're insured by Cigna, your PBM is Express Scripts. If you have Aetna, your PBM is CVS Caremark. The same companies that dictate which hospitals and doctors you can see are also deciding which drugs you can take—and profiting from both sides of the transaction.

But we'll get into that later.

PBMs were originally created to bring order and efficiency to the prescription drug market.

They emerged in the 1960s and 1970s as prescription drug benefits became a more significant part of employer-sponsored health plans. At the time, individual employers lacked the scale and expertise to negotiate directly with pharmaceutical companies and pharmacies. PBMs filled this gap by acting as intermediaries, handling claims processing and using their volume-based purchasing power to secure better rates from drug manufacturers and retail pharmacies.

This type of model isn't unique to healthcare. Group purchasing organizations (GPOs) exist in industries like retail and manufacturing, where businesses pool their purchasing power to negotiate lower prices on supplies. Travel booking platforms secure bulk discounts on hotels and airfare, offering rates that individual consumers wouldn't be able to access on their own. PBMs were positioned to play a similar role—leveraging scale to reduce costs and simplify prescription drug management for employers, insurers, and government programs.

For years, this approach appeared to work. PBMs helped streamline claims processing, created formularies to standardize drug coverage, and negotiated bulk discounts that made medications more affordable than if employers or insurers were contracting alone. Their role became even more essential in the 1990s and early 2000s, when pharmaceutical spending surged due to the introduction of high-cost brand-name drugs and the expansion of Medicare Part D. Employers and insurers relied on PBMs to contain these costs, trusting that their size and negotiating power would keep drug prices in check.

But as the prescription drug market grew, so too did the power and influence of PBMs. What began as a straightforward cost-management function evolved into a complex and opaque business model—one that no longer simply negotiated savings but found ways to profit from rising drug prices.

PBMs were no longer just middlemen securing discounts. They became some of the most powerful players in healthcare, sitting at the intersection of manufacturers, insurers, pharmacies, and

CHAPTER 27

employers—and, in many cases, using that position to extract more profit, rather than pass savings along.

Today, the three largest PBMs—CVS Caremark (CVS Health), Express Scripts (Cigna), and OptumRx (UnitedHealth Group)—control nearly 80% of the prescription drug market. They dictate which drugs are covered, how much patients pay, and which pharmacies can dispense medications—all while operating behind a veil of secrecy.

The question is: How did an industry originally designed to lower costs become one of the biggest drivers of prescription drug spending?

To answer that, we have to look at what PBMs actually do today—and how their business practices have evolved from simple cost-saving mechanisms into one of the most controversial and least understood forces in American healthcare.

Chapter 28

THE HIDDEN PROFITS OF PBMS: REBATES AND SPREAD PRICING

For years, PBMs have positioned themselves as the heroes of drug pricing, negotiating behind the scenes to secure rebates from pharmaceutical companies and drive down costs. The industry line is that these rebates—essentially, discounts that drug manufacturers pay PBMs in exchange for preferred formulary placement—are a major tool in cost containment.

But if these rebates were truly working in the way PBMs claim, why do drug prices continue to rise? Why do patients often pay more for medications in the U.S. than anywhere else in the world? The answer is simple: these rebates don't necessarily lower prices for consumers or employers. In fact, they often do the opposite.

Rather than using their negotiating power to push for lower prices overall, PBMs have structured the system so that higher list prices actually benefit them. And rebates are only one piece of the puzzle. Spread pricing—the practice of marking up prescription drugs at the employer and government level—is another major revenue driver for PBMs, hidden in the fine print of complex contracts.

Together, these two tactics have quietly turned PBMs into some of the most profitable entities in American healthcare—without most patients, employers, or even lawmakers fully understanding how they operate.

HOW THE REBATE SYSTEM ENCOURAGES HIGHER PRICES

At its core, the rebate system creates a direct financial incentive for drug manufacturers to raise prices. The higher the list price of a drug, the bigger the rebate a PBM can negotiate—and, in many cases, the more they can keep for themselves.

For example, let's say a drug manufacturer sets a list price of $500 for a particular medication. The PBM negotiates a rebate of $200 from the manufacturer, meaning the net price after rebates is $300. The PBM might then pass a portion of that rebate back to the employer or insurer, but it can also keep a share for itself.

Now imagine that same manufacturer raises the list price of the drug to $700. Suddenly, the PBM can negotiate a rebate of $400—making it appear as if they've secured even deeper "savings." But the net price after rebates is still $300—meaning no actual cost reduction has taken place. The patient, however, may now face a higher out-of-pocket cost based on the inflated list price.

This structure warps the entire pricing system, rewarding drugs with the highest initial prices rather than those that are truly cost-effective. Manufacturers know that to secure a spot on a PBM's formulary—the list of covered drugs—they have to play this game. As a result, they set their prices artificially high, with the expectation that rebates will be negotiated later.

This is why drugs like insulin, which has existed for over a century, have seen list prices skyrocket despite no meaningful change in the product itself. In the case of insulin, PBMs have reportedly received rebates so large that in some cases, they collect more revenue from insulin sales than the manufacturers themselves.

A 2021 Senate report revealed that from 2013 to 2018, insulin list prices more than doubled, even though the actual cost of producing the drug remained stable. One major insulin manufacturer admitted that it raised prices specifically to ensure it remained competitive in PBM negotiations.

It's one thing to hear that PBMs control an enormous amount of money—hundreds of billions flowing through opaque rebate accounts and pricing schemes—but it's another to grasp just how much these middlemen manipulate the system to inflate costs, obscure savings, and ultimately profit at the expense of patients, employers, and even state governments.

In 2023 alone, PBMs handled an estimated $334 billion in gross-to-net reductions for brand-name drugs. That's the difference between the sticker price of a medication and what's actually paid after behind-the-scenes negotiations. The staggering scale of these transactions reveals how much leverage PBMs wield over pricing, access, and affordability. And yet, the primary beneficiaries of this massive financial churn aren't the employers who fund these health plans or the patients who rely on these medications—it's the PBMs themselves.

This power dynamic isn't some abstract economic theory. It plays out in real life, with real consequences. Consider tadalafil, a drug used to treat pulmonary hypertension. In 2022, PBMs marked up its price by an astronomical 7,736% for commercial payers. That's not a typo. What should have been a reasonably priced medication was instead turned into a massive profit center—one where the patient and employer footed the bill, with no way to challenge it.

PBMs justify their pricing tactics by pointing to the rebates they negotiate, claiming these discounts lower costs for health plans. But the numbers tell a different story. While net prices for brand-name drugs fell by 8% from 2017 to 2020, list prices jumped by 23% over the same period. This is no coincidence. The larger the rebate, the higher the list price—because PBMs operate on a system where their fees are often tied to the size of the discount they "secure." The more a drug's price is artificially inflated upfront, the more PBMs can extract in rebates. Employers and patients don't see those savings; they're just left paying the bloated costs.

And rebates aren't even the worst offender when it comes to PBM profit schemes. Spread pricing, an even more insidious practice, allows PBMs to charge employers and government programs significantly more for a drug than they reimburse the pharmacy—pocketing the difference. It's a legalized form of skimming, hidden behind convoluted contract language and a lack of transparency.

The scale of spread pricing's impact is staggering. In just one year, Ohio's Medicaid program was overcharged by $244 million through spread pricing. Kentucky saw a similar scam play out, costing the state an estimated $123 million annually. And this isn't just a problem in government programs—employers across the country are routinely paying inflated drug costs due to PBMs manipulating the spread between what they pay and what the pharmacy receives.

If this sounds like an unsustainable business model, it is—but only for the people actually paying for healthcare. PBMs are thriving. A 2025 Federal Trade Commission (FTC) report revealed that the three largest PBMs—CVS Caremark, Express Scripts, and Optum Rx—raked in $7.3 billion in excess revenue from specialty drug markups between 2017 and 2022. They weren't just marking up prices a little; they were strategically inflating the cost of critical specialty medications to maximize profit, knowing full well that patients and employers had no choice but to pay.

Specialty drugs, in particular, have become a goldmine for PBMs, and their own mail-order and specialty pharmacies are at the center of it. The FTC report highlighted that PBM-affiliated pharmacies were charging 42% more for specialty medications compared to independent competitors. This isn't about patient care. It's about steering as much volume as possible through their own high-cost channels to extract additional revenue.

Despite these revelations, PBMs continue to operate with near-total impunity, manipulating contracts and pricing structures in ways that are nearly impossible for employers to challenge. Some states, however, have started fighting back. In California, lawmakers introduced a bill requiring PBMs to be licensed by the state Department of Insurance and pass 100% of negotiated drug rebates to health plans. This legislation aims to prevent PBMs from pocketing the savings that should, in theory, lower costs for employers and patients.

But legislation alone won't fix the problem. Employers need to recognize that PBMs are not their allies in cost management. These companies were originally created to negotiate better drug prices, but the incentives have flipped. Their profits now come from keeping prices high, securing bigger rebates, and maintaining absolute control over how prescription drugs are priced, dispensed, and reimbursed.

And the worst part? Most people still don't realize this is happening. Patients continue to wonder why their prescriptions cost so much. Employers continue to assume their PBM is working in their best interest. Meanwhile, billions of dollars are siphoned away, year after year, into a system designed not to lower costs, but to ensure they keep rising.

WHO PAYS THE PRICE?

At the end of the day, someone has to foot the bill for the games PBMs play, and it's not the PBMs themselves. It's employers, patients, and taxpayers who bear the cost—often without even realizing it.

Patients are hit first, facing higher out-of-pocket costs because PBMs structure copays and deductibles around the inflated list prices of drugs rather than their actual, post-rebate costs. A medication that should cost $50 might carry a $500 price tag at the pharmacy counter, simply because the PBM's contract demands that pricing be based on the pre-rebate list price rather than the true net cost. This isn't just a technicality—it's a carefully engineered profit strategy, one that forces patients to pay more than they should for life-saving medications.

Employers, who assume they are negotiating fair rates for their employees, are often left in the dark about the real cost of the drugs covered under their health plans. PBMs lock up rebate details and pricing arrangements behind confidentiality clauses, preventing employers from seeing how much money is flowing through these agreements and whether they're actually getting the savings they were promised. In too many cases, they're not. One report found that only 60% of large employers received the full rebate pass-through they had negotiated—meaning the PBM simply pocketed the rest.

Government programs like Medicaid and Medicare also overpay, but on an even larger scale. PBMs manipulate rebate negotiations and spread pricing arrangements to extract billions from public programs, knowing that the complexity of drug pricing makes it difficult for regulators to track the full extent of the overcharges. In Ohio's Medicaid program alone, PBMs were found to have charged taxpayers $244 million more than they reimbursed pharmacies in a single year. In Kentucky, spread pricing drained an estimated $123 million from the state's Medicaid program annually. These aren't just accounting issues. These are taxpayer dollars—money meant to provide care for vulnerable populations—being siphoned off by middlemen who add little value to the system beyond their ability to obscure financial flows.

If the problem is so clear, why hasn't anything changed? There's no shortage of legislative proposals to rein in PBM practices. Yet, every time meaningful reform gains traction, the industry proves remarkably effective at maintaining the status quo.

PBMs argue that the rebates they negotiate help lower overall drug costs, but multiple investigations have revealed that the opposite is true. The Federal Trade Commission (FTC) and state attorneys general have launched probes into PBM pricing structures, questioning whether these entities are actually driving up costs rather than reducing them. Some states have attempted to crack down, passing laws that ban spread pricing in Medicaid managed care programs, but PBMs have adapted—repackaging the same fees under different contractual terms and continuing business as usual.

At the federal level, progress has been slow. PBM executives have been called to testify before the Senate Finance Committee, the House Oversight Committee, and the House Energy & Commerce Committee, facing bipartisan criticism over their pricing tactics, rebate schemes, and formulary decisions. Numerous reports have documented how PBMs profit from high drug prices, and lawmakers have drafted multiple bills aimed at increasing transparency, banning spread pricing, and ensuring rebates flow directly to consumers. But when it comes time to pass legislation, reform efforts stall.

In late 2024, during Congress's lame-duck session, a bipartisan proposal to limit PBM practices gained momentum. Initially, the bill included provisions that would have forced PBMs to pass all negotiated savings to employers and patients. But by the time lobbyists finished working behind the scenes, key provisions had been watered down or stripped out entirely. The session ended without a final vote, and the industry emerged largely unscathed.

And as of the writing of this book, despite all the talk, hearings, and growing public frustration, PBM reform has once again been left out of the latest federal funding bill—a continuing resolution that lawmakers had originally intended to include key PBM transparency and rebate provisions. Instead, the package was quietly removed, kicking reform efforts down the road once again, proving just how powerful PBM influence remains on Capitol Hill.

This is not an isolated incident—it's a pattern. Legislation is introduced, hearings are held, and tough questions are asked, yet the fundamental structure of the PBM industry remains untouched. The reason is simple: money. PBMs, pharmaceutical companies, and their lobbying arms spend staggering amounts to shape public policy in their favor.

PhRMA, the lobbying group representing drug manufacturers, spent over $376 million on lobbying between 2017 and 2023. PBM trade groups, such as the Pharmaceutical Care Management Association (PCMA), have poured millions into campaign contributions, policy advocacy, and strategic efforts to influence legislation. Many members of Congress receive donations from PBMs, insurers, or pharmaceutical companies—creating an uphill battle for reform advocates who want to hold the industry accountable.

For all the hearings, reports, and proposed bills, the PBM system remains intact, with only minor adjustments at the state level. Some states have passed laws banning spread pricing in Medicaid managed care programs, but PBMs have adapted, changing contract terms, renaming fees, and shifting their profit centers while maintaining control over the drug pricing system.

This isn't just a bureaucratic failure—it has devastating real-world consequences. In 2019, a mother testified before Congress about how her son died while rationing insulin because he couldn't afford the medication. He was a young man with his whole life ahead of him, forced into an impossible situation by a system that placed profits above patients. Insulin manufacturers, PBMs, and insurers all pointed fingers at one another, but the end result was the same: a completely preventable death in one of the wealthiest nations in the world.

And still, the hearings continue. The outrage builds. The stories pile up. But the system? It remains unchanged.

Cole Schmidtknecht's story is yet another tragic example of how corporate decisions in the pharmaceutical supply chain can have devastating, real-world consequences. At just 22 years old, he lost his life to an asthma attack—not because treatment didn't exist, but because he couldn't afford it. For years, he had relied on an inhaler that kept his asthma under control, paying around $66 per prescription. But when OptumRx, the PBM owned by UnitedHealth Group, altered its formulary and removed his medication from coverage, the price skyrocketed to $539. Faced with an impossible choice between his inhaler and paying rent, Cole walked out of the pharmacy empty-handed. Just days later, he suffered a fatal asthma attack. His parents later learned that Optum had swapped his medication for a more expensive alternative, a move that increased PBM profits while leaving Cole without access to the treatment that had kept him stable for years. Now, his family is suing, arguing that the opaque and profit-driven decisions of PBMs are not just a matter of policy failure, but of life and death.

The frustration isn't limited to patients. Employers, too, have found themselves blocked from securing better deals for their employees. Despite being the ones footing the bill, many employers are kept in the dark about the actual costs of the prescriptions they cover, the rebates PBMs negotiate, and the terms dictating which drugs make it onto their formularies.

Employers often assume that because they are self-funding their prescription drug plans, they have full control over their costs, formulary decisions, and how rebates are handled. But buried deep in PBM contracts (or even not so deep) are carefully crafted provisions that ensure the employer never actually has full access to the real numbers, let alone the power to act on them. These provisions are designed to lock in inflated drug prices, obscure rebate pass-throughs, and prevent any meaningful audit oversight.

CHAPTER 28

Take, for instance, this type of contract language regarding rebate disclosures:

"PBM shall retain the sole and exclusive discretion to determine the allocation and application of Manufacturer Rebates, discounts, administrative fees, and other financial incentives, and shall have no obligation to disclose any such financial arrangements to Plan Sponsor. Rebate payments, if applicable, shall be remitted at PBM's discretion, and Plan Sponsor waives all rights to audit, verify, or challenge PBM's rebate methodologies."

In other words, the employer is paying the bills, but has no right to see the financial transactions driving those bills. Imagine a company handing over its corporate credit card to a third-party expense manager, who then negotiates "discounts" on business travel and office supplies—yet refuses to disclose how much was actually paid or how much of the savings were pocketed. That's the level of opacity employers are dealing with when it comes to PBMs and rebates.

Another provision often found in PBM contracts restricts an employer's ability to modify the formulary or even understand why certain drugs are covered while others are excluded:

"PBM retains the exclusive right to establish and modify the Formulary, which shall be based on PBM's proprietary clinical and financial analysis. Plan Sponsor acknowledges that Formulary decisions are confidential and proprietary to PBM and shall not be subject to review or modification by Plan Sponsor."

This means that even if an employer identifies a cheaper, equally or even more effective drug, they may have no ability to switch to it. PBMs frequently place higher-cost drugs on preferred tiers because those drugs offer larger rebates—which the PBM often keeps.

For those employers who suspect something isn't adding up, PBMs have airtight contractual clauses to keep audits limited and ineffective:

"Plan Sponsor shall have the right to conduct an audit of up to 250 randomly selected claims per contract year. PBM shall provide Plan Sponsor with only the aggregate results of such audit. Plan Sponsor agrees that any audit results may not be shared with third parties, including independent consultants or auditors, without PBM's express written consent."

To put this in perspective: A self-funded employer with 10,000 employees might process over 2 million prescription drug claims in a given year. Yet their PBM contract may only allow them to audit 250 of those claims—just 0.0125% of total spending. Oh yeah, and even if the audit shows that we're doing something wrong, you can't actually do anything about it or show anyone ... without our permission.

Imagine running a multimillion-dollar business and being told that you can only review a tiny fraction of your expense reports—and that even if you find something concerning, you can't share your findings with an outside expert to verify them. Business dinner receipts receive more scrutiny from a company's CFO than their Rx spend.

And, even when employers attempt to negotiate better deals, steer employees toward lower-cost options, or carve out certain PBM services, contractual terms often prevent them from doing so:

"Plan Sponsor agrees that PBM maintains an exclusive network of preferred pharmacies, and that all covered prescriptions shall be dispensed through said network. Plan Sponsor may not alter, carve out, or negotiate separate direct contracts with network pharmacies without PBM's prior written approval. Failure to adhere to network exclusivity shall result in immediate termination of the Agreement."

In practice, this means that even if an employer identifies a pharmacy willing to offer significantly lower prices, they may not be allowed to contract directly with that pharmacy. Instead, they are forced to use PBM-owned pharmacy networks, which often charge inflated rates.

This dynamic becomes even more pronounced when it comes to specialty pharmacy—the fastest-growing and most expensive segment of prescription drug spending. Specialty drugs, which are used to treat complex conditions like cancer, multiple sclerosis, and autoimmune diseases, often come with astronomical price tags, sometimes costing hundreds of thousands of dollars per patient per year. Given the financial stakes, one might assume that employers and patients would have flexibility in choosing where to fill these prescriptions to secure the best pricing and service. But PBMs have designed their contracts to ensure that doesn't happen.

Most major PBMs own and operate their own specialty pharmacies, and they use their formularies, network restrictions, and contract clauses to force patients to fill prescriptions exclusively through these PBM-affiliated pharmacies. This is often framed as a matter of "efficiency" or "better patient management," but in reality, it ensures that PBMs keep the profit in-house, rather than allowing competition from lower-cost specialty pharmacies.

Take this common provision found in PBM contracts:

"Plan Sponsor agrees that all Specialty Pharmaceuticals, as determined by PBM's proprietary definition, must be dispensed exclusively through PBM's designated Specialty Pharmacy Network. Plan Sponsor shall not contract with alternative Specialty Pharmacies nor direct members to external Specialty Pharmacy providers outside of PBM's network. Specialty Pharmacy terms, including dispensing fees, service charges, and reimbursement methodologies, shall remain confidential and are not subject to external audit or review."

For an employer, this means that even if another specialty pharmacy is willing to provide the exact same medication at a lower cost, they are contractually barred from working with them. Instead, they are required to use the PBM's own specialty pharmacy, which often charges inflated prices and layers on additional fees.

The impact on patients is equally frustrating. A patient with a chronic illness might have a long-standing relationship with a specialty pharmacist at a local hospital or an independent provider—but when their employer switches to a new PBM, they are forced to transfer their prescriptions to the PBM's mail-order specialty pharmacy. These pharmacies are notorious for delays, administrative hurdles, and a lack of personalized care.

The same restrictions apply to mail-order pharmacy services, which PBMs aggressively push for maintenance medications. Employers often find clauses like this embedded in their agreements:

"Plan Sponsor agrees that all maintenance medications exceeding a 90-day supply shall be dispensed exclusively through PBM's Mail-Order Pharmacy. Retail pharmacies shall not be permitted to fill such prescriptions beyond the 90-day limit. Any deviation from this policy shall result in increased cost-sharing for the member and additional administrative fees for the Plan Sponsor."

In effect, patients are forced into PBM-owned mail-order systems, even if they prefer picking up their medication locally or find better pricing at independent pharmacies. Meanwhile, local pharmacies—many of which offer lower cash prices than what PBMs charge employers and provide a better patient experience with the member—are cut out of the market entirely.

PBMs have spent decades perfecting this art of contractual entrapment—locking in opaque pricing models, limiting employer oversight, and eliminating real negotiating power. Even large, sophisticated employers with significant purchasing leverage are routinely restricted from knowing basic details about how their drug plans are managed.

The irony is that employers, as self-funded plan sponsors, are legally responsible under ERISA to act in the best interests of their employees—yet PBM contracts prevent them from fulfilling that duty. The very system that was designed to empower employers to make smart purchasing decisions instead ties their hands behind their backs, leaving them dependent on PBMs who profit from higher costs.

The question is no longer whether PBMs are taking advantage of employers—it's how long employers will continue to accept it.

Chapter 29

A BILLIONAIRE WALKS INTO A BROKEN SYSTEM: MARK CUBAN'S DISRUPTION OF THE DRUG SUPPLY CHAIN

While much of the pharmaceutical industry clings to complex rebate schemes, opaque pricing models, and a reliance on intermediaries who profit by inflating the cost of care, one of the most compelling—and unexpected—disruptors has emerged in the form of billionaire entrepreneur Mark Cuban. Known to the public as a tech mogul, media personality, and owner of the Dallas Mavericks, Cuban has recently turned his attention to one of the most opaque and exploitative corners of the healthcare market: the pharmacy supply chain.

With the launch of the Mark Cuban Cost Plus Drug Company (MCCPDC), he has attempted to strip away the complexity and expose the raw truth about drug pricing in America. His model is refreshingly straightforward and deliberately transparent: source generic medications directly from manufacturers, apply a 15% markup, add a $5 pharmacy fee, and a $5 shipping charge. That's it. No hidden rebates, no backdoor deals, no preferred placement schemes. A medication that might cost over $9,000 through traditional channels can be found on costplusdrugs.com for less than $50.

And while many initially dismissed this as a publicity stunt or niche service, the impact has been profound. By demonstrating what drugs *should* cost, Cuban has pulled back the curtain on how much the American public is being overcharged—not just by manufacturers, but by the middlemen who have built entire business empires on unnecessary complexity. He didn't just start a company—he sparked a public reckoning.

He has also been unflinching in his critique of the entire U.S. healthcare system, labeling it as "horrific" and riddled with opacity. He has remarked, "PBM contracts are like Fight Club—the first rule is you can't talk about them," highlighting the secrecy surrounding pharmacy benefit managers. Expressing his mission, Cuban stated, "I just wanna f*ck up healthcare," emphasizing his disruptive approach to reform. He also questioned the necessity of traditional health insurance, asserting, "I don't think there's a reason that health insurance should exist," advocating for more transparent and direct healthcare solutions. These statements underscore his commitment to overhauling a system he perceives as fundamentally flawed.

He is truly engaged in understanding the structural failures of the healthcare system. I was introduced to him through a mutual friend and colleague, Marilyn Bartlett—a trailblazer in public sector health reform and someone whose work in Montana helped redefine what's possible in employer-sponsored care. Through that connection, I've had the privilege of engaging directly with Mark via email. And let me be clear: this is not a celebrity vanity project. He has been responsive, engaged, curious, and entirely willing to listen. Not only that—he listens to *people who've been in the trenches*. He asks thoughtful questions. He seeks insight not from corporate lobbyists or trade associations, but from people like Marilyn, myself, and other reformers who have spent years trying to hold this system accountable.

In our conversations, I've seen firsthand his genuine desire to understand the full picture—and his openness to tackling the broader healthcare spend. While his initial focus has been on PBMs and drug pricing, I firmly believe that's only the beginning. Mark understands that the dysfunction isn't isolated to prescription drugs. It spans every corner of the system—from facility fees to hospital consolidation to the administrative waste plaguing insurers and third-party administrators. And I've been honored to be part of the early and ongoing dialogue about what might come next.

There's something deeply powerful about having someone with Cuban's platform, resources, and independence turn his attention to an industry that has remained largely immune to accountability. He's not beholden to shareholders. He's not compromised by campaign contributions. He's not interested in incrementalism. He wants results. And unlike many so-called disruptors who quietly sell out to incumbents or pivot to profit extraction, Cuban is trying to build something sustainable and transformative—something that returns pricing power and transparency to the consumer.

Will it single-handedly fix American healthcare? Of course not. But what it has already done is break the illusion that these high costs are inevitable. Cuban has shown that it *can* be done differently—and that's often the hardest part of change: proving that the impossible is actually quite feasible, once you stop listening to the people who profit from keeping it broken.

If you're an employer, a policymaker, or even a patient who has felt trapped by the current system, this should be a wake-up call. The emperor has no clothes—and Mark Cuban, of all people, is the one bold enough to say it out loud.

Chapter 30

BEHIND THE FORMULARY: WHO CONTROLS YOUR MEDICATION?

Rebates are just one piece of the puzzle. PBMs don't just negotiate prices—they control which drugs are covered, which aren't, and how much patients pay at the counter. This power is embedded in the formulary, the list of approved drugs that PBMs design for health plans.

In theory, formularies should prioritize clinical effectiveness and affordability, ensuring that patients receive the best treatment at the lowest cost. But in reality, PBMs use formularies as a tool for financial leverage, steering patients toward drugs that generate the highest profits—often at the expense of lower-cost alternatives.

And because these decisions happen behind closed doors, neither employers nor patients have any meaningful way to challenge them.

FORMULARIES: WHO DECIDES WHAT DRUGS YOU CAN TAKE?

Most people assume that when a doctor prescribes a medication, they will be able to get it filled—perhaps with a little hassle over prior authorization, but ultimately, their treatment plan will be followed. Few realize that an invisible force dictates which medications are covered,

CHAPTER 30

which require extra hurdles, and which are simply unavailable to them. That force is the formulary, a list of drugs that a pharmacy benefit manager (PBM) approves for coverage under an insurance plan.

Originally, formularies were designed to prioritize cost-effective, clinically sound medications, steering patients toward cheaper generics instead of expensive brand-name drugs whenever possible. In theory, this should help patients and plan sponsors save money. But in practice, formularies have become a profit center for PBMs, manipulated to drive rebates, inflate costs, and force patients onto drugs that may not be the best option for their health.

Doctors and patients experience these consequences every day, but the full scope of the problem is staggering. A recent study found that 55% of PBM-mandated drug substitutions are not for generics or biosimilars but entirely different medications with different active ingredients. In many cases, these substitutions are neither medically equivalent nor financially beneficial for the patient. The impact of these changes is not trivial—millions of Americans suffer real harm due to PBM-driven formulary exclusions. In the case of atrial fibrillation and venous thromboembolism treatments alone, formulary restrictions could lead to as many as one million adverse events and nearly 924,000 treatment discontinuations.

This is not a theoretical issue. It is happening to real people, every day.

Lisa, a 45-year-old teacher from Ohio, had been managing her rheumatoid arthritis with the same medication for years. It wasn't cheap, but it kept her symptoms under control, allowing her to work, care for her family, and live without crippling pain. Then one January morning, she went to refill her prescription and was told it was no longer covered.

The PBM running her employer's health plan had removed it from the formulary, replacing it with a so-called preferred alternative.

The problem? The new drug was not chemically equivalent, had a worse track record for side effects, and required months of dosage adjustments before patients typically saw relief. Lisa's doctor fought to keep her on the medication that worked, but it took weeks for the prior authorization process to play out. In the meantime, Lisa's pain returned. She missed work, struggled with daily activities, and had to go through unnecessary suffering—all because a drug manufacturer had paid the PBM a larger rebate to secure a more favorable placement on the formulary.

Lisa's case is not unique. And there are stories that end with far more tragic and life-changing consequences.

PBMs design their formularies not to promote the safest or most cost-effective treatment, but to maximize their own revenue streams through rebate negotiations with pharmaceutical companies. Drug manufacturers compete for a place on these formularies by offering steep, undisclosed rebates to PBMs, often as high as 60% of the drug's list price. In exchange, the PBM gives their drug exclusive or preferred placement, even if it is more expensive or less effective than alternatives.

This practice extends to life-saving medications, where formulary exclusions can be particularly devastating. A young woman in California suffering from chronic migraines had finally found relief with a new medication after years of debilitating pain. But when her PBM restructured its formulary, her drug was removed in favor of another that had a different mechanism of action and lower reported efficacy. Her migraines returned, sending her to the emergency room multiple times. The decision to exclude her medication had nothing to do with science or cost-effectiveness—it was a financial maneuver that resulted in more profit for the PBM, while she suffered the consequences.

MANIPULATING FORMULARIES TO INFLATE COSTS

One of the most shocking aspects of PBM-driven formulary design is that it frequently results in higher—not lower—drug prices.

For years, insulin has been at the center of this controversy. In 2020, a major PBM excluded a lower-cost generic insulin from its formulary while keeping the brand-name version, despite the two being chemically identical. The reason? The brand-name drug manufacturer paid a higher rebate.

PBMs defend these rebate-driven formularies by claiming that the negotiated discounts help lower overall drug spending. But the reality is that less than 1% of these rebates are passed on to patients. Instead, PBMs and insurers pocket the savings while forcing patients to pay out-of-pocket costs based on inflated list prices.

The impact of these exclusions is staggering. The study on formulary manipulation found that patients with atrial fibrillation, venous thromboembolism, migraines, and psoriasis could see their treatments forcibly switched, resulting in millions of discontinuations and adverse events each year.

In the case of migraine prevention, formulary exclusions could lead to nearly 900,000 patients experiencing worsened symptoms or serious adverse events. For those with atrial fibrillation, the consequences are even more dire—stroke risk increases by 45% to 85% for patients forced to switch or discontinue treatment.

EMPLOYERS ARE LOCKED OUT OF THE PROCESS

Despite being the ones paying the bill, employers have almost no say in how formularies are structured.

PBM contracts explicitly prohibit employers from auditing or questioning formulary decisions. Even if an employer discovers that their plan is paying for a more expensive drug instead of a lower-cost alternative, they are often powerless to challenge the arrangement.

Here's an actual provision found in a PBM contract:

"PBM retains sole and exclusive discretion to determine formulary placement and exclusion criteria. Plan Sponsor acknowledges that all rebate arrangements, formulary design strategies, and associated financial incentives are proprietary to PBM and are not subject to disclosure or audit."

In other words, even though employers are paying the bill, PBMs refuse to tell them why certain drugs are covered and others aren't, how much the plan is actually saving, or what the true cost of each drug is.

This lack of transparency means that many employers are unknowingly paying more for drugs than they should be and have no ability to push back.

Chapter 31

FORMULARIES, OPIOIDS, AND THE ARCHITECTURE OF HARM

The consequences of formulary exclusions and forced drug switching are not theoretical; they play out in real life, affecting patients in ways that are often invisible to the public until tragedy strikes. While these exclusions are framed as cost-saving measures, in practice, they often do the opposite—driving up patient out-of-pocket costs, forcing unnecessary medication changes, and leading to worse health outcomes.

For many patients, formulary exclusions mean their insurer will no longer cover a medication that has been working for them, forcing them onto an alternative—often a drug with a higher side-effect profile, a less convenient dosing schedule, or a different mechanism of action that doesn't work as well. This isn't just frustrating; it can be dangerous. A study published in the *Journal of Health Economics and Outcomes Research* estimated that formulary exclusions for conditions like atrial fibrillation and migraines could lead to treatment discontinuation for nearly a million patients, increasing their risk of hospitalization, complications, and even death. In many cases, the excluded drug isn't removed because it's ineffective—it's removed because another manufacturer negotiated a better deal with the PBM.

For patients managing chronic conditions, these exclusions can be especially devastating. Take the case of cancer patients who have seen their oral chemotherapy drugs suddenly excluded from coverage, forcing them to switch treatments mid-course or navigate a complex system of appeals that can take months. Or consider patients with multiple sclerosis, who have had stable, well-tolerated medications dropped in favor of alternatives that lead to new and debilitating side effects.

The financial impact is equally staggering. Between 2017 and 2020, while the net prices of brand-name drugs (the price after rebates) declined by 8%, their list prices—the price patients are charged before rebates—skyrocketed by 23%. This is by design. PBMs negotiate ever-larger rebates with manufacturers in exchange for placing high-priced drugs in preferred formulary positions. But those savings don't necessarily flow back to the patients or the employers footing the bill. Instead, patients paying coinsurance (a percentage of the drug's price) often see their out-of-pocket costs tied to the inflated list price rather than the lower net price, meaning they end up paying more even when their insurer is paying less.

Employers, meanwhile, remain largely in the dark. PBMs design formularies under layers of secrecy, preventing employers from knowing whether a covered drug is truly the most cost-effective option or simply the one with the biggest rebate kickback. One industry analysis found that only 60% of large employers received the full rebate pass-through they were promised in their PBM contracts. And while some states have begun investigating PBMs' role in drug pricing, progress has been slow. In 2022, the three largest PBMs—CVS Caremark, Express Scripts, and OptumRx—collectively excluded 1,156 unique medications from their formularies, a 29% increase from the prior year. These exclusions disproportionately affected medications for chronic illnesses, including cardiovascular disease, neurological disorders, and autoimmune conditions.

CHAPTER 31

Perhaps the most insidious part of this system is how little control patients and prescribers have. Doctors routinely find themselves fighting to get insurers to cover the medications they know work best for their patients, only to face layers of denials, prior authorizations, and step therapy requirements that delay treatment. And for patients who are forced to switch medications, the impact can be catastrophic.

Cole Schmidtknecht's story, previously discussed in this book, is just one of many examples of how formulary exclusions and price manipulation can be a matter of life and death. His inhaler was suddenly excluded from coverage, forcing him into an impossible financial decision that ultimately cost him his life. This isn't an isolated case. Across the country, insulin-dependent diabetics, cancer patients, and individuals managing rare diseases are seeing their life-saving medications yanked from formularies—not because those drugs are ineffective, but because a different manufacturer cut a better deal with the PBM.

Despite mounting evidence of the harm these practices cause, reform remains elusive. The Federal Trade Commission and multiple state attorneys general have launched investigations into PBM practices, but legislative efforts at the federal level have repeatedly stalled. In late 2024, a bipartisan PBM reform package was initially included in a larger federal funding bill, only to be stripped out at the last minute. The result? Despite years of hearings, reports, and political posturing, PBMs continue to operate with few restrictions, dictating which medications patients can access and at what price.

It is easy to think of this as a problem for lawmakers to fix, but awareness is key. Patients need to know that when their insurance stops covering a medication, it's not necessarily because there's a better option—it's because someone, somewhere, is making money off the switch. Employers need to demand transparency in their PBM contracts and push for full rebate pass-throughs. And the public at large needs to recognize that while PBMs claim to be negotiating savings, the system they've built is structured to keep drug costs high while obscuring their own profits.

This isn't just about formularies. It's about control—who has it, who profits from it, and who ultimately pays the price when the system puts financial incentives ahead of patient care.

PBMS' ROLE IN THE OPIOID CRISIS

For anyone inclined to give PBMs the benefit of the doubt—who believes that rebates and formulary management are simply tools to lower costs for employers and patients—one question remains: How do you explain this?

PBMs claim that their role in the prescription drug supply chain is to ensure that medications are affordable and accessible, steering patients toward cost-effective treatments while negotiating savings on behalf of employers, health plans, and the government. Yet when it came to one of the deadliest drug crises in American history, these same PBMs did the exact opposite.

As we've already seen, formularies are the most powerful tool PBMs have—deciding which drugs are covered, which require prior authorization, and which have usage limits. PBMs insist that these measures exist to promote safer prescribing practices, prevent unnecessary spending, and protect patients.

But when it came to opioids, PBMs actively bargained away those safeguards—not to protect patients, but because Purdue Pharma and other opioid manufacturers were paying them to do so.

The idea that PBMs are neutral, cost-saving intermediaries collapses under the weight of their own documented actions during the opioid epidemic. While government agencies, insurers, and public health advocates worked to curb the reckless overprescribing of opioids, PBMs were striking deals to keep the floodgates open—all while collecting billions in payments for doing so.

The role of PBMs in the opioid epidemic isn't a matter of speculation—it's a documented fact. Thanks to investigative reporting by *The New York Times*, we now have undeniable proof that PBMs didn't just passively allow the flood of opioids into American communities. They helped accelerate it, striking deals that made opioids more accessible, more profitable, and harder to regulate.

For years, Purdue Pharma and other opioid manufacturers paid PBMs handsomely to secure favorable placement on drug formularies—the lists that dictate which medications are covered by insurance and how easily patients can access them. These weren't small payments; Purdue alone shelled out up to $400 million per year in rebates to PBMs, ensuring that OxyContin remained not only covered but often the most accessible pain management option available. Between 2003 and 2012—right as the opioid epidemic spiraled out of control—these payments doubled.

The result was a system where opioids weren't just easy to get; they were financially incentivized at every level. PBMs eliminated prior authorization requirements, meaning doctors didn't need to justify opioid prescriptions before insurers would cover them. They removed quantity limits, allowing patients to receive dangerously high doses—sometimes in the hundreds or even thousands of pills per month. And they refused to steer patients toward safer, non-addictive alternatives, even as overdose deaths surged.

This was not a passive failure of oversight. PBMs actively structured formularies in ways that prioritized opioids over safer pain management options—not because opioids were the best medical choice, but because they were the most profitable. At the same time, PBMs worked to limit access to addiction treatments like buprenorphine, making it harder for patients to receive care once they had developed a dependency.

When Purdue and other manufacturers were finally forced to reckon with their role in the crisis, facing multibillion-dollar lawsuits and public outcry, the PBMs that enabled their rise largely escaped scrutiny. While drug companies were accused of fueling the epidemic, PBMs quietly distanced themselves, despite the overwhelming evidence that their rebate-driven formularies had shaped prescribing patterns for over a decade.

The opioid crisis is often framed as a failure of regulation, of aggressive pharmaceutical marketing, of government oversight. But it was also a failure of the very system that claims to negotiate savings and promote patient safety. PBMs were supposed to act as gatekeepers, ensuring that high-risk drugs were carefully managed and that formularies prioritized the best medical outcomes. Instead, they built a system where the most addictive, most dangerous medications were the easiest to access—so long as the price was right.

UnitedHealthcare actually considered limiting OxyContin prescriptions to 60 pills per month—after discovering that some patients were being prescribed up to 1,000 pills per month. But after its PBM, Merck-Medco (which later became part of Express Scripts), warned that such a restriction would cost them valuable rebates, the insurer backed down. Instead, they settled on a 124-pill limit—more than double what they had originally planned.

When Purdue struck similar deals with other PBMs, it openly celebrated its success in keeping insurers from imposing restrictions. An internal email from Purdue executives even boasted: "Our work behind the scenes is paying off!"

Even within PBMs, there were those who saw the harm these deals were causing and tried to push back.

In 2017, an OptumRx executive proposed immediately restricting access to Opana ER, a painkiller scheduled to be pulled from the market for safety reasons. The logic was simple: if a drug is too dangerous to remain on the market, PBMs should stop covering it.

But another OptumRx executive quickly shut him down. "We currently get rebates," he wrote in an email. "That would put our rebates at risk."

In another internal exchange, OptumRx senior vice president David Calabrese argued that the company had a moral obligation to act.

"My attitude," he wrote, "is toward the gross overprescribing and overpromotion of these medications to our country's citizens, the countless deaths, and my commitment to doing whatever is within my power to put an end to it."

His colleague's response?

"Stop with the attitude, and help us make sure we are compliant with our contracts."

PBMs had all the tools to be part of the solution. Their formularies dictate prescribing behavior nationwide—had they imposed even basic restrictions, the opioid crisis could have played out very differently.

And when public outrage finally caught up with them in 2017 and 2018, PBMs didn't implement restrictions out of a sense of responsibility or moral reckoning. Instead, Express Scripts executives calculated how much money they would lose by restricting opioid access—and decided to charge employers and insurers new fees to "make up for the rebate hit."

At OptumRx, some executives pushed to remove OxyContin from the formulary entirely, recognizing Purdue's central role in the crisis. But once again, the decision came down to rebates.

One OptumRx manager made the case plainly:

"Purdue has looked awful in the news since basically 2008. They basically caused the opioid epidemic, and we're essentially rewarding their bad behavior. From a purely PR perspective, I think it would look good on us."

His colleague's response?

"Valid point ... but the amount of utilization on OxyContin and the rebates we collect prevented us from doing it."

WHY HAVEN'T PBMS FACED ACCOUNTABILITY?

While Purdue Pharma, opioid distributors, and pharmacies have collectively paid over $50 billion in settlements for their role in the opioid crisis, PBMs have largely escaped accountability.

Despite clear evidence that they took money to keep opioid prescribing unrestricted, PBMs have managed to stay in the shadows, continuing to operate as self-proclaimed cost-cutters and drug access gatekeepers.

The consequences of these backroom deals weren't just financial—they were catastrophic. From 1999 to 2021, nearly 645,000 people in the U.S. died from an opioid overdose, with prescription opioids playing a significant role in the early years of the crisis. Entire communities were hollowed out, particularly in Appalachia, where states like West Virginia, Ohio, and Kentucky saw some of the highest overdose rates in the country. The devastation is deeply personal for families like that of Patrick Cagey, a promising young man from Maryland who was first prescribed opioids after a routine shoulder surgery. Within months, his casual use spiraled into addiction, and despite attempts at recovery, he died of an overdose at just 24 years old.

Or the story of Emily Walden's son, T.J., a bright, ambitious 21-year-old who was prescribed opioids for a minor back injury. What started as a short-term prescription turned into dependency, and eventually, he was introduced to stronger formulations. T.J. overdosed on extended-release opioids—formulations that PBMs helped keep easily accessible—leaving his mother to become one of the most outspoken advocates against these corporate-driven policies. Their stories are just two among thousands, a brutal reminder that these corporate decisions had real, irreversible consequences.

The opioid epidemic is one of the clearest examples of how PBMs have prioritized profit over patient well-being. If their own contracts forced them to keep deadly opioids widely available in exchange for cash, what does that say about how they manage access to other life-saving drugs today?

And perhaps more importantly—if PBMs could do this with opioids, what else are they doing right now that we don't know about?

Chapter 32

THE PHARMACEUTICAL MACHINE: INNOVATION OR EXPLOITATION?

If PBMs have perfected the art of manipulating access to prescription drugs for profit, pharmaceutical companies have mastered the game of pricing them. PBMs blame drug manufacturers for setting sky-high list prices, while pharma points the finger back at PBMs for demanding ever-larger rebates and playing formulary games that keep costs inflated. But as we've seen, neither side is innocent. And nowhere is this more apparent than in the pharmaceutical industry's pricing strategies—where life-changing innovations are often accompanied by staggering, seemingly arbitrary price tags.

THE PHARMACEUTICAL MACHINE: INNOVATION OR EXPLOITATION?

Few industries carry the same moral weight as pharmaceuticals. A breakthrough drug can mean the difference between life and death, between suffering and relief. But alongside genuine innovation lies a stark reality: the business of medicine is just that—a business. And like any other industry, pharmaceutical companies are driven by profit, often at the expense of those who need their products the most.

CHAPTER 32

The United States spends more on prescription drugs than any other country in the world, with annual expenditures exceeding $600 billion and rising. Drug manufacturers argue that high prices are necessary to fund research and development, particularly for novel therapies targeting rare and complex diseases. Meanwhile, critics point to profit margins that far exceed those of other industries and question whether the cost of innovation is being artificially inflated.

The tension between groundbreaking therapies and exploitative pricing is perhaps best seen in two areas: the manipulation of drug patents to extend monopolies—known as evergreening—and the astronomical prices attached to the latest generation of treatments, from GLP-1 medications for weight loss to high-cost cancer therapies.

Pharma, like PBMs, claims it is merely responding to market forces. But as we examine their pricing tactics, the question remains: are we paying for true medical advancements, or are we simply feeding a system designed to extract maximum revenue at every turn?

For patients diagnosed with diseases that once meant certain death or debilitating illness, modern pharmaceuticals have been nothing short of miraculous. A child born with cystic fibrosis today has access to drugs that can dramatically slow disease progression, adding decades to their life expectancy. A person with HIV, once facing a grim prognosis, can now live a near-normal lifespan thanks to antiretroviral therapy. And for those with previously untreatable cancers, breakthrough immunotherapies and gene-targeting drugs have offered newfound hope.

These success stories underscore the extraordinary value of pharmaceutical innovation. But alongside these medical triumphs, another trend has emerged: the relentless rise in drug prices.

The cost of prescription medications in the United States has skyrocketed at a pace far exceeding inflation, wages, and even overall healthcare expenditures. What was once a system designed to fund research and deliver lifesaving treatments has evolved into a profit-maximizing machine that often prioritizes financial gain over patient access.

A BRIEF HISTORY OF THE PHARMACEUTICAL INDUSTRY AND DRUG PRICING

In the early 1900s, the pharmaceutical industry was primarily composed of small, independent drugmakers focused on producing basic remedies and vaccines. Penicillin, the first true antibiotic, was discovered in 1928 but wasn't mass-produced until World War II, when the U.S. government played a crucial role in its development and distribution. During this era, drug prices remained relatively stable, as many medications were either developed in government-funded labs or manufactured by multiple companies, keeping costs in check.

The landscape began to shift in the 1950s and 1960s as pharmaceutical companies grew larger and more powerful. The passage of the 1962 Kefauver-Harris Drug Amendments required companies to prove that new drugs were both safe and effective before marketing them. While this was a major step forward for patient safety, it also increased the cost and complexity of bringing new drugs to market.

Then came the Bayh-Dole Act of 1980, a pivotal moment that allowed universities and private companies to patent drugs developed with federal research dollars. This legislation was intended to spur innovation by incentivizing private investment in drug development, but it also led to the explosion of patent monopolies that now dominate the industry.

In the decades that followed, drug prices began an exponential rise. Consider these figures:

- In 1960, the U.S. spent $2.7 billion on prescription drugs.

- By 1980, that number had grown to $12 billion.

- In 2000, drug spending had soared to $122 billion.

- Today, Americans spend more than $600 billion per year on prescription medications.

What changed? A combination of factors, including patent evergreening, the rise of blockbuster drugs, and the introduction of direct-to-consumer advertising, which fueled demand for high-cost medications.

THE COST OF RISING DRUG PRICES

The impact of soaring drug costs is felt across every sector of the economy:

- **Government Programs**: Medicare and Medicaid are now among the largest purchasers of prescription drugs. In 2022, Medicare Part D spent over $216 billion on prescription drugs, while Medicaid's drug spending topped $80 billion. The federal government has struggled to rein in costs, with pharmaceutical lobbying often blocking attempts at reform.

- **Employers**: Companies that provide health insurance to their workers are paying the price as well. Employers now spend an average of $1,600 per covered employee per year on prescription drugs, a figure that has nearly doubled in the past decade. These rising costs contribute to higher premiums and increased cost-sharing for employees.

- **Individuals**: The financial burden on patients is staggering. A recent study found that one in four Americans struggle to afford their medications, with many resorting to skipping doses, rationing pills, or going without treatment altogether.

For those with chronic conditions, the cost of staying healthy can mean choosing between paying for medicine and covering basic needs like rent and groceries.

At the heart of this crisis is a fundamental question: Are the astronomical prices of today's drugs truly reflective of innovation and research costs, or are they the result of a system engineered to extract as much profit as possible from Americans?

If you were to cross the border into Canada, fly to Europe, or visit just about any other developed nation, you'd find something striking: the exact same medications, manufactured by the same companies, often cost a fraction of what they do in the United States. The numbers are staggering. A vial of insulin that costs nearly $100 in the U.S. is available for just $8 in Germany. Humira, a best-selling drug used to treat autoimmune conditions, costs nearly $3,000 per injection in the U.S. but less than $600 in the U.K. Even newer, high-demand drugs like Ozempic are affected—Americans pay over $900 per month for the medication, while patients in Japan pay just $169.

This pricing disparity isn't due to differences in quality, production costs, or even supply chains. It comes down to a single factor: the way drugs are priced and negotiated. In nearly every other high-income country, governments regulate drug costs, often using purchasing power to set price ceilings. The U.S., in contrast, allows pharmaceutical companies to set their own prices with virtually no restrictions. The result? Americans are subsidizing the rest of the world's access to affordable medication, while patients, employers, and taxpayers at home foot an ever-growing bill.

The enormous price discrepancies between the U.S. and other nations have been the subject of repeated congressional hearings. Lawmakers have dragged pharmaceutical executives before Congress, demanding explanations for the soaring cost of life-saving drugs. In 2019, the CEOs of seven major drug companies testified before the Senate Finance Committee, insisting that high U.S. prices were necessary to fund research and development. They pointed to the billions spent each year on innovation, suggesting that without these high prices, the pipeline of groundbreaking treatments would dry up.

That argument, however, doesn't hold up under scrutiny. A House Oversight Committee report released in 2021 found that many of the biggest drugmakers were spending far more on stock buybacks, executive bonuses, and marketing than on research and development. Between 2016 and 2020, 14 major pharmaceutical companies spent $577 billion on dividends and stock buybacks—$56 billion more than they spent on R&D during the same period.

Despite these revelations, little has changed. Congress continues to hold hearings, release reports, and introduce bills to lower drug costs, but the pharmaceutical lobby remains one of the most powerful in Washington. Lawmakers from both parties have received millions in campaign contributions from pharmaceutical companies and their trade groups, ensuring that while outrage over drug prices makes for good soundbites, meaningful reform remains elusive.

HOW OTHER COUNTRIES KEEP DRUG PRICES IN CHECK

Unlike the U.S., most developed nations use aggressive negotiation tactics to control drug prices. In Canada, the government's Patented Medicine Prices Review Board ensures that new medications aren't priced beyond reasonable limits. In the U.K., the National Institute for Health and Care Excellence evaluates whether a drug's cost is justified based on its clinical benefits. Germany allows pharmaceutical companies to set their own prices for the first year after a drug is introduced, but after that, insurers negotiate prices based on real-world data and international comparisons.

Meanwhile, in the U.S., Medicare—the largest purchaser of prescription drugs—is legally barred from negotiating most drug prices. This prohibition, inserted into the Medicare Modernization Act of 2003 at the urging of the pharmaceutical industry, has cost taxpayers billions. While Congress recently passed a measure allowing Medicare to negotiate prices on a small selection of high-cost drugs, the scope is limited, and the pharmaceutical industry is already fighting it in court.

THE SYSTEM ISN'T BROKEN—IT'S WORKING EXACTLY AS DESIGNED

If the goal of the U.S. pharmaceutical pricing system was to ensure that medications were affordable and accessible, it would be failing. But that was never the goal. The system was built to maximize profits, and by that measure, it's functioning exactly as intended. Pharmaceutical companies justify high prices by blaming the costs of research, but the reality is that much of that research is subsidized by government funding and taxpayer dollars. The National Institutes of Health, for example, plays a critical role in early-stage drug development, often funding the research that leads to blockbuster drugs. But once those drugs hit the market, pharmaceutical companies alone reap the financial rewards.

As noted in previous chapters, the blame isn't limited to drug manufacturers. Pharmacy benefit managers (PBMs), the powerful middlemen that determine which drugs are covered by insurance plans, play their own role in driving up prices. PBMs demand steep rebates from drugmakers in exchange for favorable placement on formularies, which often leads to artificially inflated list prices. The pharmaceutical industry points to PBMs as the real culprits behind high drug costs, while PBMs shift the blame back to drug companies.

Meanwhile, patients, employers, and taxpayers are left paying the price.

A SYSTEM DESIGNED TO EXTRACT MAXIMUM REVENUE

When Americans hear about high drug prices, they often assume the money is going toward scientific breakthroughs, but the truth is more complicated. The industry does produce life-saving innovations—but at what cost? The same companies that develop groundbreaking treatments also game the system to keep prices high, using tactics like patent evergreening to block competition. As a result, the U.S. continues to spend more on prescription drugs than any other country in the world, with no signs of slowing down.

In the next section, we'll examine one of the most common tactics drug companies use to maintain their monopolies: manipulating the patent system to extend exclusivity well beyond the original expiration date. Some of the most expensive drugs on the market today should have been subject to generic competition years ago—but thanks to legal loopholes and aggressive lobbying, their manufacturers have found ways to keep prices high indefinitely.

Chapter 33

THE PHARMACEUTICAL INDUSTRY'S GREATEST TRICK: THE ILLUSION OF EXPIRING PATENTS

Most people assume that when a drug's patent expires, competition will take over, driving down prices and making medications more affordable. That's how the system is supposed to work—after a 20-year exclusivity period, the patent expires, allowing lower-cost generic or biosimilar alternatives to enter the market. But in the pharmaceutical industry, that's more of a theoretical concept than a reality.

For many of the best-selling drugs in the world, pharmaceutical companies have mastered the art of what is known as patent evergreening—a series of legal, regulatory, and business tactics that allow them to extend their monopolies far beyond the original expiration date. These maneuvers block competition, keep prices high, and ensure that drug companies continue to extract billions from the healthcare system long after their initial exclusivity period was supposed to end.

Take Humira, a drug that has become the poster child for patent gaming. First approved by the FDA in 2002 to treat autoimmune diseases like rheumatoid arthritis and Crohn's disease, Humira was originally scheduled to face competition by 2016. Instead, its manufacturer, AbbVie, built a fortress of 165 overlapping patents—many of them minor variations of existing patents—ensuring that competitors were locked out of the market for years. The result was that Humira continued generating massive profits, raking in over $200 billion in total revenue before biosimilar alternatives were finally allowed to hit the U.S. market in 2023.

During this extended monopoly, the price of Humira skyrocketed. In 2003, a single dose cost around $500. By 2023, that same dose was priced at more than $3,000—a 500% increase, despite the fact that the drug itself had not fundamentally changed. While other countries, including those with robust pharmaceutical markets, saw Humira's price remain relatively stable, American patients were left paying exponentially more for the exact same medication.

Humira is not an isolated case. The same playbook has been used across the industry. Enbrel, another autoimmune drug first approved in 1998, was supposed to lose its patent protection in 2010. Instead, through a series of patent extensions on minor modifications—such as slight adjustments to its molecular structure and injection method—manufacturer Amgen managed to extend its monopoly until at least 2029. That's a 30-year exclusivity period, far beyond the intent of the original patent laws.

Another example is Revlimid, a chemotherapy drug that has been a lifeline for cancer patients—but at a steep cost. Originally set to face generic competition years ago, its manufacturer, Celgene (now owned by Bristol Myers Squibb), cut exclusivity deals with generic manufacturers that technically allowed some competition but heavily restricted the supply of lower-cost alternatives. This arrangement allowed Celgene to maintain its market dominance and keep prices artificially high, ensuring that the company continued profiting while patients and insurers were left footing the bill.

These examples illustrate a fundamental problem in the pharmaceutical industry. Patent laws were designed to balance the need for innovation with the public's right to affordable medications. Drugmakers would get a temporary monopoly to recoup their investment and fund future research, but eventually, competition would lower prices. Instead, evergreening has allowed companies to turn that temporary monopoly into an indefinite one.

One of the most common tactics is filing new patents on slight modifications of the drug. A company might tweak the formulation from a twice-daily pill to a once-daily extended-release version, even if there is no significant benefit to patients. They might change the method of delivery, such as moving from an injectable solution to a prefilled pen or inhaler, and patent the new device. Some companies patent specific manufacturing processes, preventing competitors from using similar production methods even if the drug itself is no longer under patent.

Insulin manufacturers have been particularly aggressive in using this strategy. Despite insulin being over a century old, drugmakers have continuously reformulated their products just enough to extend their exclusivity. While the core molecule remains largely unchanged, new delivery systems—pens, pumps, and other devices—have kept insulin prices far higher in the U.S. than in almost any other country.

Perhaps the most notorious example of reformulation for financial gain is OxyContin. Purdue Pharma's blockbuster painkiller became a central figure in the opioid crisis, in part because of how easily the original formulation could be crushed and abused. Facing the expiration of its original patent in 2010, Purdue made a calculated move—it reformulated OxyContin into an "abuse-deterrent" extended-release version, then withdrew the original formula from the market entirely.

This maneuver not only extended Purdue's monopoly but also blocked generic competitors from producing lower-cost versions of the original OxyContin. The result? Purdue was able to continue charging exorbitant prices while reinforcing the company's public narrative that it was taking action to curb opioid abuse—despite its role in fueling the epidemic in the first place.

A similar strategy played out with Namenda, a drug used to treat Alzheimer's disease. Originally sold as Namenda IR, an immediate-release twice-daily pill, the drug's patent was set to expire in 2015. To sidestep generic competition, its manufacturer, Allergan, introduced Namenda XR, an extended-release once-daily version.

While patients and doctors weren't necessarily demanding a once-daily version, the change allowed Allergan to secure a new patent and block generic competitors from entering the market for an additional several years.

But the company didn't stop there. In a move that drew public outrage and legal scrutiny, Allergan pulled Namenda IR from the market altogether, forcing doctors and patients to switch to Namenda XR—the version that only the brand-name manufacturer could sell. The result? A multi-billion-dollar windfall for Allergan and higher costs for Alzheimer's patients and their caregivers.

Another common evergreening strategy is shifting a drug's delivery method from oral to topical, which allows companies to rebrand an existing medication as a "new" product with patent protection.

Consider diclofenac, a nonsteroidal anti-inflammatory drug (NSAID) commonly used to treat arthritis pain. Originally available as an inexpensive oral pill, its manufacturer reformulated it into a topical gel (Voltaren Gel) and a patch (Flector Patch)—both of which were granted new patents and sold at many times the price of the original pill.

The irony? The gel and the patch delivered the same active ingredient as the original diclofenac pill—just at a significantly higher cost to patients and insurers. And because the reformulated versions were classified as new drugs, they remained under patent protection for years longer than they otherwise would have.

These maneuvers don't represent genuine medical breakthroughs; they are legal and business strategies designed to prevent price competition.

Despite growing awareness of this issue, meaningful reform has remained elusive. Congress has held hearings, and the Federal Trade Commission has launched investigations, but pharmaceutical lobbying efforts have been incredibly effective at stalling legislative action. The U.S. Patent and Trademark Office continues approving new patents without requiring companies to prove that their modifications provide any substantial medical benefit. Meanwhile, the Food and Drug Administration, which regulates drug safety and effectiveness, has no authority over patents, leaving it powerless to prevent these abuses.

The burden falls on generic drug manufacturers to challenge these patents in court—an expensive, time-consuming process that many smaller companies simply can't afford. Even when generics do win lawsuits, major drugmakers often reach settlements that delay competition in exchange for financial incentives, further extending their control over the market.

The consequences of this strategy weren't just financial—they were human.

In the years Humira's monopoly was extended, many patients couldn't afford their medication, especially those with high-deductible health plans or who fell into the Medicare donut hole, where out-of-pocket costs soared. Employers that provide health insurance saw their drug spending skyrocket, forcing them to pass those costs onto employees through higher premiums, copays, and deductibles.

In one particularly egregious example, an independent pharmacy in Minnesota reported that a patient was being charged $77,000 for a single year's supply of Humira—a price that was entirely avoidable had biosimilars been allowed onto the market sooner.

Even Medicare and Medicaid, which collectively cover tens of millions of Americans, were forced to overpay due to Humira's extended monopoly. A 2022 study found that had biosimilars been available in 2016 as originally planned, Medicare alone would have saved $7.2 billion in drug costs—a staggering amount that instead went directly into AbbVie's pockets.

HUMIRA WASN'T THE FIRST, AND IT WON'T BE THE LAST

McKinsey's consulting work wasn't limited to Humira. They have advised other pharmaceutical companies on similar life-cycle management strategies, helping drugmakers extend monopolies on everything from insulin to cancer drugs.

And the pharmaceutical industry isn't slowing down. More than 80% of the top-selling drugs in the U.S. today have multiple patents extending their monopolies well beyond their original expiration dates.

The playbook McKinsey helped refine is being replicated across the industry, ensuring that Americans continue to pay the highest drug prices in the world.

The implications are clear: as long as these tactics remain legal, drug companies will keep using them. The Humira case should have been a wake-up call for policymakers, yet efforts to close the patent loopholes remain stalled. Pharmaceutical lobbying power is simply too strong, with billions spent on campaign donations, advertising, and legal battles to maintain the status quo.

Meanwhile, as policymakers debate piecemeal solutions, patients, employers, and taxpayers remain trapped in a system where the price of staying healthy is dictated by corporations focused more on Wall Street than on medicine.

The pharmaceutical industry frames itself as the driver of medical innovation, but as the Humira case demonstrates, sometimes its greatest innovation isn't in medicine—it's in finding new ways to keep prices high.

In the next section, we'll look at how the pharmaceutical industry doesn't just use patents to protect profits, but also exploits a labyrinth of financial incentives, backdoor deals, and rebate schemes—all of which ensure that the people who can least afford it continue paying the most.

The cost of these monopoly protections is staggering. Medicare spent over $10 billion on Humira alone over a five-year period simply because it couldn't access cheaper alternatives. Employer-sponsored health plans now allocate a growing share of their budgets to expensive specialty drugs, while patients struggle with sky-high out-of-pocket costs. A 2022 study found that more than 40% of cancer patients delay or skip treatments due to financial hardship—many of these drugs should have had lower-cost generics available years earlier.

And I fear that this is just the beginning, especially with the introduction and massive uptake of GLP1s for weight loss. If Medicare and Medicaid were to cover GLP-1 weight-loss drugs, which was proposed by the Biden administration in 2024 just before he left office, even under conservative cost estimates, the financial implications would be massive. With obesity rates in the U.S. at approximately 42%, a significant portion of enrollees in these programs would likely qualify for treatment. Given that Medicare covers 65 million Americans and Medicaid provides coverage for 85 million, the potential number of patients is substantial. Even if you were to assume a 50% discount off of today's list price, either due to negotiations, rebates, or increased competition, that number sits at an eye-popping $4.1 trillion over the next decade.

While lawmakers have proposed some reforms, such as allowing Medicare to negotiate drug prices and preventing manufacturers from filing overlapping patents for minor modifications, the pharmaceutical industry has proven adept at working around these measures. In contrast, some European countries have already rejected many of the evergreening tactics that are routinely approved in the U.S. However, pharmaceutical companies have fiercely resisted similar efforts here, arguing that limiting patent protections would stifle innovation and slow the development of new treatments.

But that argument doesn't always hold up. Many of the industry's biggest cash cows—drugs that have generated tens of billions in revenue—were initially developed with significant government funding. The National Institutes of Health (NIH) plays a critical role in early-stage research, often laying the groundwork for drugs that companies later bring to market at exorbitant prices. Yet, once those drugs become profitable, it is the private companies—not the taxpayers—who reap the financial rewards.

Patent evergreening is just one piece of the puzzle. While drugmakers fight to extend monopolies on existing drugs, they are simultaneously setting unprecedented prices for new treatments. The next generation of therapies—gene editing, cell therapy, and personalized medicine—holds enormous potential for patients, but at what cost?

Consider Zolgensma, a gene therapy designed to treat spinal muscular atrophy. It's a revolutionary treatment, offering a potential one-time cure for a devastating disease. But it comes with a price tag of $2.1 million per patient, making it one of the most expensive drugs in the world.

Or take CAR-T cell therapy, a cutting-edge cancer treatment that modifies a patient's immune cells to attack tumors. While these therapies represent incredible medical advances, they also come at a staggering cost—often exceeding $500,000 per treatment.

Are these prices justified by the true cost of research and development? Or are they simply the numbers that pharmaceutical companies believe the market will bear?

As evergreening keeps older drugs expensive and new therapies push pricing into uncharted territory, the financial burden on patients, employers, and taxpayers continues to grow. The pharmaceutical industry insists that these costs are necessary to sustain innovation. But at what point does the pursuit of profit outweigh the public good?

In the next section, we'll explore how pharmaceutical companies set prices for new drugs, the enormous profits they generate, and whether the industry is truly focused on medical breakthroughs—or just maximizing its bottom line.

If you were to ask a pharmaceutical executive why a particular drug costs what it does, you'd likely hear a well-rehearsed response about research and development costs, regulatory hurdles, and the high cost of bringing a drug to market. Yet, if that were truly the determining factor, why do Americans pay so much more than patients in other developed countries for the exact same medications?

The truth is drug pricing is far more about strategy than science. The process of setting a drug's price is not based on a simple equation of development costs plus a reasonable profit margin. Instead, it's an opaque and highly calculated exercise, guided by what the market will tolerate, what insurers and pharmacy benefit managers (PBMs) will accept, and—most importantly—what will generate the highest return for shareholders.

Chapter 34

THE MYTH OF RESEARCH AND DEVELOPMENT COSTS

Pharmaceutical executives love to tell a story. It's a familiar one, repeated in congressional hearings, press releases, and whenever drug pricing comes under scrutiny. They paint a picture of an industry taking enormous financial risks, investing billions into research, and racing against time to develop lifesaving drugs. They argue that without sky-high prices, innovation would dry up, and medical breakthroughs would slow to a trickle.

It's a compelling narrative. But like most corporate storytelling, it leaves out some inconvenient details—starting with the fact that much of the real investment in drug discovery doesn't come from pharmaceutical companies at all. It comes from the American taxpayer.

For decades, the U.S. government, primarily through the National Institutes of Health (NIH), has played the most critical role in funding biomedical research. The NIH pours over $40 billion a year into scientific studies, much of which lays the foundation for the blockbuster drugs that pharmaceutical companies eventually bring to market. Between 2010 and 2019, every single one of the 356 new drugs approved by the FDA was linked to NIH-funded research. Every single one.

Yet once these drugs make it to pharmacy shelves, it is private corporations—not taxpayers—who reap the financial rewards.

THE REAL COST OF "RESEARCH AND DEVELOPMENT"

We've all heard the explanation for why drug prices in the U.S. are so high: Research and Development (R&D). It's a phrase repeated by pharmaceutical executives in congressional hearings, plastered across industry-funded studies, and parroted by pundits and even well-meaning friends. It's a quick and easy way to shut down a conversation—because who wants to be the person arguing against innovation? The implication is clear: If we don't pay these prices, life-saving treatments won't get developed.

It's an argument designed to create fear. What if cancer drugs stopped being developed? What if treatments for rare diseases dried up? If we squeeze pharmaceutical profits, won't we be dooming future generations to a world without medical breakthroughs? This is the industry's most powerful defense—and they've spent billions making sure we all believe it.

But what does "R&D" actually mean? When drugmakers claim that it costs upwards of $2.6 billion to bring a new drug to market, what exactly are they counting? Most people assume it refers to things like laboratory research, clinical trials, and FDA approval processes—the essential steps to discovering and proving the safety and effectiveness of a new drug. But the reality is much murkier.

A significant portion of R&D spending has nothing to do with groundbreaking discoveries. It includes legal fees for patent disputes, the cost of acquiring smaller biotech firms that have already developed promising drugs, and even marketing tactics disguised as research. In many cases, drugmakers don't spend their R&D budgets inventing new medicines—they spend them tweaking existing drugs just enough to extend their monopolies. Minor changes, like reformulating an injectable into a pill or introducing a slow-release version of the same medication, can secure years of additional exclusivity without

CHAPTER 34

delivering any real medical benefit. And yet these efforts are counted as R&D investments.

Then there's the matter of what pharmaceutical companies don't pay for—but still take credit for. The U.S. government, primarily through the National Institutes of Health (NIH), funds much of the early-stage research that leads to blockbuster drugs. In fact, between 2010 and 2019, every single drug approved by the FDA was connected to taxpayer-funded research. But once those drugs become commercially viable, it's private companies—not the taxpayers—who reap the financial rewards.

And it's not just direct funding. NIH research grants come with something called indirect cost reimbursements, meant to cover the administrative and operational expenses of universities, hospitals, and research institutions. But some of the most prestigious universities and research hospitals in the country receive indirect cost rates as high as 50%—meaning that for every $1 million in federal funding, half a million dollars might be spent on things like executive salaries, luxury office space, and high-end amenities. When the Trump administration proposed capping these indirect reimbursements at 15%, elite universities fought back hard, arguing that it would cripple research efforts. But critics pointed out that these institutions were already receiving hundreds of millions of taxpayer dollars annually, much of which was being funneled into administrative overhead rather than scientific discovery.

So while drug companies claim that high prices are the cost of innovation, the reality is far more complicated. The public is already footing the bill for much of the real research—yet when these drugs finally reach the market, it is the pharmaceutical companies that claim ownership and set prices however they see fit.

If this system were truly designed to reward innovation, wouldn't it ensure that the public—who funds the discoveries—benefits from affordable access to the medicines they helped create? Instead, the system is structured to privatize profits while socializing costs, allowing pharmaceutical companies to charge whatever the market will bear while shifting the risks and expenses onto taxpayers.

A great example of this—one that nearly everyone is familiar with—is the COVID-19 vaccines. While pharmaceutical companies raked in billions from their distribution, the research and development that made them possible was largely funded by the U.S. government and taxpayers. The very foundation of these vaccines—the mRNA technology used in both Pfizer-BioNTech and Moderna's shots—was developed with NIH grants and decades of federally funded research. Yet when the time came to bring these vaccines to market, pharmaceutical companies claimed ownership, set their own prices, and reaped unprecedented profits.

Take Moderna, for instance. Before the pandemic, the company had never successfully brought a product to market, despite receiving nearly $10 billion in U.S. government funding to develop and manufacture its COVID-19 vaccine. By 2022, Moderna had reported $39 billion in vaccine sales, transforming it from an obscure biotech company into one of the most profitable pharmaceutical firms in the world. Pfizer, which partnered with the German company BioNTech, earned $75 billion from COVID-related products in 2022 alone.

And yet, despite these record-breaking profits, both Pfizer and Moderna have dramatically raised prices on their vaccines since the government stopped purchasing them in bulk. During the pandemic, the U.S. government bought Pfizer's vaccine for $19.50 per dose—but as soon as the shots hit the commercial market, Pfizer announced a staggering price hike to $110–$130 per dose. Moderna followed suit, raising its vaccine price from $15 to around $130 per dose, even though taxpayers had already footed the bill for its development.

The price increases weren't tied to higher production costs or new innovations—they were simply a reflection of what the market would bear. The companies justified these hikes by pointing to the costs of manufacturing, distribution, and continued research. But critics argued that these price increases were a textbook example of corporate greed, particularly given the fact that the vaccines would not have existed without decades of public investment.

And let's not forget the pandemic itself—a global crisis that led to emergency use authorizations, expedited regulatory pathways, and unprecedented sales volumes. Unlike traditional drug development, where companies face years of uncertainty and high failure rates, the COVID-19 vaccines had a guaranteed global market and billions in advance government contracts before they even hit the shelves. The risk to these companies was almost nonexistent.

Even after making tens of billions, Moderna infamously attempted to patent key aspects of its vaccine without crediting the NIH scientists who contributed to its development. The government had to step in and demand recognition for its role, a rare but telling sign of how pharmaceutical companies operate—they will happily take public funding but fight tooth and nail to maintain sole ownership of the profits.

The COVID-19 vaccine rollout was a once-in-a-lifetime example of just how deeply intertwined government funding and pharmaceutical profits really are. And yet the industry still clings to the narrative that high prices are the inevitable cost of innovation. But if that were true, why did taxpayers pay for the research upfront, only to be charged again when the final product was released?

This isn't an isolated case. The same pattern repeats across the pharmaceutical industry—where the public shoulders the risk, but the private sector reaps the reward. And when these companies aren't profiting off taxpayer-funded research, they're using the next tool in their arsenal: gaming the patent system to lock in monopolies and keep drug prices high for decades.

Chapter 35

HOW DO COMPANIES DECIDE A PRICE?

So, if R&D costs don't actually dictate prices, what does?

A pharmaceutical company's pricing strategy is often determined by a few key factors:

What will insurers and PBMs tolerate? Drugmakers don't set prices in isolation; they negotiate with PBMs and insurers, who have enormous power over which drugs make it onto formularies. This is why new drugs are often launched with a high list price—so that PBMs and insurers can demand steep rebates and still come out with a deal that looks favorable to them.

One of the clearest examples of PBM influence over drug pricing is the case of insulin, which has seen decades of price increases despite being available for over a century. Insulin manufacturers like Eli Lilly, Novo Nordisk, and Sanofi have steadily raised list prices—not because production costs increased, but because PBMs demanded ever-larger rebates in exchange for formulary placement. This created a vicious cycle: manufacturers inflated prices so they could offer bigger rebates, allowing PBMs to claim they were securing "savings" for insurers and employers. But those rebates rarely made their way to patients, who were left paying ever-rising out-of-pocket costs.

What will the market bear? Drug companies conduct extensive market research to determine how much a new medication can be priced

CHAPTER 35

before pushback becomes too strong. This is why orphan drugs (those that treat rare diseases) often have astronomical price tags—because patients and insurers have no alternative, they will pay whatever is necessary.

Consider Zolgensma, a $2.1 million gene therapy for spinal muscular atrophy (SMA). Novartis, the drug's manufacturer, defended the price by pointing to the devastating nature of SMA and the fact that the drug is a potential one-time cure. With no direct competition and an extremely vulnerable patient population, the company set a price that was not based on the drug's development costs, but on what insurers and Medicaid programs could be forced to pay.

How does it compare to existing treatments? One of the most egregious examples of a high-cost drug with questionable added value is Aduhelm, the Alzheimer's drug developed by Biogen. Initially priced at $56,000 per year, Aduhelm was approved despite conflicting clinical trial results and widespread skepticism from the medical community. A major independent review by the Institute for Clinical and Economic Review (ICER) concluded that the drug's benefits did not justify its cost, estimating that a fair price for Aduhelm should be between $3,000 and $8,400 per year—a fraction of what Biogen originally charged. Yet, because the FDA granted accelerated approval based on biomarker evidence rather than clear clinical improvements, Biogen was able to launch at a price many times higher than what independent cost-effectiveness analyses suggested.

Similarly, the cancer drug Revlimid, produced by Celgene (later acquired by Bristol Myers Squibb), saw its price skyrocket from $6,000 per month in 2005 to over $20,000 per month by 2021. The drug is an analog of thalidomide, an older and significantly cheaper drug, yet Celgene was able to justify its price increases by making minor changes to dosing, formulations, and market positioning. A 2020 study in JAMA found that nearly 50% of all new cancer drugs approved by the FDA between 2009 and 2017 showed no significant survival benefit over existing treatments, yet they were often priced at levels far above older alternatives.

Another example is Sovaldi, Gilead's hepatitis C treatment, which debuted in 2014 at $84,000 for a 12-week course. While it was a significant medical breakthrough—a cure rather than a long-term treatment—Gilead's pricing strategy ignited a national debate. A Senate Finance Committee report later revealed that Gilead had deliberately set an exorbitant price, not based on development costs, but based on what the company believed payers would tolerate. The report uncovered internal company documents showing that Gilead executives were fully aware of the public outrage the pricing would trigger but proceeded anyway, prioritizing revenue maximization over patient access.

It is worth remembering that while most patients—and even many doctors—assume that a newly approved drug must be superior to what's already available, that is not necessarily true. The FDA's approval process does not require new drugs to be more effective than existing treatments—only that they meet safety and efficacy benchmarks. A 2017 study published in *The BMJ* found that among new cancer drugs approved between 2003 and 2013, nearly two-thirds entered the market without evidence of improving overall survival or quality of life compared to existing options. Yet, these drugs were often priced substantially higher than older treatments.

A stark example of this is the arthritis drug Xeljanz (tofacitinib), which was approved in 2012. While positioned as a more convenient oral alternative to injectable biologics like Humira, clinical trials later showed that it was associated with higher risks of serious side effects, including blood clots and cancer. Yet, it was priced at a premium, and pharmaceutical marketing heavily promoted it as an innovative alternative, despite lacking evidence of superior efficacy.

The reality is that pharmaceutical companies use FDA approval as a marketing tool, leveraging the public's assumption that "new"

CHAPTER 35

means "better." But with no regulatory requirement to demonstrate superiority over existing drugs, companies can launch products at dramatically higher prices without offering any real improvements for patients.

The problem is compounded by aggressive direct-to-consumer advertising, which is legal in the U.S. but banned in most other developed countries. A 2022 study in *JAMA Internal Medicine* found that drug ads often exaggerate benefits while downplaying risks, making patients more likely to demand expensive new drugs even when cheaper, equally effective alternatives exist.

How high can we start? Pharmaceutical companies have learned that the initial launch price of a drug is critical—it sets the tone for what insurers, government programs, and patients will expect to pay in the future. That's why many companies deliberately start high, knowing they can always adjust downward if public or regulatory pushback becomes too strong.

Take Sovaldi, the $84,000 per treatment course Hep C drug. The backlash against its $84,000 launch price was swift—state Medicaid programs, insurers, and even Congress scrutinized the cost, and public outrage forced Gilead to offer discounts and rebates to some payers. But by setting the price sky-high from the outset, Gilead ensured that even with concessions, it would still make billions in profit. A Senate Finance Committee investigation later revealed that Gilead executives explicitly modeled various price scenarios, concluding that they could afford to take some heat if it meant maximizing revenue in the long run.

Another example is EpiPen, which saw its price surge more than 500% after Mylan Pharmaceuticals acquired it in 2007. The company initially tested the waters with gradual price hikes, then pushed it to over $600 per two-pack by 2016. The public outrage that followed forced Mylan to introduce a half-priced "authorized generic" at $300, but that was still a dramatic increase from the roughly $100 price tag when they first acquired the drug. The initial high price gave Mylan a cushion to "walk back" its pricing while still raking in profits—a strategy that has since been widely adopted by other pharmaceutical companies.

This strategy also explains why drug companies rarely, if ever, lower the price of a drug once it's set. If a drug is launched at a relatively low price, increasing it later risks public scrutiny and regulatory intervention. This is why companies frequently use "price anchoring"—starting at an exorbitant number to make any later reductions seem like a generous concession, even when the final price remains dramatically inflated.

It also helps explain why the U.S. sees far steeper price hikes on existing drugs than other countries. In 2022, an analysis of Medicare Part D drugs found that over 1,200 medications had their prices increased above the rate of inflation, with some rising by more than 500% over a five-year period. Unlike other countries where price increases must be justified based on manufacturing costs or added clinical value, pharmaceutical companies in the U.S. have no regulatory limits on how high they can raise prices once a drug is established in the market.

By setting prices as high as possible at launch, pharmaceutical companies give themselves the flexibility to adjust later—but always in a way that maximizes their bottom line. And because insurance companies and PBMs negotiate based on percentage discounts rather than actual costs, a drug that starts out expensive remains a revenue machine for all involved—even when those "discounts" are later applied.

Chapter 36

WHY ARE DRUG PRICES SO MUCH HIGHER IN THE U.S.?

In almost every other developed nation, governments negotiate drug prices directly with manufacturers. Countries like Canada, Germany, and the United Kingdom conduct cost-effectiveness analyses, evaluating how much a drug improves a patient's quality of life relative to its price. If a drug doesn't demonstrate a meaningful benefit, it won't be covered—or it will only be reimbursed at a set price.

For example, in Germany, drugmakers can set their own price for the first year after launch, but then insurers negotiate the price down based on international comparisons and real-world data. In the UK, the National Institute for Health and Care Excellence (NICE) uses a cost-per-QALY (quality-adjusted life year) metric to determine how much the National Health Service (NHS) will pay for a drug. If a drug is deemed too expensive relative to its benefits, the NHS simply won't cover it.

The U.S., in contrast, has no such system. Medicare—the single largest purchaser of prescription drugs—is legally barred from negotiating most drug prices due to the Medicare Modernization Act of 2003, a law written with heavy influence from the pharmaceutical industry. This means that while other countries force drugmakers to justify their prices, the U.S. allows them to charge whatever the market will bear.

In 2022, the Inflation Reduction Act (IRA) marked a significant, albeit limited, shift in this policy. For the first time, Medicare was granted the authority to negotiate prices on a small selection of high-cost drugs. This was heralded as a breakthrough in the fight against pharmaceutical price gouging, with the potential to save billions in taxpayer dollars over time. However, the reality is far less transformative than its proponents suggest.

The law's impact is constrained by several key limitations. First, the negotiated prices won't take effect until 2026, giving drug manufacturers years to prepare countermeasures—such as increasing prices before negotiations begin or shifting costs to other parts of the healthcare system. Second, the number of drugs subject to negotiation is shockingly low: in its first year, only ten drugs will be affected, with additional drugs phased in over the coming years. Given that Medicare Part D covers thousands of medications, this barely makes a dent in overall drug spending.

Even more concerning is the fact that only older drugs—those that have been on the market for at least nine years for small-molecule drugs and thirteen years for biologics—are eligible for negotiation. This means that pharmaceutical companies can still rake in a decade or more of inflated profits before any government intervention kicks in. It also provides an incentive for manufacturers to avoid price reductions by making slight modifications to their drugs to extend their monopoly period—a tactic they have long perfected through patent evergreening.

The pharmaceutical industry has, unsurprisingly, responded with fierce opposition and legal challenges. Drugmakers and their lobbying groups, including PhRMA, have filed lawsuits arguing that price negotiations amount to unconstitutional government price controls that stifle innovation. They claim that reduced revenue from Medicare negotiations will force companies to cut back on research

— CHAPTER 36 —

and development—though, as previously discussed, much of that "R&D" spending goes toward executive bonuses, marketing, and shareholder buybacks.

While the Inflation Reduction Act represents a long-overdue step toward reining in drug prices, its limited scope and delayed implementation mean that the U.S. pharmaceutical market will remain one of the most expensive in the world. Without broader reforms—such as expanding negotiation power, capping out-of-pocket costs, or addressing the root causes of inflated pricing—the burden will continue to fall on patients, employers, and taxpayers, who will keep paying exorbitant sums for medications that cost a fraction of the price in other developed nations.

Chapter 37

WHAT HAPPENS WHEN PRICES ARE TOO HIGH?

When drug prices spiral out of control, the consequences are real and often devastating. Patients are forced to ration essential medications, employers struggle with soaring healthcare costs, and taxpayers continue to subsidize an increasingly unsustainable system. While policymakers debate reforms and pharmaceutical executives defend pricing strategies, real people are caught in the crosshairs—people whose lives depend on medications that are simply too expensive.

Consider the case of Trikafta, a breakthrough drug for cystic fibrosis (CF) that has transformed the lives of many patients. Approved in 2019, the drug has been hailed as one of the most significant medical advances for those suffering from the disease. But with a price tag of more than $300,000 per year, access to this life-changing medication remains out of reach for many patients.

For years, CF advocates have fought to make Trikafta more widely available, arguing that its cost makes it impossible for some families to afford treatment even with insurance. In the U.K., where the government negotiated a lower price, the drug is far more accessible. But in the U.S., many patients have faced insurance denials, massive out-of-pocket costs, or bureaucratic obstacles that make it nearly impossible to stay on the medication. Some have even turned to crowdfunding to cover their prescriptions—an absurd and heartbreaking reality in one of the wealthiest countries in the world.

For patients with multiple sclerosis (MS), the price of treatment has skyrocketed beyond reason. Drugs that once cost $8,000 per year in the 1990s now carry annual price tags exceeding $100,000. A 2022 study published in *JAMA Neurology* found that MS drug prices in the U.S. are nearly four times higher than in comparable nations, despite being produced by the same manufacturers.

Take the case of a woman named Julie, who was diagnosed with MS in her late 20s. For years, she relied on a medication that kept her condition stable. But when her insurance plan changed, she was suddenly left with a $7,000-per-month bill for the same drug she had been taking for years. Unable to afford the cost, she was forced to stop treatment. Within months, her symptoms worsened, and she lost mobility in one of her legs. Her experience is not unique—neurologists across the country report that many MS patients delay or stop taking their medication due to cost, increasing the likelihood of severe relapses and permanent disability.

Cancer drugs are among the most expensive medications on the market, and one of the starkest examples is Gleevec, a revolutionary leukemia drug introduced in 2001. Initially priced at $26,000 per year, Gleevec's cost inexplicably rose to more than $120,000 annually over the next decade—even as its production costs remained stable.

The manufacturer, Novartis, justified these price hikes by citing the need to fund future innovation, but critics point out that the drug had already paid for itself many times over. Meanwhile, patients with chronic myeloid leukemia (CML) were left scrambling for ways to afford treatment. Some maxed out credit cards or drained retirement savings just to stay alive. Others, unable to cover the exorbitant cost, rationed doses or skipped treatment altogether—putting their lives at risk.

Even after generic versions of Gleevec became available, the price didn't drop as expected. Instead, the cost of generics remained stubbornly high, largely due to a lack of competition and exclusive deals between drugmakers and pharmacy benefit managers (PBMs) that kept prices inflated.

These cases illustrate a disturbing pattern: life-saving medications exist, but their cost puts them out of reach for many who need them most. While pharmaceutical companies claim that high prices are necessary to fund future innovation, the reality is that much of the research behind these drugs was publicly funded, and the profits generated far exceed what is needed to sustain new drug development.

A PERFECTLY DESIGNED SYSTEM, JUST NOT FOR PATIENTS

After everything we have explored—the incentives baked into our system, the ways in which pharmaceutical companies and PBMs manipulate pricing, and the consequences for patients, employers, and taxpayers—the fundamental question remains: *At what point does the pursuit of profit become a ransom demand?*

This isn't just a rhetorical question. It plays out in real decisions every day, in health plans across the country. I know because I've been in that position. But before I share my own experience, let me tell you another.

A patient, diagnosed with cancer, needed Keytruda, a breakthrough immunotherapy drug that could save his life. But unlike a one-time treatment, he would need it for a long time—potentially indefinitely. His nurse advocate, working on his behalf, called the hospital to get approval for the course of treatment, but also to ask a question most people don't realize can even be asked: *Can the price be lowered?*

Hospitals acquire drugs at wholesale prices, but what they bill insurers and patients is another story entirely. The nurse advocate knew this, and she also knew that this hospital had acquired Keytruda at around $6,000 per dose—but was charging over $75,000 per dose.

She pressed them: *Why? How is this justifiable?*

The response wasn't just cruel—it was revealing. The woman on the other end of the line, without hesitation, flatly said, "Well, the price isn't going to matter when he's dead, is it?"

Not just what she said—but *how* she said it. Matter-of-fact. Unbothered. Almost bored. As if to say: *So what? What are you going to do about it? Not take the drug that could save your life? Not pay whatever it takes to keep your child alive? Not do everything possible to prevent a heart attack, a stroke, a disease progressing beyond the point of no return?*

That conversation is a microcosm of everything that's wrong with the American healthcare system. It is not built to serve patients—it is built to extract the highest possible revenue from them, knowing they have no choice.

I know this all too well because I've faced decisions just like it. When you are responsible for the healthcare coverage of over 800,000 people, every choice carries immense weight. Behind every policy decision, every formulary placement, every cost-containment strategy, is a real person—someone waiting for treatment, someone making impossible trade-offs, someone whose life could be upended by a single decision.

One case still lingers with me. A new drug had just come to market, carrying a staggering price tag of over $100,000 per dose. The PBM suggested implementing a six-month post-launch waiting period before covering it—a common strategy meant to allow time for additional data collection, price negotiations, or potential competitor drugs to enter the market. On paper, six months didn't seem unreasonable.

But then I thought: *What if this were my son? My daughter? My mother or father?*

If you have never lived with a life-threatening condition, six months might sound like a reasonable pause. But for those who are suffering, six months might as well be 60 years. The difference between immediate access and a six-month delay could mean irreversible progression of disease, loss of function, or even death.

Yet what made this decision especially enraging wasn't just the price—it was the blatant inequity. That same drug, from the same manufacturer, was being sold in Europe for less than half of what was being charged in the U.S. And the company was still turning a profit overseas.

So what was the choice, really? Delay access and hope that the cost would come down? Or approve it immediately, knowing full well that by doing so, we were reinforcing a system that allows pharmaceutical companies to hold lives hostage to profit?

We covered it immediately. And in doing so, we—like every other plan forced into these decisions—rewarded a system that has lost all moral grounding.

That's the real crisis. These are not just abstract policy debates or theoretical budget calculations. They are decisions that determine who gets to live and who is left behind.

CONCLUSION: THE CHOICE WE FACE

We've spent this book peeling back the layers of a healthcare system that, for all its complexity, really comes down to a simple truth: it wasn't built to serve patients—it was built to extract as much money as possible from them.

You've seen how hospitals inflate prices with no justification, how insurance companies profit whether they pay for care or deny it, and how pharmaceutical companies and PBMs manipulate the system to

CHAPTER 37

keep costs high while blocking competition. At every turn, the people who are supposed to be "paying the bills" for healthcare—employers, taxpayers, and patients—are shut out, misled, or outright exploited.

So where do we go from here?

This final section isn't about more problems—it's about what happens next.

This is where we talk about what's at stake if we continue down this path, what we stand to gain if we change course, and most importantly, who holds the power to do something about it. Because make no mistake—despite what the industry wants you to believe, the American healthcare system is not some immovable force of nature. It is a business, shaped by the choices we allow it to make.

The question is: Will we finally demand better?

As you read these final pages, I want you to think about the people in your life—your family, your employees, your neighbors—who are one diagnosis or surprise bill away from financial catastrophe. Then ask yourself: Is this really the best we can do?

Because the truth is, we don't have to accept this.

The path forward isn't easy, but it is clear. And it starts with understanding the system and understanding that we are not powerless.

Chapter 38

THE HIGH STAKES: WHAT HAPPENS IF WE DO NOTHING?

Every year, reports come out detailing the relentless rise of healthcare costs; we see the headlines, we hear the warnings, and yet, year after year, the problem only gets worse. Employers shake their heads at double-digit premium increases, workers watch more of their wages eroded, and policymakers hold hearings that lead nowhere. We've sustained the "unsustainable" for decades—how much longer can we keep this up?

At what point do we stop treating this as just a healthcare problem and start recognizing it as the economic crisis that it is?

The United States spends more on healthcare than any other country—nearly 20% of our GDP—yet our outcomes are nowhere near the best. Instead, Americans are saddled with higher costs, worse health outcomes, and increasing financial strain on families, businesses, and government programs. We pour billions into a system that fails to deliver value, while other nations spend far less and still manage to provide universal coverage, lower drug prices, and longer life expectancy.

And it's not just individuals who are struggling—this system is crushing American competitiveness. The consequences of these rising costs go beyond just benefits. Money spent on skyrocketing healthcare expenses is money not spent on raises, hiring, or business expansion. It's a hidden tax on every worker, reducing take-home pay and squeezing household budgets.

While American employers struggle to compete under the weight of these expenses, U.S. businesses are put at a massive disadvantage. The idea that healthcare costs are undermining U.S. economic competitiveness is not new. Princeton economist Uwe Reinhardt spent years warning that our broken system would eventually become an "albatross around the neck of American businesses." In 2017, during Berkshire Hathaway's annual shareholder meeting, Buffett stated: "Medical costs are the tapeworm of American economic competitiveness." He argued that while corporate taxes were often viewed as the biggest drag on U.S. business, it was actually healthcare spending that posed a greater long-term threat. Unlike other nations where healthcare costs are controlled at a national level, in the U.S., employers shoulder a massive and ever-growing burden—making it harder for them to compete globally.

Buffett, along with Jeff Bezos (Amazon) and Jamie Dimon (JP Morgan Chase), attempted to tackle this issue head-on by launching Haven, a joint venture aimed at reducing healthcare costs for their employees. However, despite their influence and financial backing, Haven shut down in 2021—a testament to just how deeply entrenched and resistant to reform the current system is.

Buffett's analogy of healthcare as a "tapeworm" is particularly apt. Like a parasite, rising healthcare costs feed off the economy, draining resources that could otherwise go to wages, retirement security, education, and business investment. Every extra dollar spent on bloated healthcare costs is a dollar not spent on innovation, job creation, or worker prosperity.

His words reinforce the larger argument: if we do nothing, healthcare costs will continue to eat away at America's economic future, crippling businesses, families, and government budgets alike.

And here we are.

If the U.S. spent the same amount on healthcare as other high-income nations, we would save nearly $1 trillion annually. That's money that could be used to reduce the deficit, invest in infrastructure, or put toward tax cuts that would actually help middle-class families. Instead, we continue throwing money into a healthcare system designed to extract profits rather than improve care.

Employer-sponsored health insurance enjoys a massive tax break, exempt from payroll and income taxes. That's $384 billion in lost federal revenue each year—a subsidy that primarily benefits high-income workers while starving public programs of funding. At the same time, non-profit hospitals—many of which behave like for-profit conglomerates—pay no taxes despite being some of the largest landowners in major cities. These tax-exempt entities sit on billions of dollars in real estate, yet cities and states see little benefit in return.

We don't just lose dollars to this system—we lose opportunities.

If health premiums had risen at the same pace as inflation rather than far outstripping it, American families would have far more financial security. Let's put it in real terms:

- **Retirement Savings:** If the average family had been able to invest their premium increases in a 401(k) over the last five years instead of funneling that money into healthcare costs, they'd have an extra $113,848 for retirement.

- **College Savings:** Had those same dollars gone into a 529 plan for a child's education, growing over 18 years, it would amount to $86,383—enough to send a child to college without massive student loans.

- **Homeownership:** Even if those premium increases were simply placed in a savings account, it would total $38,292—a down payment on a home that many families now can't afford.

This isn't just about healthcare—it's about the American dream slipping further out of reach for millions of families.

THE NATIONAL DEBT AND HEALTHCARE COSTS: A COLLISION COURSE

Healthcare is already the largest share of the federal budget, consuming $1.6 trillion annually between Medicare, Medicaid, and other public programs. But it's not just government spending—it's also one of the biggest drivers of our growing national debt.

The federal government now spends as much on interest payments for the national debt as it does on Medicare. And with healthcare costs projected to keep rising, those pressures will only worsen.

As health spending grows unchecked, it threatens every other national priority. Rising costs will continue to drain resources from public health, medical research, and disease prevention. It will make it harder to invest in the things that truly improve health outcomes—like education, housing, and social services.

And yet, instead of addressing the problem, Congress throws money at it while protecting the very industries driving costs higher. The pharmaceutical lobby remains one of the most powerful forces in Washington, and as long as politicians benefit from the status quo, meaningful reform will remain elusive.

WHEN HEALTHCARE FAILS THE PEOPLE IT'S SUPPOSED TO SERVE

It's one thing to talk about healthcare in terms of dollars and percentages—rising costs, unsustainable spending, the burden on businesses. But what often gets lost in these discussions is the human toll—the lives that are shortened, the families that are devastated, the people who fall through the cracks of a system that values profit over well-being.

For all the money we spend—nearly $4.5 trillion a year—Americans are getting a raw deal. Life expectancy in the U.S. has declined for three straight years, an unprecedented backslide for a developed nation. A baby born in the United States today can expect to live, on average, 76.1 years, putting us behind at least 50 other countries—including not just high-income nations like Japan (83.7 years), Switzerland (83.9 years), and Australia (83.4 years), but also places like Costa Rica, Lebanon, and Chile. In some U.S. states, life expectancy is lower than in Bangladesh or Algeria.

The gap is even starker when you break it down by race. Black Americans have a life expectancy of 70.8 years, nearly six years shorter than white Americans and nearly a decade shorter than Asian Americans (83.5 years). Indigenous Americans fare even worse—life expectancy among Native populations has dropped to 65.2 years, putting them on par with developing nations like Myanmar and Madagascar.

Why? The same preventable chronic diseases that the U.S. healthcare system claims to treat—heart disease, diabetes, hypertension, and obesity—are instead becoming more deadly, not less. Sixty percent of American adults now have at least one chronic disease, and 40% have two or more. While other wealthy nations have made progress in reducing deaths from these conditions, the U.S. continues to fall behind because the system isn't built to prevent illness—it's built to treat it for as long as possible, at the highest price possible.

The crisis extends to maternal and infant health as well. The U.S. maternal mortality rate is the highest of any developed country, with 32.9 deaths per 100,000 live births—more than double the rate of Canada, nearly four times the rate of Germany, and ten times higher than countries like Sweden or Norway. Black women are at even greater risk, dying at 2.6 times the rate of white women, a disparity that has persisted for decades. Yet rather than invest in maternal healthcare, hundreds of hospitals have closed labor and delivery units, particularly in rural and predominantly Black communities. Between 2014 and 2022, nearly 300 hospitals shut down their maternity wards, leaving millions of women without access to prenatal or emergency obstetric care. The result? More deaths. More stillbirths. More unnecessary suffering.

Even infants who survive birth face worse odds in the U.S. than in other wealthy nations. The U.S. infant mortality rate is 5.4 per 1,000 live births, making an American baby twice as likely to die before their first birthday as a baby born in France or Finland. And again, race plays a role—Black infants die at more than twice the rate of white infants. The cause isn't just lack of access to care—it's also medical neglect, institutional bias, and the financial disincentive for hospitals to invest in unprofitable but life-saving services.

And then there's obesity—the most visible example of our system's failure. Nearly 42% of American adults are obese, up from just 30% in 2000. Obesity fuels heart disease, stroke, diabetes, and cancer—four of the leading causes of death in the U.S. Yet rather than investing in prevention, nutrition, and lifestyle interventions, the healthcare industry is pouring billions into GLP-1 weight loss drugs like Ozempic and Wegovy—at a cost of over $10,000 per patient, per year.

The weight-loss drug market is projected to hit $100 billion by 2030. Do we really think these companies want to solve obesity? Or do they want to keep people on expensive medications for life rather than tackling the root causes—the food deserts, the processed food industry, the lack of primary care access, and the economic instability that drives unhealthy habits in the first place? The incentives are clear: there's more money in treating a lifetime of obesity than in preventing it.

And if obesity drugs are the latest billion-dollar bonanza, opioids are the ultimate cautionary tale. More than 600,000 Americans have died from opioid overdoses since 1999—a crisis manufactured by Purdue Pharma, fueled by reckless prescribing, and enabled by a healthcare system that incentivized pain management over holistic care. Today, more than 2.1 million Americans suffer from opioid use disorder, and while Purdue has been sued into oblivion, the cycle continues. The same industry that flooded the country with opioids is now profiting from "solutions" like Suboxone and addiction treatment centers—raking in billions from the crisis they created.

Even for those lucky enough to access healthcare without financial ruin, the system itself is riddled with waste and harm. Studies show that at least 30% of hospital admissions involve unnecessary procedures or treatments. Spinal surgeries, knee replacements, cardiac stents, and even C-sections are often performed not because they're medically necessary, but because they're highly profitable.

And then there's medical error—the third leading cause of death in the U.S., behind only heart disease and cancer. More than 250,000 Americans die every year due to preventable mistakes, yet hospitals fight every attempt to make patient safety data public.

If you're lucky enough to survive the system, you may not survive the bill that follows. Two-thirds of bankruptcies in the United States are tied to medical debt. Nearly one in five Americans has an unpaid

CHAPTER 38

medical bill in collections. This is uniquely American—no other wealthy country forces its citizens into financial ruin just for getting sick.

And yet those who benefit from this system—the health insurers, the hospital executives, the pharmaceutical giants—see any attempt at reform as an existential threat. That's because it is—for them. The truth is, for as much as they claim to care about patients, they are fighting to protect an industry that thrives on our collective suffering.

But here's the paradox: The U.S. also has some of the most advanced, groundbreaking, and truly lifesaving medical care in the world. Our surgeons perform miracles. Our physicians and nurses are among the best trained anywhere. From trauma centers to cutting-edge cancer treatments, American medicine can be extraordinary—when you can access it. But shouldn't that be the goal? Shouldn't we demand a system that delivers world-class care without bankrupting families or forcing people to ration their medications? Shouldn't we ensure that when people need treatment, they can trust that they're getting the right care—not the care that is most profitable?

Because in almost every example above—maternal mortality, chronic disease, obesity, opioid addiction, medical errors—the common denominator isn't bad medicine, bad doctors, or bad patients. It's bad incentives. The system isn't broken—it's functioning exactly as designed. We pay for treatment, not for health. We reward sickness, not prevention. We fund crisis response, not crisis avoidance.

And the result? A nation that spends more on healthcare than anyone else, yet is sicker, dying younger, and going bankrupt trying to stay alive.

The question is not whether we can afford to change—the question is whether we can afford not to.

Chapter 39

THE PATH FORWARD: DO WE HAVE THE WILL TO CHANGE?

Healthcare is deeply personal. The people who deliver care—our nurses, doctors, technicians, and even administrators—are not villains. In fact, many of them entered the field because they wanted to heal, to help, to save lives. And many of them do just that, every single day. But good people working within a broken system does not make that system any less broken.

What may have started as noble, mission-driven institutions have, over time, morphed into something unrecognizable. The industry that once prided itself on patient care has been overtaken by financial incentives, where revenue maximization too often takes precedence over health outcomes. The mission statements still talk about compassion and service, but the reality is clear to anyone who looks closely—this is a system built not to deliver the best care at the best price, but to extract the highest possible revenue from patients, employers, and taxpayers.

There is no need to rehash the full parade of horribles. If you've made it this far, you understand the scale of the problem. The real question now is: What do we do about it?

The good news is that the fight isn't over. The greatest untapped resource in this battle isn't another government task force or corporate initiative. It's the American people.

An informed, engaged, and active public is the last, best hope for real change. No industry—no matter how powerful—can withstand sustained pressure from the people it claims to serve. That's where you come in.

What happens next depends on whether we allow this system to continue unchecked, or whether we demand something better. The solutions exist—but they won't happen without a public willing to fight for them.

EMPLOYERS: THE POWER THEY DON'T REALIZE THEY HAVE

Corporate America has spent years griping about healthcare costs but has done surprisingly little to challenge the system siphoning billions from their bottom line. These are companies that negotiate *everything*—from supply chains to IT contracts to corporate travel—down to the last cent. And yet, when it comes to their second-largest expense after payroll, many employers roll over the moment their broker delivers bad news about yet another double-digit increase.

I've seen CEOs fight tooth and nail over minuscule cost overruns in procurement, aggressively renegotiating vendor contracts, pushing for transparency in every corner of their business. But when their consultant tells them, "It's going to be another tough year," they shrug and accept it. They take the renewal as if it's an inevitable act of nature rather than the result of opaque pricing schemes, misaligned incentives, and outright manipulation by the very firms that claim to be advocating on their behalf.

It doesn't have to be this way. Employers have enormous leverage—they just have to stop playing by rules designed to keep them in the dark. The moment they start asking tough questions, demanding real answers, and refusing to sign blank checks, the entire game changes.

If you're an employer, the next few sections are written with you in mind. They're designed to help you ask sharper questions, demand greater accountability, and ultimately take back control of your health plan.

If you're an employee with employer-sponsored coverage, this part can help you understand how decisions are made about your benefits — and how to ask the right questions when something doesn't add up.

CONSULTANTS & BROKERS: WHO DO THEY REALLY WORK FOR?

Every employer with a health plan has a consultant or broker. And most employers assume that these intermediaries are working exclusively on their behalf, helping them navigate the complexities of the healthcare market. But in reality, many of these firms are deeply entangled with the very insurance carriers and pharmacy benefit managers (PBMs) they're supposed to be negotiating against.

Before signing off on another recommendation from your consultant, ask them:

- Are you getting paid by the insurance carriers or PBMs you're recommending? What commissions, bonuses, or override payments do you receive? (Hint: If they won't provide a *full* disclosure, assume the worst.)

- What happens if I move my plan to a different TPA or insurer? Will you still represent me? If not, why not?

- What's your financial incentive for steering me toward a fully insured plan instead of self-funding? Have you quantified the savings I'd see from self-insuring versus taking the carrier's renewal?

- How do you benchmark what I'm paying compared to similar employers? If you don't have real market comparisons, how do you know we're not being overcharged?

- If I need to audit my plan—claims, network contracts, PBM arrangements—will you help? Or will you tell me it's too complicated?

Push for documentation. Would you let an employee expense thousands of dollars for a corporate retreat without an itemized receipt? Of course not. So why would you let your broker or TPA tell you they *can't* provide a fully unredacted claims file?

The bottom line: If your consultant isn't fighting for transparency, they're not working for you. They're working for the system that's profiting off your ignorance.

PBMS: THE BLACK BOX OF DRUG PRICING

If there's any part of the healthcare supply chain that should raise immediate red flags, it's PBMs. These entities control which drugs are covered, how much employers pay, and what patients ultimately pay at the pharmacy counter. They claim to lower costs, but in reality, they profit from the *spread*—the difference between what they pay the pharmacy and what they charge the plan sponsor.

Employers should be asking:

- What percentage of manufacturer rebates are you keeping, versus passing on to us? If it's not 100%, why?

- How do you decide which drugs are placed on the formulary? Are lower-cost generics or biosimilars being excluded because you make more money from higher-priced brand-name drugs?

- Can I audit all invoices from drug manufacturers? If they refuse, that's a giant red flag.

- What's my *real* net cost per script, including all fees? If they can't give you a straight answer, they don't want you to know.

- Why am I paying more for some generics than a cash-paying patient at a retail pharmacy? If PBMs were actually reducing costs, this wouldn't happen.

Employers *will* get pushback on these questions. But that's exactly how you know you're pressing in the right place.

TPAS: WHO CONTROLS THE CLAIMS DATA CONTROLS THE MONEY

Third-party administrators (TPAs) are supposed to process claims on behalf of self-insured employers. But in reality, many are aligned with big insurance carriers or health systems, meaning their loyalty is split between the employer they serve and the industry they depend on.

Here's what employers should be asking their TPAs:

- Who owns the network you're contracting with? If the answer is a major insurer, your plan is likely being repriced in ways you can't see.

- Will you provide a fully unredacted claims file? If not, why?

- Can I see a direct comparison between what our plan pays for hospital services and the hospital's cash price? If there's a significant difference, you're being overcharged.

- How are you auditing claims for errors or overbilling? If they don't have a clear answer, assume it's not happening.

- What percentage of our total spending is going toward administrative fees versus actual care? If they won't break it down, there's a reason.

Employers need to own their data. If you don't control your claims data, you don't control your health plan. Period.

THE LEGAL RECKONING: WHY EMPLOYERS NEED TO PAY ATTENTION

If all of this sounds like something *someone else* should be worrying about—think again. The legal landscape for employer-sponsored health plans is shifting fast, and companies that fail to act could find themselves on the receiving end of lawsuits similar to the ones that reshaped the 401(k) industry.

The JP Morgan case, the Wells Fargo case, and the Johnson & Johnson case all center around the same basic argument: Employers failed in their fiduciary duty by allowing excessive healthcare costs to go unchecked.

Just as corporations were sued for mismanaging retirement plans—resulting in hundreds of billions in settlements—employers are now being held accountable for failing to protect employees from overpaying for healthcare.

And the standard is clear: If you *could have* asked tough questions and *didn't*, you may be legally responsible for the financial harm to your employees.

IF YOU'RE AN EMPLOYER, THIS BOOK WON'T FIX YOUR HEALTH PLAN—BUT IT'S A STARTING POINT

I'm not pretending this book is a step-by-step guide to fixing your health plan overnight. There's no easy button here—there never is for things that matter. But if you're serious about taking back control, here's where you start:

1. Take these questions and ask them. Call your consultant, your PBM, your TPA—demand answers.

2. Refuse to accept vague responses. If they tell you, "It's too complicated," push harder.

3. If you suspect you're being overcharged, investigate. Hire an independent auditor, benchmark against other plans, pull claims data and analyze it.

If you do even *one* of these things, you'll be ahead of 95% of employers who just take what they're given. And if enough businesses start doing this, we'll stop being price-takers and start being price-setters.

The system won't change because it wants to. It will change because the people paying the bills—you—start demanding better.

Chapter 40

LABOR UNIONS & WORKER ADVOCACY: THE SLEEPING GIANT IN THE HEALTHCARE FIGHT

For more than a century, labor unions have fought for fair wages, safe working conditions, and benefits that allow their members to retire with dignity. Healthcare has always been central to that fight. Yet even as unions negotiate stronger contracts, many have unknowingly allowed their health plans to be infiltrated by the same predatory middlemen driving costs higher for everyone.

No wage increase can outpace the relentless rise of healthcare costs. When premiums jump 8% to 12% annually—far exceeding inflation—every dollar secured at the bargaining table is eroded before it even reaches a worker's paycheck. Healthcare isn't just a benefits issue—it's a wage issue, a pension issue, a worker-rights issue. And for too long, unions have been sold the myth of "good union healthcare," assuming that because they have negotiated plans, they must be getting the best deal. In reality, many union plans are just as vulnerable to hidden fees, spread pricing, and outright manipulation as corporate plans.

PBMs pocket millions in undisclosed rebates, hospitals overcharge for routine procedures, and insurers bake profit margins into administrative fees under the guise of cost control. Unions must ask themselves: Are we truly providing the best possible healthcare to our members, or are we simply providing the most expensive version of it? If union leaders aren't scrutinizing healthcare spending with the same intensity they negotiate wages and pensions, they are leaving money on the table. And that money isn't going to patient care—it's going to PBMs, insurance executives, and hospital administrators whose salaries have soared while workers' deductibles and out-of-pocket costs climb.

The good news is that unions have the power to change this. But they must be willing to ask tough questions of their vendors—questions that, in many cases, employers have only recently started asking themselves.

Who's profiting off our members' medications? Are we getting 100% of the manufacturer rebates on prescription drugs, or is our PBM skimming a cut? Can we see a breakdown of spread pricing, or are we paying massive markups on generic drugs that should cost pennies? How much are we being charged for specialty medications, and are there lower-cost alternatives? PBMs dictate formularies, but that doesn't mean their decisions are in the best interest of workers—it often means they are maximizing their own revenue streams.

What about hospital and health system contracts? What are the top ten most expensive claims in the plan, and how do those charges compare to what a cash-paying patient would owe? If union leaders discovered their members were paying five times more for the same procedure than an uninsured patient off the street, would they stand for it? Do we have direct contracts with hospitals, or are we relying on a carrier's network—one that takes a cut of every hospital reimbursement, driving costs even higher? Are we being hit with outrageous "facility fees" for routine outpatient services?

Then there's the role of consultants, brokers, and third-party administrators. Are our consultants receiving kickbacks from

CHAPTER 40

insurers, TPAs, or PBMs? If they are, whose interests are they really representing? Can we audit our claims in real time, or is the TPA making money from hidden administrative fees buried in contracts? How does our plan compare to others of a similar size—are we overpaying compared to national benchmarks?

Union leaders must take these questions seriously—not just for their members, but for their own legal protection. Recent lawsuits against JP Morgan, Wells Fargo, and Johnson & Johnson have made one thing clear: organizations that knowingly allow their employees to be overcharged for healthcare can be held legally responsible. If corporations are now facing lawsuits for failing to act in the best financial interest of their employees, how long before multi-employer union plans find themselves in the same position?

The legal pressure is mounting, but more importantly, so is the moral obligation. Union funds manage billions of dollars in healthcare spending. That is money deducted from workers' wages with the promise of providing the best possible care. If unions allow those dollars to be siphoned into hidden fees, inflated hospital charges, and PBM profiteering, they are failing their members.

This is not a lost cause. In fact, unions are uniquely positioned to lead the fight for real reform. Unlike individual employers, which often operate in silos, labor has the ability to mobilize across industries, across states, and across political divides. And history has proven that when labor moves, politicians follow.

That means refusing to sign contracts that don't allow full claims data access. If you can't see what you're paying for, you're being robbed. It means moving away from carrier-controlled networks that limit competition and drive up prices. It means exposing PBM price manipulation—the three largest PBMs control 80% of all prescriptions in the U.S., and their pricing practices are designed to benefit themselves, not patients. It means being willing to file lawsuits when necessary, holding vendors accountable for the billions being extracted from workers' wages.

Healthcare should be a benefit, not a burden. But as long as unions allow their plans to be manipulated by middlemen, it will continue to be a tax on wages, pensions, and economic security. It's time for labor to wake up to the reality of what's happening. The industry wants unions distracted—fighting for 3% raises while quietly siphoning thousands per worker per year into a broken system.

But once unions start pushing back—asking the right questions, refusing bad contracts, demanding transparency—the balance of power shifts.

Because at the end of the day, unions don't just represent workers. They represent the last great force capable of breaking the stranglehold that corporate healthcare has on the American economy.

Chapter 41

THE POLITICIANS AND POLICYMAKERS: THE ARCHITECTS OF THE SYSTEM THEY REFUSE TO FIX

It would be easy to believe that policymakers are simply overwhelmed by the complexity of healthcare—that they haven't reformed the system because they don't know how. But that's not the truth. The truth is far simpler, far uglier: they know exactly what's wrong, and they've chosen not to fix it.

That's not to say politicians are inherently corrupt or malicious. Many of them care deeply about their constituents. Many genuinely want to do the right thing. But in a system where every elected official is looking toward their next election, where hospital systems and pharmaceutical companies are some of the largest employers in their districts, and where campaign donations keep the wheels turning, making the right choice is rarely the easy choice.

It takes courage to challenge the financial interests that have embedded themselves so deeply into the political structure. It takes bravery to stand up to a hospital system when you know it employs thousands in your state. It takes resolve to push back against a pharma-backed lobbying group when you know they're already drafting attack ads against you. And yet—this is the job they signed up for. Leadership isn't about avoiding hard decisions. It's about making the right ones.

The reality is the system won't change unless lawmakers make different choices. And those choices start with a willingness to stop protecting industry profits at the expense of patients, taxpayers, and businesses.

WHAT POLICYMAKERS CAN—AND MUST—DO

The federal government is the biggest customer and financier of the healthcare industry, yet it has failed to use its purchasing power to demand better prices or more accountability. For decades, Congress has funneled billions into the industry with almost no strings attached—propping up monopolistic hospital systems, handing out research subsidies to pharmaceutical giants who then turn around and charge Americans the highest prices in the world, and refusing to hold insurers accountable when they rake in profits while denying care. If there's one thing that's clear, it's that the industry sees any effort to rein in costs as an existential threat. And why wouldn't they? The U.S. healthcare system is a $4.5 trillion business. When that much money is at stake, you don't just give it up without a fight.

But what about the existential threat to patients? To taxpayers? To the businesses that are being crushed under the weight of rising healthcare costs? Congress cannot continue to pretend that these interests don't matter. They cannot continue to throw taxpayer dollars at the problem while ignoring the root cause: a system designed to maximize revenue rather than health outcomes. The first step toward real reform is ending the cycle of unchecked financial incentives that allow industry players to extract wealth from the system with impunity.

CHAPTER 41

One of the biggest culprits is the revolving door between government and the healthcare industry. Time and again, we see lawmakers and regulators transition seamlessly into high-paying roles at insurance companies, hospital lobbying groups, and pharmaceutical firms—sometimes within months of leaving office. The conflicts of interest are staggering. Former health officials help shape drug pricing policies, then go on to sit on the boards of the very companies that benefit. Executives from major PBMs and hospital systems land influential advisory positions, guiding the very regulations meant to keep their industries in check. And it's not just an occasional occurrence; it's a well-worn path, a built-in feature of the system rather than a bug.

Take the electronic health record (EHR) mandate, for example. The government essentially forced hospitals and providers to adopt EHR systems, a move that should have improved efficiency and patient care. But the biggest beneficiary? Epic Systems, whose CEO, Judy Faulkner, was conveniently seated on the federal committee that helped craft the rules. The result was a massive windfall for Epic, whose software became the dominant system in U.S. hospitals, even as providers complained about its usability, high costs, and lack of interoperability. This is the kind of policymaking that happens when industry insiders are allowed to write the rules.

If Congress and state legislatures are serious about reform, they need to break this cycle. There must be strict cooling-off periods preventing lawmakers and regulators from cashing in immediately after leaving office. There must be transparency requirements forcing full disclosure of financial ties between policymakers and the industries they regulate. And there must be real accountability for those who continue to put corporate profits above public health.

Beyond tackling corruption and conflicts of interest, policymakers need to fix the broken incentives that drive up costs. Hospitals should not be allowed to charge facility fees that turn routine outpatient care into multi-thousand-dollar bills simply because they own the building. PBMs should not be profiting by inflating drug prices rather than lowering them. Medicaid and Medicare funds should not flow freely to organizations that refuse to comply with basic price transparency measures. The government has an obligation to stop subsidizing inefficiency and waste.

And yet, instead of addressing the root cause of rising costs, Congress continues to pour money into a failing system. Healthcare is already the largest share of the federal budget, consuming $1.6 trillion annually between Medicare, Medicaid, and other public programs. And it's only going to get worse. The federal government now spends as much on interest payments for the national debt as it does on Medicare, and healthcare costs are one of the biggest drivers of that debt. If lawmakers fail to rein in spending, it won't just threaten the stability of healthcare programs—it will threaten the country's entire fiscal future.

So, what will it take for policymakers to act? Another financial crisis? Another round of employer lawsuits exposing how broken the system is? The collapse of a major hospital chain that suddenly can't sustain itself under its own bloated cost structure? Or will it take a public that finally refuses to accept the status quo?

Because at some point, politicians will have to choose. Do they continue protecting an industry that exploits patients, bankrupts families, and erodes trust in the system? Or do they finally do their jobs and fight for the people they were elected to represent?

The time for excuses is over. The solutions exist. The problem isn't a lack of knowledge, and it isn't a lack of options. It is a lack of will. If lawmakers refuse to act, then it falls to the public—to voters, to businesses, to labor groups—to force them.

Politicians are always looking toward their next election. If they won't fix this system because it's the right thing to do, they need to be made to fix it because their careers depend on it.

The Final Chapter

A SYSTEM THAT BREAKS US BEFORE IT HEALS US

If you've made it this far, you understand the gravity of what we're up against. You've seen the numbers, the corruption, the staggering inefficiencies, and the relentless drive for profit that has warped a system that was meant to heal. But if you really want to understand how broken American healthcare is, you don't need a white paper. You don't need a study. You just need to live through it.

I learned that lesson early.

I was in college, drowning under the weight of expectations I had placed on myself—expectations that, over time, had manifested in something far darker: an eating disorder that I could no longer control. I had pushed myself to the breaking point, and when I finally realized I couldn't pull myself out alone, I did the hardest thing anyone struggling with mental illness can do: I asked for help.

With the help of my roommate at the time, I managed to see a counselor at GW, someone who would help me find the care I needed. I thought this was the beginning of getting better. I thought the system would work the way it was supposed to.

Instead, I was about to get my first real introduction to the grim realities of American healthcare.

The counselor wasted no time recommending a treatment facility in Naples, Florida—a well-regarded inpatient program that, she assured me, could take me immediately. I trusted her. I had no reason not to. It wasn't until much later that I learned she had a financial relationship with the hospital, earning referral fees for every patient she sent their way. I wasn't just a student in crisis. I was a commission.

The facility itself? On the surface, it looked exactly as I had imagined—a quiet place to heal, with therapy sessions, nutrition plans, and a regimented schedule designed to help people like me regain control of their lives. But once I was inside, I started to see the cracks. This was definitely not the four seasons, with peeling wallpaper, a drained and dirty swimming pool, stained carpeting and bad food (oh, the irony).

I was placed in a double room, stripped of anything that could be used for self-harm, and sent to group therapy with the other patients. And that's when I realized something wasn't right. While some of the group was what you would expect—thin, struggling, but determined to get better—there were some unexpected surprises that I tried not to prejudge. First, there was Ed.

Ed was a tall, heavyset black man, soft-spoken and kind, the type of guy who would hold the door for you even when you were still ten feet away. But it was clear from the start that he didn't quite fit. Sitting in our group therapy sessions, while the rest of us talked about our struggles with food, control, and body image, Ed mostly sat in silence. It wasn't that he was rude or uninterested—he just had nothing to say. And then I learned why.

Ed didn't have an eating disorder.

He had been addicted to drugs. His Medicaid coverage for addiction treatment had run out, and the only way the hospital could keep billing was to give him a new diagnosis—an eating disorder he didn't have. This wasn't care. This was billing manipulation. And Ed? He just wanted a roof over his head. He didn't complain. He played along because the alternative was being discharged with nowhere to go.

Then there was Beth, a model from New York. And by that, I mean she made sure we all knew she was a model from New York. She carried herself with the kind of effortless arrogance that made it clear she considered herself better than the rest of us. And she wasn't there for "treatment" in the way that the rest of us were.

Beth came every year for a month-long reset. She wasn't interested in recovering. She wasn't even pretending to be. She was bulimic, sure, but she wasn't there to stop bingeing and purging. She was there because the hospital offered a controlled environment where she could restrict her calories and lose a few pounds in peace. And unlike the rest of us? She was private pay. She could afford to come and go as she pleased, and she did—year after year.

Then there was Sally.

Sally was a grandmother, always smiling, always knitting. She radiated a kind of cheerful calm that made you wonder if she even belonged there. While the rest of us were fighting to claw our way out of whatever personal hell had landed us in treatment, Sally seemed ... relaxed. Happy, even. And then I found out why.

Sally also came every year, just like Beth. But her reason was different.

Her stated diagnosis? Sugar addiction.

Every year, Medicare paid in full for her to come stay at the hospital for a month. She rented out her house while she was in treatment, giving her much needed extra cash on her fixed income retirement.

And then there was Kelly.

Kelly was in her mid-thirties, a mom, and for her first three days in treatment, she did nothing but cry.

She wasn't like Beth, or Sally, or even me. She wasn't there for an eating disorder—she was there because she was an alcoholic.

But not the stereotype. She wasn't drinking out of a brown paper bag under a bridge. She was a suburban mom with a beautiful little girl. She drank wine at night. Then during the day. Then all the time. And when she got a DUI just days before arriving at the hospital, she knew she had to do something before she lost everything.

Her insurance? It didn't cover alcohol rehab.

But it did cover eating disorder treatment.

So that's what she was there for.

And then there was me.

Three weeks into my stay, I had gained just enough weight for Aetna to declare me "cured." The insurance company was done paying. My parents weren't prepared to continue covering the costs, and I was a college student with no means of my own. So home I went—back into the world, where I was expected to just pick up the pieces and figure it out with no discharge planning or outpatient services. My coverage had run out.

A few weeks later, a bill arrived: $2,500. Turns out I had overstayed Aetna's allotted time. My parents, unimpressed with my apparent failure to recover on Aetna's timeline, decided I should pay it myself. Maybe, they reasoned, if I had "skin in the game," I wouldn't make the mistake of developing an eating disorder again.

And so, at nineteen years old, I was also introduced to "the concept of" medical debt.

THE SYSTEM THAT EXPLOITS EVERYONE—JUST DIFFERENTLY

Ed was a casualty of a system that needed to keep billing.

Beth was wealthy enough to use it to her advantage.

Sally found a loophole and made it work for her.

Kelly was forced to lie just to get help.

And I was declared "better" because my weight hit an algorithmic threshold.

This wasn't healthcare. This was business.

And it was just the tip of the iceberg.

How many people have been denied care they desperately needed because an insurance company arbitrarily decided they were "well enough"?

How many hospitals have stretched billing codes past the point of recognition just to keep revenue coming in?

How many families have been financially ruined by a system that treats them like ATMs rather than patients?

This was my introduction to the American healthcare system.

But here's what I want you to understand: I was lucky.

So many people aren't.

This fight isn't about policy. It's not about numbers. It's about real people, living real lives, and suffering in a system designed to exploit them.

For years, I have fought to expose the failures, the corruption, the broken incentives of the American healthcare system. First as a state official, then as a consultant, and now as an advocate. I've sat in rooms with hospital executives who pretended not to understand why their prices were so high. I've gone head-to-head with insurance companies that fought transparency at every turn. I've watched as policymakers—people who could *actually* do something—looked the other way, too afraid or too compromised to take on the industry.

And yet, through all of it, I have never stopped believing that something in the American healthcare system is worth saving. Because beneath the greed and dysfunction, beneath the profit-driven schemes and bureaucratic waste, there is something real. There are doctors, nurses, and surgeons who perform miracles every day. There are hospitals and research institutions that are unparalleled in their ability to save lives.

This became painfully clear to me a few months ago.

I was waiting for my son to get out of soccer—football to the real fans—when I heard it. That sickening thud, the kind that makes your stomach drop before your brain even registers what happened. I turned just in time to see a young boy—no more than 11—hit by a car going at least 40 mph. His small body crumpled onto the pavement. Time slowed.

I ran to him, dialing 999 with shaking hands. He was unconscious but breathing. His face was pale, his body eerily still except for the shallow rise and fall of his chest. His legs were shattered, bent at unnatural angles that made it clear the human body was never meant to bend that way. I knelt beside him, speaking softly, holding his hand because his mother wasn't there yet. I knew nothing about him, but in that moment, it didn't matter. He was just a child, and no child should be alone in a moment like this.

I stayed with him, waiting what felt like an eternity for the ambulance. And in those agonizing minutes, another thought crept in—one that I couldn't shake. *Would he get the best care?* I was told the children's hospital here was good. But it wasn't as good as the hospitals in the U.S. It wasn't CHOP. It wasn't Dallas Children's. It wasn't Boston Children's. Would they be able to save him? Would the right specialists be available? Would the system move quickly enough?

Two days later, he was gone.

I will never know if things would have been different had he been in a U.S. hospital. Maybe nothing could have saved him. Maybe the outcome was already written the moment that car made impact. I am sure the doctors and nurses did everything they could, and I have no doubt they were skilled and compassionate. But that question—could it have been different?—has stayed with me.

It revealed something I instinctively knew, something that all my years in healthcare policy had never shaken. Despite everything I have fought against, despite the corruption, the profiteering, the greed—when it comes to actually delivering care, the U.S. healthcare system is unmatched. That belief is not born out of patriotism or nostalgia; it is rooted in reality. If my children were sick, if I received a life-altering diagnosis, I wouldn't hesitate—I would want to be on the first flight back to the U.S. if possible. That tells me something. That tells me that what we have is worth saving.

That is why this fight matters.

Because if I, if we, still believe in what American healthcare *can* be, then we owe it to ourselves—and to every patient, every family, every business struggling under its weight—to make it better. To strip out the corruption, the greed, the waste. To ensure that the system that provides world-class care isn't also the system that bankrupts families, closes hospitals in rural communities, and prioritizes shareholders over patients.

We have the best healthcare in the world—now we must summon the courage to fix the system around it, so that it heals instead of harms, uplifts instead of exploits, and fulfills its promise to every patient who places their trust in it.

Resources

American Hospital Association, *Survey: Premiums for Employer-Sponsored Coverage Up 4% in 2021*, November 10, 2021. (https://www.aha.org)

Ars Technica, *Things Aren't Looking Good for the Infamous CEO of Health Care Terrorists*, 2024. (https://arstechnica.com/health/2024/11/things-arent-looking-good-for-infamous-ceo-of-health-care-terrorists)

Associated Press, *Federal Investigation into Steward Health Care Fraud and Corruption*, 2024. (https://apnews.com)

Bates White, *Hospital Merger Price Effects Studies*. (https://www.bateswhite.com)

Business Wire, *Steward Health Care and Medical Properties Trust Reach Settlement Agreement*, 2024. (https://www.businesswire.com)

California Attorney General's Office, *Settlement on Hospital Merger Price Effects*. (https://oag.ca.gov/news/press-releases/attorney-general-becerra-state-unions-employers-and-workers-reach-settlement)

Centers for Medicare & Medicaid Services (CMS), *National Health Expenditure Data*. (https://www.cms.gov/Research-Statistics-Data-and-Systems/Statistics-Trends-and-Reports/NationalHealthExpendData)

Center for Equitable Growth, *Hospital Consolidation Matters*. (https://equitablegrowth.org/research-paper/hospital-consolidation-matters)

CBS News, *Steward Health Care Lawsuits and Hospital Closure*

Rumors, 2024. (https://www.cbsnews.com/boston/news/steward-health-care-lawsuits-millions-hospital-closure-rumors/)

Commonwealth Fund, *Global Perspective on U.S. Health Care*, January 31, 2023. (https://www.commonwealthfund.org)

Commonwealth Fund, *High U.S. Health Care Spending*, October 4, 2023. (https://www.commonwealthfund.org)

Commonwealth Fund, *Mirror, Mirror 2017: International Comparison Reflects Flaws and Strengths*, 2017. (https://www.commonwealthfund.org)

Commonwealth Fund, *Mirror, Mirror 2024: An International Comparison of Health Systems*, September 19, 2024. (https://www.commonwealthfund.org/publications/fund-reports/2024/sep/mirror-mirror-2024-international-comparison-health-systems)

Commonwealth Fund, *Mirror, Mirror: Comparing Health Systems Across Countries*, June 23, 2010. (https://www.commonwealthfund.org)

Commonwealth Fund, *U.S. Health Care from a Global Perspective, 2019*, January 30, 2020. (https://www.commonwealthfund.org)

Congressional Budget Office (CBO), *Federal Subsidies for Health Insurance*. (https://www.cbo.gov/publication/59278)

Futurism, *UnitedHealth and Optum Inhaler Lawsuit*. (https://futurism.com/neoscope/unitedhealth-optum-inhaler-lawsuit)

Health Affairs, *It's the Prices, Stupid: Why the United States is So Different from Other Countries*. (https://www.healthaffairs.org/doi/10.1377/hlthaff.22.3.89)

Health Affairs, *Articles on U.S. Health Costs and Inequities*. (https://www.healthaffairs.org)

Health System Tracker, *Health Spending Explorer*. (https://www.

healthsystemtracker.org/health-spending)

Health System Tracker, *How Does Health Spending in the U.S. Compare to Other Countries?*, January 23, 2024. (https://www.healthsystemtracker.org)

Health System Tracker, *How Does the Quality of the U.S. Health System Compare to Other Countries?*, October 9, 2024. (https://www.healthsystemtracker.org)

Health System Tracker, *How Do Healthcare Prices and Use in the U.S. Compare to Other Countries?*, May 8, 2018. (https://www.healthsystemtracker.org)

Health System Tracker, *What Drives Health Spending in the U.S. Compared to Other Countries?*, August 2, 2024. (https://www.healthsystemtracker.org)

Johns Hopkins Public Health, *U.S. Health Care Spending Highest Among Developed Countries*, January 7, 2019. (https://publichealth.jhu.edu)

JAMA Network, *Employer-Sponsored Health Insurance Premium Cost Growth and Its Associations*, January 16, 2024. (https://jamanetwork.com)

Kaiser Family Foundation (KFF), *2021 Employer Health Benefits Survey*, November 10, 2021. (https://www.kff.org)

Kaiser Family Foundation (KFF), *Employer Health Benefits Survey 2023*. (https://www.kff.org/health-costs/report/2023-employer-health-benefits-survey/)

Kaiser Family Foundation (KFF), *Health Spending Explorer*. (https://www.healthsystemtracker.org/health-spending)

Kaiser Family Foundation (KFF), *International Comparison of Health Systems*, May 28, 2024. (https://www.kff.org)

Kaiser Family Foundation (KFF), *Poll on Public Views of Prescription Drug Costs.* (https://www.kff.org/health-costs/poll-finding/public-opinion-on-prescription-drugs-and-their-prices/)

Lown Institute, *Fair Share Spending Report 2023.* (https://lowninstitute.org/2023-fair-share-spending)

Lown Institute, *How Non-profit Hospitals Inflate Costs and Avoid Taxes.* (https://lowninstitute.org/hospital-index/)

Marshall Allen, *Never Pay the First Bill: And Other Ways to Fight the Health Care System and Win.* (https://www.marshallallen.com/book)

Marty Makary, *The Price We Pay: What Broke American Health Care—and How to Fix It.* (https://www.martymd.com/book)

Marty Makary, MD, *Unaccountable: What Hospitals Won't Tell You and How Transparency Can Revolutionize Health Care.* (https://www.penguinrandomhouse.com/books/310122/unaccountable-by-marty-makary-md/)

MedPAC, *March 2024 Report to Congress on Medicare Payment Policy.* (https://www.medpac.gov)

National Bureau of Economic Research (NBER), *Various Working Papers on Healthcare Spending, Hospital Mergers, and Cost Sharing, 2021–2024.* (https://www.nber.org)

New York Post, *Bankrupt Hospital Chain Paid Private Equity Giant $700M Dividend*, 2024. (https://nypost.com)

New York Times, *PBMs and Opioid Epidemic Links*, December 17, 2024. (https://www.nytimes.com)

OCCRP, *How Private Equity and an Ambitious Landlord Put Steward Healthcare on Life Support*, 2024. (https://www.occrp.org/en/investigation/how-private-equity-and-an-ambitious-landlord-put-steward-healthcare-on-life-support)

OpenSecrets.org, *Healthcare and Pharmaceutical Lobbying.* (https://www.opensecrets.org)

PatientRightsAdvocate.org, *Hospital Price Transparency Report.* (https://www.patientrightsadvocate.org/hospital-price-transparency-report-july-2023)

PBS, *Health Costs: How the U.S. Compares with Other Countries,* October 22, 2012. (https://www.pbs.org)

PBS NewsHour, *Investigation Reveals How Investors Made Millions as Steward Health Care Collapsed,* 2024. (https://www.pbs.org/newshour/show/investigation-reveals-how-investors-made-millions-as-steward-health-care-system-collapsed)

Peterson Foundation, *How Does the U.S. Healthcare System Compare to Other Countries?,* August 16, 2024. (https://www.pgpf.org)

RAND Corporation, *Hospital Price Transparency Reports.* (https://www.rand.org/pubs/research_reports/RR4394.html)

Reuters, *Bankrupt Steward Health Approved to Sell Six Massachusetts Hospitals at Loss,* 2024. (https://www.reuters.com)

Statista, *Healthcare Spending as a Percentage of GDP by Country 2023.* (https://www.statista.com)

The Guardian, *Opioid Epidemic and FDA Oversight,* 2017. (https://www.theguardian.com)

The Wall Street Journal, *How Health Insurance Costs Outpace Inflation, in Charts,* October 9, 2024. (https://www.wsj.com/articles/how-health-insurance-costs-outpace-inflation-in-charts-612812ed)

The Wall Street Journal, *Steward's Ownership of Massachusetts Hospitals Ends in Shutdowns and Bailouts,* 2024. (https://www.wsj.com)

About the Author

Chris Deacon is a healthcare reform advocate, attorney, and former public official known for saying what others won't—especially when it comes to holding powerful institutions accountable. The daughter of two military veterans, Chris grew up moving from place to place, an upbringing that sparked her curiosity and gave her an early education in adaptability. She fell in love with policy and politics during college in Washington, D.C., then earned her law degree from Rutgers and settled in New Jersey with her husband.

Chris began her career clerking and practicing law before entering public service, first as Deputy Attorney General and later as Counsel to Governor Chris Christie. She went on to lead the State Health Benefits Program (SHBP) within New Jersey's Department of the Treasury—one of the largest public health plans in the country—where she pushed for aggressive reforms to rein in costs and expose waste.

Since leaving government in 2021, Chris has become a nationally recognized voice for health plan transparency and employer empowerment. She's testified before Congress, state legislatures, and business coalitions, earning a reputation for cutting through industry spin and saying the uncomfortable things others are afraid to say—often because their jobs or contracts depend on their silence.

Now living in northwest England due to her husband's work, Chris continues her advocacy while exploring other healthcare systems up close. She is an avid reader of European history, passionate about mental health, and outspoken about her own experiences to help break the stigma. When she's not writing or traveling for work, she plays the part of chauffeur, tutor, cook, trainer, and coach to her three kids—roles she takes on with both exhaustion and joy.

Anyone who knows Chris can feel her energy and her deep sense of purpose. This work isn't just professional—it's personal.

www.ingramcontent.com/pod-product-compliance
Lightning Source LLC
Chambersburg PA
CBHW030312150825
31016CB00005B/9